Write It .5

A Process Approach to College Essays with Readings

Linda Strahan
Kathleen Moore
University of California-Riverside

Kendall Hunt
publishing company

Cover image © Shutterstock, Inc.

Kendall Hunt
publishing company

www.kendallhunt.com
Send all inquiries to:
4050 Westmark Drive
Dubuque, IA 52004-1840

Copyright © 2013 by Kendall Hunt Publishing Company

ISBN 978-1-4652-2591-7

Printed in the United States of America
10 9 8 7 6 5 4 3 2 1

Contents

Preface

John Briggs
Professor of English
McSweeny Chair of Rhetoric and Teaching Excellence
Director, the University Writing Program
University of California, Riverside

What is success in higher education? It depends, more than anything, upon your academic literacy—your ability to read, write, and speak on a level appropriate to your college or university. Reading, writing, and speaking in higher education are not only skills. They depend upon your *preparation*, not only your academic background but also your *dedication* to the course that assigns this textbook. You must read more, and more widely, than you have before. You will need to participate in class. Writing must be your daily task. Repeated practice is just as important in your academic work as it is in making music or competing in an athletic event. More learning, practice, and performance—perhaps more than you can now imagine—will be necessary for you to pass and prosper in this course and succeed in your studies.

This book will help you if your preparation is persistent. You will need to learn more, including how to *perform* what you know in speaking and writing. You will need to read more, and reread. To become a better reader, you will need to speak in class, and write for your instructor and your classmates, over and over. You must learn how to practice well, and to *seek* what you need to understand.

Write It .5 is a book that will assist you in these endeavors. Without your energetic investment in studying this book, however, you will be less likely to succeed. Make this book your companion and guide. Take it with you, and it will repay your attention. Invest in it. Use it to learn how to succeed in this class and in your higher education.

Acknowledgments

This book would not have been possible without the inspiration and support of the instructors in the University Writing Program at the University of California, Riverside and the exemplary support team at Kendall-Hunt. We want to thank all of them for their encouragement and help.

Our special thanks go to our editor, Lindsay Wubben, and our project manager, Amanda Smith, for their dedicated attention to this project. We want to especially acknowledge our colleagues Kim Turner and Rochelle Gold for their willingness to talk through some of the issues that confronted us as we developed this book.

Finally, our gratitude and thanks to our colleague Benedict Jones for his tireless and inspired editorial work. His corrections, suggestions, and additions always originated from his long experience working with students, and his contributions have significantly improved the quality of this book.

Becoming More Familiar with Academic Culture

In order to do well in this class and in all of your college classes, it is important that you understand a few basics that most instructors assume you already know. Read and complete the activities in Part I so that you have a sound awareness of some of these basics.

Here is an overview of the skills and guidelines presented in Part I:

- how to read a course syllabus to prepare for writing assignments
- some common English idioms
- guidelines for avoiding plagiarism
- tips for using a dictionary
- using the writing process
- the interdependence of three basic skills: reading, speaking, and writing

Reading a Syllabus

A *syllabus* is a document that provides students with information regarding the plan and design of a college-level course. The instructor for each course offered in your college or university will make a syllabus available in some form, hard copy or electronic, to his or her students. It is the students' responsibility to become familiar with the syllabus and use it to guide their study and preparation for each class meeting, assignment, and exam.

In order to participate productively in a course, you will have to understand the way a syllabus is to be read. Ordinarily, a syllabus will contain detailed information about the following topics related to the course:

1. a course description—

   The course description offers an overview of the class. It explains the topics, skills, and expected learning outcomes of the course. It identifies any prerequisites for the course. Sometimes it will include some information about the format of the class meetings, discussion, workshop, lecture, or lab.

2. the texts for the course—

   The syllabus lists all the books related to the course. Some of the books will be labeled "required texts." If a book appears on the "required" list, then students are expected to purchase or have a copy of that text available to them for study throughout the quarter or semester.

   Other books on the syllabus will be listed as "optional texts." An optional book is one that the instructor feels will be a valuable resource for students taking the course, but whose information will either review material from preparatory courses or offer useful supplemental material to the present course. Students need to make their decision regarding the purchase of "optional texts" on the basis of their own familiarity with the subject of the course, or their personal interest in learning more about the subject.

3. requirements for the course—

   The requirements for a course can include the names and types of exams (quizzes/midterms/final), the amount of reading, the number of papers, the types of homework assignments, and an explanation of the other kinds of assignments students must complete in order to receive a credit-bearing grade in the course.

4. other pertinent information for the course—

   If the instructor expects students to follow other instructions, information, rules, or guidelines in the class, they will be addressed on the syllabus. In the syllabus, students might also find a discussion of the use of computers and cell phones or university and instructor policy regarding plagiarism. It is important that students read this information carefully because it can have an impact on successful completion of the course.

5. tentative schedule of readings and assignments for the course—

   The syllabus includes a chronological plan for the class. It lists the dates of all exams and the due dates for all papers and assignments. Most often in undergraduate classes, the syllabus contains a daily plan. It lets the students know the topic or activity for each class meetings. Readings to be covered during a class are listed for the date of the class; however, students are expected to come to class prepared; this means that any readings or assignments listed for that day are to be completed **before** attending the class.

Sample Syllabus

Study the sample syllabus below and answer the discussion questions that follow it.

BW3 Lecture: Basic Writing
Fall 2012

Basic Writing 3 is a grammar-intensive writing course designed to help students strengthen their reading, critical thinking, and writing skills. Successful completion of this class with a grade of "S" ("C" or better) will qualify you to enroll in English Writing 4, a course that fulfills the Entry Level Writing Requirement.

Note: BW3 is designed as a multi-quarter course to help students prepare most effectively for the demands of English 4. Thus, students should expect to require two quarters or more of BW3 before earning an "S" for the class.

BSWT003 Components

1. **An online lab**—To receive a satisfactory grade for BW3L, students must pass weekly quizzes related to grammar and reading comprehension. This work is found on the BW3L Blackboard site, and the grade awarded for this 1-unit course is NOT part of this lecture course. Contact Information: Keith Vance (lashv@ucr.edu).

2. **A journal project**—To receive a satisfactory grade for the journal, students must complete entries each week. The journal has its own iLearn page, where you will find instructions. If you have questions about this component of BW3 or you do not see the journal in your list of classes on iLearn, contact Kim Turner (kimbert@ucr.edu).

3. **A lecture**—The lecture component is our class! Assignments and grading for this component of BW3 are described in the remainder of this syllabus.

Lecture Class Policies

Attendance and Participation

You need to be in class on time every day. You may not make up any work that you miss if you are absent or tardy unless you present a doctor's note or are required at a university event. Please avoid being late to class. It is a distraction to the entire class and may adversely affect your grade; you cannot make up work you miss when you are tardy. **Bring your books to class every day!**

Plagiarism

If you are not already familiar with the University's policies concerning academic dishonesty, get that way! Plagiarism will not be tolerated in this class. You will receive a zero for any work that contains plagiarized material, even if that material amounts to less than 1% of your paper. You simply will not pass if you use someone else's ideas or words as if they are yours or without proper citation. Moreover, I will report cases of academic misconduct to the Student Conduct Office. (See for reference: http://senate.ucr.edu/bylaws/?action=read_bylaws&code=app&section=06.03).

(Continued)

Required Materials

1. *Write It*, 3rd ed., by Strahan, Moore, & Heumann (*WI*) 9780757589782
2. *Understanding and Using English Grammar*, 4th ed., by Azar & Hagen (*UUEG*) 9780132333313
3. *Thousand Pieces of Gold*, by McCunn 9780807083819
4. College-level dictionary
5. Internet access

Class Etiquette

1. No cell phones or other electronic devices (including headphones).
2. Rudeness or personal attacks against members of the class will not be tolerated.
3. No sleeping.
4. If you don't follow these class rules, I will ask you to leave class for the day.

Evaluation Process: 73% needed to pass the class	
Essay 1: "In Praise of Margins"	10%
Essay 2: *Thousand Pieces of Gold*	20%
Essay 3: In-class essay	20%
Homework, class assignments, quizzes, group work, participation	20%
Final Exam	30%
See the description of General Grading Standards for Essays below	

Essays—General Policies

- **Paper format:** All essays must follow MLA formatting—that is, typed and double-spaced with one inch margins on all sides. Use Times New Roman, 12 point font. (See the resources on iLearn for help with MLA format.)
- **Workshops:** There will be draft workshops for essays 1 & 3. You are expected to bring <u>COMPLETE</u> drafts of your essays to class on the days of the workshops. In other words, rough ≠ short. Failure to bring an adequate draft will lower your essay grade by ½ letter grade; failure to come to class on the workshop day will result in the same penalty.
- **Paper Submission:** When an essay is due, you must submit a printed out paper to me so that I can write comments and suggestions for you. All essays must also be submitted to SafeAssign on the iLearn site on the day the paper is due. I won't grade your paper until you have submitted it in both forms.

Late Work Policy

- **Late Essays:** All essays are due at the <u>beginning of class</u> on the day assigned. <u>If you are late to class, your paper is counted one day late.</u> Except in verified cases of emergency or serious illness, your final paper grade will be lowered if your paper is turned in late. Specifically, I will take off ½ letter grade (5%) for each class day that it is late. If a paper is more than 1 calendar week late, I will not accept it. You must complete all essays in order to pass the class.
- **Late Homework:** Students always want to know if I accept late homework. I know that sometimes you cannot help missing a class period or two if you are sick, so I will accept

late homework up to two times; after that, I will not accept it. If you are absent, it is your responsibility to complete the work that is due the day you are returning. Some homework is listed on the syllabus, but you should always double-check with a classmate.

Class & Group Participation: Guidelines for Evaluation

- **Outstanding Contributor (A):** Contributions in class and/or groups reflect exceptional preparation. Ideas offered are always substantive, and they provide one or more major insights as well as direction for the class/group. If this person were not a member of the class/group, the quality of discussion and work would be diminished markedly.

- **Good Contributor (B):** Contributions in class and/or groups reflect thorough preparation. Ideas offered are usually substantial and provide good insights. If this person were not a member of the class/group, the quality of discussion and work would be diminished.

- **Adequate Contributor (C):** Contributions in class and/or groups reflect satisfactory preparation. Ideas offered are sometimes very helpful and provide generally useful insights. If this person were not a member of the class/group, the quality of discussion and work would be diminished somewhat.

- **Non-Participant (D):** This person says little or nothing in class and/or groups. Hence, there is not an adequate basis for evaluation. If this person were not a member of the class/group, the quality of discussion and work would not be changed.

- **Unsatisfactory Contributor (F):** Contributions in class and/or groups reflect inadequate preparation. Ideas offered are seldom helpful and provide few if any insights for the class/group. If this person were not a member of the class/group, valuable airtime would be saved.

> Reading assignments MUST be done on or before the day listed below. You must bring your books to class.

Course Schedule:

Subject to Change

Week Zero			**Friday, Sept. 28** • Introduction to the course

Week One	**Monday, Oct. 1**
	• **Read:** *Write It*, pp. 1–11
	• **HW due:** Assignment #1 on iLearn (grammar diagnostic)
	• **Read:** *UUEG*, Chapter 1
	• **HW due:** *UUEG*, Chapter 1, Exercises 4, 6, 8, 10, 11
	• **Lecture:** Basic Verb Tenses
		Wednesday, Oct. 3
		• **Read:** *Write It*, pp. 18–27
		• **HW due:** Assignment #2 on iLearn (Reading comprehension questions)
		• **Read:** *UUEG*, pp. 439–441 (Basic Grammar Terminology)
		• **HW due:** *UUEG*, Chapter 1, Exercises 16, 17, 18
		• **Lecture:** Basic Essay Structure
			Friday, Oct. 5
			• **Read:** *Write It*, pp. 29–32
			• **Read:** *Write It*, pp. 51–54
			• **HW due:** *Write It*
			  1. "Vocabulary Check" pp. 55–56
			  2. "Questions to Guide Your Reading," pp. 57–58
			• **Read:** *Thousand Pieces of Gold*, Chapters 1–5
			• **Lecture:** Basic Essay Structure, continued

(Continued)

	Monday, Oct. 8	Wednesday, Oct. 10	Friday, Oct. 12
Week Two	• **Read:** *UUEG*, Chapter 2 • **HW due:** *UUEG*, Ch. 2, Exercises 1, 4, 10 • **HW due:** *Write It*, pp. 59–60 • **HW due:** Reading Log #1 (instructions on the iLearn site) • **Lecture:** Effective Thesis Statements	• **Read:** *Thousand Pieces of Gold*, Chapters 6–9 • **HW due:** *UUEG*, Chapter 2, Exercises 11, 19, 27, 38 • **Lecture:** Effective Body Paragraphs (the 4 Cs)	• **Read:** *UUEG*, Chapter 3 • **HW due:** *UUEG*, Chapter 3, Exercises 4, 7, 13, 16, 19 • **HW due:** Reading Log #2 (instructions on the iLearn site) • **Read:** *Write It*: "The Shallows" (pp. 76–79) & "Hitting Pay Dirt" (pp. 81–83) • **Lecture:** Incorporating Support
Week Three	**Monday, Oct. 15** • **HW due:** *UUEG*, Ch. 3, Exercises 23, 30, 31, 34 • **Read:** *Thousand Pieces of Gold*, Chapters 10–14 • **Read:** *Write It*: "The Dance within My Heart" (pp. 84–86), "Blue-Sky Research" (pp. 87–90) & "Everyday Playtime for Adults" (pp. 92–95)	**Wednesday, Oct. 17** • **HW due:** *Write It*, pp. 61–63 (prewriting) • **HW due:** Reading Log #3 (instructions on the iLearn site) • **In-class:** Review for Test #1	**Friday, Oct. 19** • **Test 1:** Verbs #1 (Chapters 1, 2 & 3, *UUEG*) • **Read:** *Thousand Pieces of Gold*, Chapters 15–18
Week Four	**Monday, Oct. 22** • **HW due:** *Write It*, pp. 64–68 (Outline) • **HW due:** Reading Log #4 (instructions on the iLearn site) • **Read:** Student Essays 1 & 2, pp. 430–434 (*Write It*) • **Lecture:** Assessing your work and the work of others	**Wednesday, Oct. 24** • **Read:** *Thousand Pieces of Gold*, Chapters 19–25 • **Read:** UUEG, Chapter 4 • **HW due:** *UUEG*, Ch. 4, Exercises 1, 2, 10, 11, 14, 15 • **Read:** Student Essays 3 & 4, pp. 435–439 (*Write It*) • **HW due:** Assessment questions for Student Essay 1–4 (*Write It*, pp. 430–439)	**Friday, Oct. 26** • **Due:** Completed Draft for Draft Workshop for Essay #1 (bring a typed, printed out copy to class)
Week Five	**Monday, Oct. 29** • **HW due:** *UUEG*, Chapter 4, Exercises 18, 19, 23, 25, 26 • **HW Due:** Reading Log #5 (instructions on the iLearn site) • **Lecture:** Revision Strategies (bring your new drafts to class)	**Wednesday, Oct. 31** • **Read:** *Thousand Pieces of Gold*, Chapters 26–33 • **Read:** *UUEG*, Ch. 6 • **HW due:** *UUEG*, Chapter 6, Exercises 3, 4, 5, 8, 9 • **Lecture:** Subject-Verb Agreement	**Friday, Nov. 2** • **HW due:** Reading Log #6 (instructions on the iLearn site) • **HW due:** *UUEG*, Ch. 6, Exercises 11, 14, 15, 19, 26, 27 • **Essay #1:** Final Draft Due
Week Six	**Monday, Nov. 5** • **Read:** *Thousand Pieces of Gold*, Chapters 24-Epilogue • **Discussion:** *Thousand Pieces of Gold*	**Wednesday, Nov. 7** • **HW due:** Reading Log #7 (instructions on the iLearn site) • **HW due:** Vocabulary & Prewriting for Essay 2 • **Test 2:** Verbs #2 (Chapters 1–4 and 6, *UUEG*)	**Friday, Nov. 9** • **Quiz:** *Thousand Pieces of Gold*

Week Seven	**Monday, Nov. 12** **Holiday: No Class**	**Wednesday, Nov 14** • **HW Due:** Outline for Essay 2 • **Read:** *UUEG*, Ch. 7 • **HW Due:** *UUEG* Chapter 7, Exercises 21, 22, 23, 27, 29, 30 • **Lecture:** Nouns and Articles	**Friday, Nov. 16** • **Read:** *Write It*, pp. 102–104
Week Eight	**Monday, Nov. 19** • **Draft Workshop, Essay 2** (bring a complete, typed draft to class)	**Wednesday, Nov. 21** • **Read:** *Write It* (Read any two essays from the "Extended Activities" section that look good to you from pages 125–156) • **HW Due:** The discussion questions for the two essays you chose (emailed to me)	**Friday, Nov. 23** **Holiday: No Class**
Week Nine	**Monday, Nov. 26** • **In-Class Essay:** Day 1 • **HW Due:** *UUEG* Chapter 7, Exercises 32, 33, 34, 37, 38, 42, 43	**Wednesday, Nov. 28** • **Essay 2 Final Draft Due** • **In-Class Essay:** Day 2	**Friday, Nov. 30** • **HW Due:** *UUEG* Chapter 7, Exercises 45, 50 • **In-Class Essay:** Day 3
Week Ten	**Monday, Dec. 3** • **Test 3:** Nouns, Articles & Determiners (Ch. 7 of *UUEG*)	**Wednesday, Dec. 5** • **Read:** Support Essays for the final	**Friday, Dec. 7** • **In-Class:** Discussion of Final Exam
Final Exam	**Monday, Dec. 10** **11:30–2:30** **Location to be announced**		

Follow-Up Activity

1. In this class, what are the consequences of turning work in late? Discuss whether or not you think this policy is reasonable.

2. Identify the specific dates for the in-class essay. Why do you think the amount of time given to complete this assignment is enough or not enough? What is the percentage of your final grade for this essay?

3. Explain everything you will need to have done to prepare for class on Oct. 10. What is different about the work you are required to submit (amount, type, etc.) on Oct. 8 compared to Oct. 10?

English Idioms

Idioms are expressions and phrases whose meanings are not determined by the definitions of their parts. They can be understood only by context and familiarity. When you come across a sentence where you know the meaning of each individual word but still cannot understand the meaning of the sentence, there is a good chance that you have encountered an idiom.

There are two categories of idioms. *Standard idioms*, the first kind of idioms, are those expressions that convey a meaning unrelated to the sum of their parts. To help you appreciate the way idioms function, here are some examples with their definitions of common idioms in American English:

IDIOM	DEFINITION
fall in love	care about romantically
burn the midnight oil	stay up late
make ends meet	balance income and expenditures
hold your tongue	be quiet
all set	ready to start
common ground	shared beliefs or interests
down-to-earth	showing good sense; practical
draw to a close	come to an end
every now and then	fairly often; repeatedly
face up to	bravely confront or challenge
find out	learn or discover
figure out	find an answer by thinking
follow-up	additional work or research that will make something better
frame of mind	one's mental outlook
get across	explain clearly
get at	reach an understanding of; find out the meaning
get away with	do something wrong and not get caught
get to the bottom of	find the real cause of
hit the books	study
in general	usually; very often
kill time	waste time
leave out	skip or omit
let pass	disregard or overlook
make sense	sound reasonable
on the fence	in doubt; undecided
on the contrary	exactly the opposite; rather
resign oneself	accept something that cannot be changed

Related to the standard idiom is a category of expressions know as *phrasal verbs*. Phrasal verbs are verbs whose meaning is changed by the addition of a preposition. There are two kinds of phrasal verbs: separable and inseparable. Separable phrasal verbs allow other words to come between the verb and its preposition. When using an inseparable phrasal verb, however, the preposition must directly follow its verb. To understand the difference, look at the sentences below.

Separable Phrasal Verbs

Verb	Preposition	Sentence
ask	out	Tim asked Jennifer out on a date.
hand	in	Nan handed her homework in late

Inseparable Phrasal Verbs

Verb	Preposition	Sentence
run	into	John ran into the wall.
look	out	Look out for the sharp edges.

To be fluent in a language, you must understand the concept of idioms and be acquainted with many common idioms. Of course, you may still in your reading find sentences whose meaning you cannot comprehend. To learn whether words and phrases are being used idiomatically, you will need to rely on the dictionary. The best resource in this case is a dictionary of American idioms, but any good standard dictionary usually lists some of the idiomatic uses of a word at the end of the entry. When you are writing, the dictionary can also help by informing you whether the phrasal verb you wish to use is separable or inseparable.

Follow-Up Activity

Use your dictionary to learn the meaning of any of the idioms below whose grammatical usage or meaning is unfamiliar to you. Explain the meaning of the expression or phrase and use it in a sentence. Then share your sentences with a classmate by reading them aloud.

bite the bullet

Definition: _____

_____

Sentence: _____

_____

hit the sack

Definition: _____

_____

Sentence: _____

_____

come across

Definition: _____

_____

Sentence: _____

_____

get the ball rolling

Definition: _____

_____

Sentence: _____

_____

proud of

Definition: _____

_____

Sentence: _____

_____

Academic Integrity: Guidelines for Avoiding Plagiarism

You may be aware of the rule that all work you turn in for credit must be your own, but sometimes students unintentionally commit plagiarism because they are unclear about what qualifies as plagiarism or infringement of copyright laws. Review the following definitions and rules and check to see that your own paper meets all the requirements of intellectual and academic honesty.

Copyright refers to the legal ownership of published material. Any writing—a play, an essay, a pamphlet, a website—is the intellectual property of the person who wrote it. If, in your paper, you borrow that property by quoting, summarizing, or paraphrasing, you must give credit to the original author. The *fair use* laws allow you to borrow brief passages without infringing on copyright, but you must credit the source and document it properly. Your handbook will show you the correct form to use for each and every source.

Plagiarism can occur when students make poor choices—for example, when a student turns in another student's work as his or her own. Institutions of higher learning have strict policies regarding this type of plagiarism, and the consequences for this action can be significant.

Plagiarism may also be committed by oversight; a student may have forgotten where he or she found the particular material or even that the material was not his or her own. It is important during your research that you include all the source information in your notes so that you will not accidentally commit plagiarism and be held accountable for it.

Remember to acknowledge the following:

Ideas—any idea or concept that you learned elsewhere that is not common knowledge

Words and Phrases—exact reproduction of another author's writing

Charts/Tables/Statistics/Other Visuals—other forms of work done by an author or artist

Your Own Work—work of your own, done for a different assignment or purpose

Intellectual property is the result of work done by a person with the head rather than the hands; nevertheless, the result of that work still belongs to the person who did it. If a carpenter made a chair, that chair is owned by its maker. You would consider taking that chair an act of theft. Try to think of printed material as a similar object and show that property the same respect you would any other. By doing so, you will avoid plagiarism and copyright infringement.

Follow-Up Activity

1. Look up "plagiarism" in a dictionary and then find and read the explanation it gives. Be sure to study carefully the importance of avoiding plagiarism when you summarize or paraphrase from a book, magazine, newspaper, or article.
2. Go online to the University's web site and find its official statement regarding academic honesty and the definition of plagiarism. You are responsible for knowing the rules and regulations the University has posted regarding academic honesty.

Using a Dictionary

A good dictionary is an essential tool for reading and writing that both students and professional writers find helpful. A dictionary provides much useful information beyond the simple definition of a word. The dictionary tells you alternative spellings for the word, the division of the word into syllables (which guides the use of hyphens when the word appears at the end of a line and needs to be broken in two), common pronunciation of the word, other meanings of the word, and the ways a word can be used in different parts of speech, as well as related words that are formed from the main word.

Finding Words in an English Dictionary

- Words appear in the dictionary in alphabetical order. This order is strictly letter by letter. No differentiation is made between single words, names, or multiple word phrases. If the name of a person or place begins with an abbreviation, it will be alphabetized as the letters appear in the name, not as if the abbreviation were spelled out.

  For example: "St. Louis," a city, would be alphabetized as beginning with "st," not as the unabbreviated "sa" for the word "saint."

- If an entry begins with a numeral, the term is listed as if the number were spelled out.

  For example: A listing for the 4 Seasons, a musical group, would be alphabetized under the letter "F."

- If two words with completely different definitions and uses share a single spelling (*homophones*), they are often given two separate listings. You will have to consider the context in which the word is used to discover which meaning is applicable to the sentence you are reading.

  For example: The word "bowl," a noun meaning a rounded dish, would be followed by a separate listing for the word "bowl," a verb meaning to play a game with a ball and pins.

- Some dictionaries contain foreign words and phrases that have not yet been assimilated into English but are still often used and understood by English speakers. These words will appear in the main body of the dictionary but will be distinguished by a change in type face, such as bold italics. In other dictionaries, foreign words will appear alphabetically in a separate list in the back of the dictionary. Some dictionaries will not include foreign words at all.

  For example: The French word "voilà," though commonly used by speakers of English, would still be considered a non-English word and would be given special treatment if included in the dictionary.

Word Meanings

The entry for a word that has more than one meaning, as most words do, will list the various meanings in order of usage from most common to least common. These meanings will be separated numerically.

For example: A dictionary might list the meanings for the word "globe" in the following manner:

1. a solid depiction of the planet earth
2. anything spherical

Pronunciation

Directly following each entry, marked letters and symbols appear within parentheses. The information within the parentheses offers a phonetic guide for the correct pronunciation of the word. In other words, the word is represented by a spelling that reflects how it sounds. Every dictionary contains in its introductory material a *pronunciation key* that explains the way vowels and consonants sound in English. The various kinds of lines over the letters and the other icons are called "diacritical marks." These marks are standard and have the same meanings in any dictionary. The most common of these marks are a line over the letter to show that a vowel is long ($\bar{o}$), and the schwa (ϑ) to indicate a neutral vowel sound made in English.

For example: In the word "manatee," which is defined as a kind of aquatic mammal, the entry for "manatee" would be followed by the following information to guide your pronunciation: (man ϑ tē).

You should familiarize yourself with the marks used most frequently in English dictionaries. Use the Internet and a search engine such as Google to find one or more of these useful charts.

Syllabification

Words are divided into syllables according to certain rules. Usually the division into syllables is phonetic and follows standard pronunciation. In that case, the word is broken after an open syllable, one with a long vowel or an unstressed vowel, or after a consonant in syllables where the vowel is short or stressed.

For example" The word "halo" would be divided into "hā-lō," but the word "halogen" would be divided as "hal-o-gen" because in the second word the "a" is not pronounced as a long vowel.

There are instances, however, where syllable division does not correspond with the way a word is pronounced. Affixes, common syllables added to a word to alter its part of speech, are not usually divided at the end of a line of type, nor are acronyms, words formed from initials.

For example: In the word "utilitarianism," the word would be divided as "u-til-i-tar-i-anism."

For another example: The acronym "UNICEF" (the United Nations International Children's Fund) cannot be divided in any way.

Word Variants

Many times in English a word will have more than one acceptable spelling. When this is the case, the dictionary will include both spellings in a single entry. The most common spelling will be given first; however, if the two spellings are used with almost equal frequency, the dictionary will precede the second spelling with either the word "or" or "also."

For example: The color word "gray" would appear as **gray** or **grey** to indicate that both spellings are in common usage.

Grammatical Usage

Before the definition or sets of definitions, the dictionary uses abbreviations that show the part of speech the word is used as for the following definition(s). These abbreviations are standard, and you can find them listed in the introductory material of your dictionary, your handbook, or your grammar text.

When a new definition is used as a different part of speech, a new abbreviation will appear before the number for that definition.

For example: The word "ice" has multiple meanings as various parts of speech. Though the dictionary entry would include other meanings in addition to the following, the change in part of speech would be indicated as "n. [or noun] **1.** Water in its solid form; v. [or verb] **2.** To frost a cake."

At the end of an entry, the dictionary will also give form changes in the word necessary to turn it into some other parts of speech. The new word will appear in bold face type in the conclusion of the entry and will be followed by the abbreviation for its part of speech.

For example: The word "slant" means to angle away from a particular level. To change "slant" into an adjective or an adverb, the word alters. The dictionary would show this new form at the end of the entry for "slant" as **slantwise**, adv. adj.

Additional Information

Dictionaries also contain other kinds of relevant information about a word to different extents depending on the size and function of the particular dictionary, but all give some amount of historical information about the entry. The history of a word is called its "etymology." It can include facts about the word's origin, its language derivation, its earliest dates of usage, earlier spellings, and other relevant material. This information is presented in square brackets after the definition itself.

For example: The simple word "dog" can be traced over a thousand years back, predating Middle English. The dictionary entry indicates its history as [bef. 1050 ME doggy, OE docga].

Follow-Up Activity

Use a good English dictionary to find the answers to the following questions:

1. Where in the dictionary would you find the entry for "3-D"?
2. What diacritical marks are used to show the difference in the pronunciation of the vowel in the words "hat" and "hate"?
3. Show the way the word "antiparliamentary" is divided into syllables.
4. What is another acceptable spelling for the word "theater"?
5. Mark the pronunciation you would choose for the words "bowie knife" and "Caribbean."

Using the Writing Process

The process of trying to write down your ideas, of getting them straight in your thoughts and then clear in your writing, takes time and hard work. When you sit down to write, you may have a vague idea of what you want to say, but your ideas will not be fully developed until you try to write them down because your thoughts take a clearer shape as you put them into sentences. This is why good writers know the importance of the *writing process* and use it. **Thinking and writing work together.** Good writing is produced through persistent thinking, and good ideas are only fully uncovered through writing. If you remember this one rule, you will be able to create clear, developed, and interesting papers.

Sometimes, an idea you have sounds unconvincing when you attempt to recreate it in written form. To create the most successful essays you can, you will have to use the writing process to uncover what you want to say and then develop your thoughts so that your readers can fully understand your ideas. If you are writing an essay that responds to a reading selection, you will also have to return frequently to read parts or all of the selection; each time you do, you will understand it better and thereby respond to its ideas in a more complex and interesting way.

Steps of the Writing Process

- prewriting
- drafting
- revising
- editing

Prewriting can include a variety of activities you do with your pen in hand, or your hands on the keyboard. You may like to list or diagram your ideas and observations about the subject of your paper. Sometimes clustering ideas or freewriting about your thoughts can help you get a good beginning as you explore and develop your ideas. In this stage of the writing process, you use writing to give shape to your thoughts and uncover new ideas. You will likely begin working on a writing assignment by prewriting, but it can come in handy at any time as you work on completing your paper.

Drafting refers to those times when you try to write out large sections of your paper. You won't have a full draft until you have a complete version, including the introduction, body paragraphs, and conclusion. Sometimes drafting includes cutting and pasting from prewriting activities to fill in the introduction or a body paragraph.

Don't think of the drafting stage as a linear task in which you write out the paper from the beginning straight through to the end. You may prefer to draft easier parts of the paper first, parts where you capture your thoughts and try to give them shape. You may want to begin with a working thesis and then try to draft paragraphs that support it in order to test its validity for yourself. Because the writing process is recursive, that is, it is circular and starts over perhaps several times, you will go back to these early pieces of draft and revise them once your thesis statement and ideas are more clearly shaped.

Revising happens when you allow your thoughts to influence your draft—perhaps reshaping or adding to it so that it is clearer and more compelling. You might decide to add more appropriate evidence, or to reword the thesis statement so that it overarches the body paragraphs you have written. Or you may discover that the essay does not make sense in a section or sections because you have used supporting evidence that is weak or unrelated.

Before you finish a paper, it should go through several revisions if it is to be as successful as you can make it. You will have to allow plenty of time for revision, so begin working on all of your writing assignments as early as possible.

Don't forget to read your draft aloud, either to yourself or to a friend. This will help you find places where more revising is needed.

Editing should be saved for last because it is the stage where you check your sentences to be sure that you do not have any grammar, punctuation, or spelling errors. Don't spend time checking the spelling of your sentences or your choice of vocabulary words until you are in the last stage of the process because your draft will likely change several times before you are ready to turn it in. Wait until the paper is complete and then read it once more to check the form of your sentences.

Remember that the stages of the writing process are *recursive*, meaning they are used over and over again to complete a writing assignment. If the process is used to its full potential, it ensures that you are always open to the discovery process and the refinement of ideas, even when a first draft has been written. Using the writing process will give you greater control over your writing because your thoughts take clearer shape as you work within its stages.

Follow-Up Activity

Working with another person in the class, describe to one another the steps each of you takes to complete writing assignments. How and when do you begin? What do you do next? What are some of the other strategies you use to complete your paper? How do they compare to the steps outlined above?

Now tell each other how the writing process you have studied here could change the way you habitually write a paper. What might you do differently? How might that change help improve the way you complete a writing assignment? Offer each other any suggestions you might have.

Reading, Writing, and Speaking in an Academic Setting

Reading, writing, and speaking form an important part of academic culture. It is only when these three elements work together that great insights can be discovered, shared, and built upon by the academic community as a whole. Our society ultimately benefits. We hope you will push yourself to work with all three of these learning strategies as you complete the assignments in this book, and in all of your course work throughout your college studies. You will see that each of the three strategies supplements and strengthens the other two. If you use all three diligently, you will see how your reading, writing, and speaking ability work together to make you a better, more successful student.

This text will guide you to use reading to develop your writing. But some of the book's activities and lessons will include opportunities not only to read, but to read *aloud* and to listen to others read aloud. Researchers and educators widely agree on the important role that reading aloud plays in your educational development, whether you are a relatively new English language learner or a native speaker of English. Perhaps you have never read aloud, or been read to, especially in a formal setting such as a classroom. But your persistence and determination will soon have you feeling comfortable reading aloud, and your literacy skills will certainly improve. Studies show that reading aloud:

- promotes literacy and language development
- builds a large vocabulary
- aids achievement in school
- develops reading comprehension skills
- develops a rich imagination
- helps associate reading and enjoyment
- improves listening and reading skills
- strengthens mental and verbal skills
- sharpens focus
- internalizes language and the meaning of words
- improves the ability to speak with clarity and precision
- improves memory of what is read
- develops awareness of English language patterns, promoting proper grammar and sentence structure
- improves writing
- helps in revising and editing

Perhaps the first important step in a class such as this one is to learn to associate reading with pleasure or fun. Especially if you have not done much reading, or if English is not your first language, you may resist opportunities to read because you associate it with unpleasantness and struggle. Read the essay below; it finds reading aloud an enjoyable activity.

Some Thoughts on the Lost Art of Reading Aloud

Essay

VERLYN KLINKENBORG

Sometimes the best way to understand the present is to look at it from the past. Consider audio books. An enormous number of Americans read by listening these days—listening aloud, I call it. The technology for doing so is diverse and widespread, and so are the places people listen to audio books. But from the perspective of a reader in, say, the early 19th century, about the time of Jane Austen, there is something peculiar about it, even lonely.

In those days, literate families and friends read aloud to each other as a matter of habit. Books were still relatively scarce and expensive, and the routine electronic diversions we take for granted were, of course, nonexistent. If you had grown up listening to adults reading to each other regularly, the thought of all of those solitary 21st-century individuals hearkening to earbuds and car radios would seem isolating. It would also seem as though they were being trained only to listen to books and not to read aloud from them.

It's part of a pattern. Instead of making music at home, we listen to recordings of professional musicians. When people talk about the books they've heard, they're often talking about the quality of the readers, who are usually professional. The way we listen to books has been desocialized, stripped of context, which has the solitary virtue of being extremely convenient.

But listening aloud, valuable as it is, isn't the same as reading aloud. Both require a great deal of attention. Both are good ways to learn something important about the rhythms of language. But one of the most basic tests of comprehension is to ask someone to read aloud from a book. It reveals far more than whether the reader understands the words. It reveals how far into the words—and the pattern of the words—the reader really sees.

Reading aloud recaptures the physicality of words. To read with your lungs and diaphragm, with your tongue and lips, is very different than reading with your eyes alone. The language becomes a part of the body, which is why there is always a curious tenderness, almost an erotic quality, in those 18th- and 19th-century literary scenes where a book is being read aloud in mixed company. The words are not mere words. They are the breath and mind, perhaps even the soul, of the person who is reading.

No one understood this better than Jane Austen. One of the late turning points in *Mansfield Park* comes when Henry Crawford picks up a volume of Shakespeare, "which had the air of being very recently closed," and begins to read aloud to the young Bertrams and their cousin, Fanny Price. Fanny discovers in Crawford's reading "a variety of excellence beyond what she had ever met with." And yet his ability to do every part "with equal beauty" is a clear sign to us, if not entirely to Fanny, of his superficiality.

I read aloud to my writing students, and when students read aloud to me I notice something odd. They are smart and literate, and most of them had parents who read to them as children. But when students read aloud at first, I notice that they are trying to read the meaning of the words. If the work is their own, they are usually trying to read the intention of the writer.

It's as though they're reading what the words represent rather than the words themselves. What gets lost is the inner voice of the prose, the life of the language. This is reflected in their writing, too, at first.

You can easily make the argument that reading silently is an economic artifact, a sign of a new prosperity beginning in the early 19th century and a new cheapness in books. The same argument applies to listening to books on your iPhone. But what I would suggest is that our idea of reading is incomplete, impoverished, unless we are also taking the time to read aloud.

Follow-Up Activity

Form small groups to discuss the following topics. Then report your conclusions to the class.

1. Tell the group your most recent memory of reading aloud or being read to. What was the book? Who did you share it with? How would you describe the experience?

2. Discuss the benefits connected to reading and listening aloud, according to Verlyn Klinkenborg, the writer of the essay?. Does her essay convince you? Explain.

3. If you haven't already done so, read the essay aloud. Then describe the difference between the two experiences—when you read it to yourself versus when you read it aloud or listened to someone read it aloud.

Writing Basics

The particular argument essay that you will study in *Write It .5* will help you gain practice in critically analyzing issues, formulating logical arguments, and persuasively expressing your opinions by using the conventional rules of written English and a conventional essay structure. The thesis-centered essay is the most commonly assigned essay format in college. Its purpose is to persuade. Its formal parts are established by convention and provide a structure for presenting an argument. These parts include an introduction that orients the readers to the essay's subject, a thesis statement that presents the argument, body paragraphs that develop and support the argument, and a conclusion that closes the essay. Study Part II carefully because it gives you an overview of the process of essay writing and other helpful information to help you succeed in this course and in other college courses that include writing. Spend some time with these pages before moving to Part III, where you will be asked to put them into practice. As you engage with the writing assignments in Part III and use the stages of the writing process to develop an essay within a particular writing context, you will want to turn back to Part II for guidance.

Part II gives you a set of strategies for critical reading, thinking, and writing, strategies that take you through the writing process as you build your response to a writing topic. As you work through the units in Part III, turn back to these basic strategies because they will help you complete those assignments. Here is a list of the basic strategies you will learn in Part II:

- techniques for doing a thoughtful reading of an essay
- a diagram of an academic essay's structure
- strategies for developing your ideas on a subject
- guidelines for responding to a writing topic
- suggestions for writing the introduction and a well-developed thesis statement
- a basic structure for writing supporting paragraphs
- a rubric for evaluating student essays

Steps for a Thoughtful Reading of an Essay

With an Example

In our everyday lives, we read on a daily basis. We live in a literate society, so we read things like signs, emails, and menus without much effort and without thinking about them very much. In an academic setting, however, reading becomes an activity that requires effort and thought.

In order to respond appropriately to a reading selection, you will have to spend some time rereading, identifying, and analyzing the reading selection's argument and supporting evidence. Here are some guidelines to help you develop sound strategies for understanding what you read. You will need to analyze any reading selection before you can discuss its argument and respond with an argument of your own.

When you follow the steps below, your reading will become focused and productive.

1. **Read the title of the reading selection.**

   The title will tell you something about the main topic of the reading. It may also tell you something about the writer's opinion on the topic. Think about what you already know about the topic and what else you want to know before you will be ready to write an essay that presents your informed opinion about it.

2. **Learn about the author.**

   If the reading selection contains information about the writer, take note of how the writer's life or work might connect with the topic of the reading. The writer's experience with the topic might indicate his or her reliability or knowledge regarding the topic of the selection.

3. **Read through the selection once quickly.**

   This first time you read the selection, read it right through so that you get a general impression of what it is about and what the writer's attitude is toward the topic. Notice the things—people, places, experiences, concepts, for example—that the writer brings up to develop and support his or her opinion about the topic.

4. **Read again to identify the thesis.**

   Read the selection a second time, but more slowly and carefully, and with a pen or highlighter in your hand. Find the thesis and underline it. Remember, the thesis states the author's overall opinion on the topic of the reading. Often, the thesis is contained in a single sentence, but, in some cases, it takes several sentences to make the main argument of the reading selection clear. There are times, too, when the author does not state his or her thesis explicitly, but, if you read the selection carefully, you should be able to state it and then write it in the margin. The thesis is often found in the last line of the introduction, but it can also come in the middle or even the end of an essay. To help, ask yourself, "What does this author seem to want readers to think about his or her topic?"

5. **Read slowly and methodically through the rest of the material.**

   Now find and underline the evidence that the writer uses to support his or her thesis. Look carefully at each body paragraph one at a time. Often, each paragraph develops a single idea that the writer brings up because it supports his or her thesis. Look in each body paragraph for a *topic sentence*—a sentence that both presents an idea and tells how it gives support to the reading's overall opinion. As you read and study the selection, be sure to write down any thoughts you have about the writer's opinion and supporting evidence. It is your job to evaluate this evidence for its logic and validity, so be sure to make notes in the margins as you read. Mark the points that you found interesting or convincing and a few words explaining your thoughts. Note, too, any weaknesses you found. When you look back at the notes you made in the selection's margins, you should have a general idea of how convincing you found the reading and what you found to be its strengths and weaknesses.

6. Read again for review.

Once you have thought through the reading selection, read it once more, looking for places where you don't quite understand what is being said. Underline any terms that you aren't familiar with, and look them up in a dictionary. Mark any places in the reading that don't fit with your understanding of the reading as a whole. Decide whether this is something the author should have revised, or whether it is something that you need to read again because you don't understand it. You may find that you need to go back to Step 4 and begin working through the reading again. Once you are certain that you understand the entire selection, you are prepared to discuss, summarize, and/or respond to the reading with your own essay.

Now use the six steps for a thoughtful reading of an essay to uncover the argument and supporting evidence of the following essay.

Sibling Rivalry

Essay

KELSEY O'NEILL

Kelsey O'Neill is a college student majoring in business. She was a high school honors student and gave the graduation speech for her senior class. The following essay is based on that speech.

Whether your generation grew up watching *The Simpsons* (when Lisa was the perfect child and Bart was the troublemaker) or the *The Brady Bunch* (when Cindy would always get her way and Peter would be blamed for mischief), you are aware of favoritism. This feeling is evident when you reflect on who in your family got the prime seat on the couch, who got the best room in the house, and who would get ice cream for dessert even though they didn't finish all their dinner.

No parent will admit to it. However, studies show that 70% of mothers and fathers exhibit a preference for a single child. Fathers gravitate toward their youngest daughter, while mothers connect with their oldest son. Parents are also inclined to prefer the oldest child. In the business sense, older children are seen as "sunk costs" and a product further down the assembly line—with more time, resources, and effort invested into their development. We inevitably walk down the store aisles and come across birthday cards to give to our brother that advertise the idea that "mom liked me better" or "I'm the favorite." If this idea of favoritism weren't true, then Hallmark wouldn't have developed an entire product line on that exact premise. Even though we won't get a direct answer if we ask our parents who they like better, siblings know, and parents know, who the "golden child" is. However, even with parental favoritism and the inevitable rivalry that results, siblings have proven to be valuable to one another in teaching a multitude of life lessons.

In every language, in every country across the world, families have siblings that pester each other every minute of every day. That is just the nature of the relationship. We would be foolish to think that brothers and sisters will get along 100%, all the time, with no quarrels. In fact, sibling rivalry has been a part of some of our oldest texts. One of the first stories in the Bible talks of a rivalry between two brothers, Cain and Abel. Cain is the older sibling who repeatedly asks his parents, "Am I my brother's keeper?" Unfortunately, since nothing is done about this rivalry, the story ends with the tragic death of Abel, who is killed by his brother out of aggravation. But some siblings absolutely get along better than others, even when they compete. Take, for example, President George W. Bush and Governor Jeb Bush, who have been trying to outdo each other since they

(continued)

were old enough to talk. Jeb was supposed to be the more studious of the two, the one who was expected to bring the family business to success. Both sons have undoubtedly been trying to win the attention and admiration of their famous parents, much like the Kennedy family with Joe Jr. and John F. Kennedy. Even as recently as this summer, the royal wedding would not have been complete without subtle sister comparisons, when Kate Middleton, the bride, was a bit upstaged by her younger sister Pippa because the cameras and media couldn't stop photographing her and talking about her. And within the royal family, there have been clear tensions. For instance, Prince William and Prince Henry are both royal by blood, but Prince William gets to become king simply because he is the eldest. Similarly, Michael Jackson and Janet Jackson were both famous. However, Michael was more famous and rose to superstardom.

Taking a closer look at the actual structure of sibling relationships, we can draw a few conclusions. The closer in age, the closer the relationship; however, if the siblings are the same gender, there is more conflict. In general, girls are the authorities in the domestic setting. Sisters have proven to have the closest relationships, whereas brothers have the most rivalry. For brothers, it is more natural even from the beginning to compare their accomplishments, such as who walked first or spoke first. Carrying on into their adult life, they compare things like who is the better athlete, who went to the better college, or who has the best job. Siblings are a dress rehearsal for our lives; they are there for the entire ride.

But there are also instances where siblings worked together and benefitted from each other. For example, Wilbur and Orville Wright created an airplane—the first machine of its kind that was able to fly a human being. Venus and Serena Williams are tennis superstars who had to practice long hours together to achieve the status they have today. The Olsen twins were together in TV shows when they were younger, and more recently, they have established a business franchise and are known as billion dollar teens. They are ranked #48 on the list of 100 highest paid celebrities, and they landed on the list of richest people under age 40, according to *Fortune Magazine* ("40 Under 40"). Now try telling me that those sisters don't work well together. When siblings can put aside the constant bickering they endured when they were younger, they can influence society and make great contributions. Brothers and sisters actually spend more time together than they do with their parents.

Because parents leave our lives too early and spouses come too late, social skills are gained from our brothers and sisters more than anyone else in life. People may be surprised to know that 65% of teens reported feeling close to a sibling. In another study with the elderly, exactly 65% also said they felt "close" or "extremely close" to their siblings (Cicirelli 46). This proves once again the timeless bond that siblings create from a young age.

If rivalry is handled well, it doesn't have to be a problem, and can teach children valuable life lessons. Sharing, cooperating, and compromising are all gained from this experience. Is sibling rivalry really so bad? Think about it. In our society, it could be an advantage. We compete for school, recognition, jobs, awards, friendship, and relationships. Younger siblings learn more charismatic skills and charm in order to get what they want. This is known as the "low power strategy" since the youngest child is the most vulnerable and needs the most care. This is the way for them to get attention and resources in a large family. One study at the University of Southern California found that children who were born second were friendlier, more playful, and more sociable as judged by their elementary school teachers. Conversely, older siblings learn empathy and patience from caring for and nurturing a younger sibling. Shockingly, a study declared that siblings have a greater influence on how we develop as a person than parents do.

In fact, Jeffrey Kluger, the author of *The Sibling Effect* and senior writer for *Time Magazine*, associated the influence of parents as providing a broad stroke of values and morals. He compared it to the likes of a hospital, with the parents as doctors doing Grand Rounds and checking briefly on all their patients, while the nurses work 24/7 on the ward, similar to the influence of the siblings. In other words, siblings do exert a great deal of effect on the person we become.

Parents must understand the cause of sibling rivalry in order to minimize its potentially negative effects. Older children begin to feel threatened by a new baby, since the introduction of him or her will deflect all the parent's love, acknowledgement, and attention from the older sibling. If the parents portray their newborn as beneficial to the other siblings, comparing the older siblings to a teacher for the newborn and giving them praise for helping their younger sibling learn to crawl, play, or cooperate, siblings are sure to grow up with a strong and healthy relationship.

The lasting effects of having a sibling have proven throughout history to advance social skills in preparation for the "real world." Exposure to this hearty competition allows for the maintenance of friendships, expression of feelings, management of conflict, and negotiation of solutions in early stages that will continue for a lifetime. As parents age and young siblings enter adulthood, they must interact and rely on each other once more, assuming the similar positions they had carried in their earlier years. As Jane Leder said, "Our siblings push buttons that cast us in roles we felt sure we had let go of long ago—the baby, the peacekeeper, the caretaker, the avoider. . . . It doesn't seem to matter how much time has elapsed or how far we've traveled."

Works Cited

Cicirelli, V. G. *Sibling Relationships Across the Life Span*. New York: Plenum Press, 1995. Print.

"40 Under 40." *CNNMoney*. Cable News Network, 17 Oct. 2012. Web. 30 May 2012 <http://money.cnn.com/gallery/magazines/fortune/2012/10/11/40-Under-40.fortune/index.html>.

Kluger, Jeffrey. "Why Mom Liked You Best: The Science of Favoritism." *Time Magazine* 14 Nov. 2011: n. pag. Print.

Leder, Jane Mersky. Web. 30 May 2012. <http://www.searchquotes.com/quotes/author/Jane_Mersky_Leder/.>

Writing Topic

According to Kelsey O'Neill, how does sibling rivalry effectively prepare children for adult life? Do you think her positive assessment of the effects of sibling rivalry is accurate? You can support your answer by using personal examples, your own observations, and evidence from this essay as well as other readings and materials.

Follow-Up Activity

For Discussion

1. Share with the class what you identified as the thesis of this reading selection. Then read aloud the paragraph that contains it.

   Tell everyone one comment you wrote in the reading's margin and explain what in the reading led to your comment.

   Identify at least two pieces of supporting evidence for the thesis of this reading. How strong are they as support? Did they help convince you that this writer's argument makes sense? Explain.

2. Prepare and present to the class a story about one time when you and a brother or sister interacted in a way that was memorable. If you don't have a sibling, tell a story about a memory you have related to being an only child. Be sure that your presentation includes an explanation of why you chose the story you told. In other words, tell the class what was important about the experience.

3. Use the six steps for a thoughtful reading that you learned above to analyze "Sibling Rivalry." Then make a list of the reading's strengths and weaknesses. Share your lists with the class and discuss the group's overall evaluation of "Sibling Rivalry."

Strategies to Help You Analyze a Reading Selection and Develop Your Ideas for Writing a Response

Students often say that they know *how* to write an essay—that is, they know they need to write an introduction, a thesis, the body of the essay, and a conclusion—but they don't know what to write *about*—that is, they think they have no ideas to put into the essay. In fact, students have many ideas about the topic; they just need a few techniques for accessing and clarifying their ideas.

Questioning

You will have already taken the first step toward writing your essay when you did a careful reading of the reading selection and the writing topic. Looking back at your annotations is a good way to remind yourself about things in the essay you thought were important. Now you need to enter the *question phase* of your prewriting. At this point, you can ask yourself several kinds of questions:

- Questions about the highlighting:
  - Why did I highlight/underline this part of the essay?
  - How is this information important to the author's point?
  - What is the relationship between this information and the question I am being asked to write about?

- Questions about your comprehension of the reading, such as:
  - What things in this essay do not make sense to me?
  - Where do I think the author should have explained further?
  - How do the examples in the essay relate to the author's point?

- Questions about the author's ideas, such as:
  - What are some of the things that the author says that I am happy to hear someone say?
  - What things that the author says seem true to me?
  - What things that the author says seem wrong to me?
  - What thing that the author says is most important to me?
  - What idea in this essay is completely new to me?

These strategies will prompt you to analyze the ideas in a reading and form your own viewpoint. Try them out now on the essay "Sibling Rivalry" above. The answers to these questions will help you understand your own thoughts about the topic of the reading and help you see how you want to respond to the writing topic.

In addition to using questions like the ones listed above to analyze, there are several other kinds of prewriting strategies you can use. Here are two of them. Use them to decide how you would respond to the writing topic that follows "Sibling Rivalry."

Freewriting

A further step in the prewriting process that you may want to take is *freewriting*. After having answered for yourself a number of the questions about the reading and question, you still may be having trouble expanding on your initial reaction to the author's position on the topic. Pick one or more of your answers to the questions you have already answered, and just begin to write about it. While you are doing this writing, do not stop or censor yourself; just let the words come. Do this for about five or ten minutes without thinking about spelling, grammar, word choice, or even the sense of what you are saying. When you have completed this activity, you will want to take a break.

After your brief break, come back and read what you have written. Most of what you now have down on paper will not end up in your essay, but, as you read through your freewriting, you will find one or more sentences or ideas that seem interesting, important, or even compelling to you. Highlight these points and ideas.

Listing

Next, you may decide to make a list of the points that you highlighted in your freewriting. *Listing* is another technique for finding the ideas you want to write about. Be sure to list all the items from your freewriting that you thought were interesting. As you make this list, other ideas may come to you. Put them on your list as well.

Study your list. Connect with some kind of mark all the ideas that seem related to each other. When you are done, one related group of ideas will probably be longer than the others. This group should provide insight into a topic for your paper.

Follow-Up Activity

Questions for Discussion

1. Use questioning, freewriting, and listing to analyze "Sibling Rivalry" and develop some ideas of your own about the subject of sibling relationships.

2. You have used several prewriting strategies to understand "Sibling Rivalry," and you have developed some of your own ideas about sibling relationships. Now that you have followed these steps, make a list of ideas that you could use if you were to write an essay that responds to the writing topic that follows "Sibling Rivalry."

3. Share with the class your list of things you could talk about in your essay, and invite classmates to give you feedback.

Prewriting strategies such as annotation, freewriting, and listing are important steps in the writing process because they lead you to form an argument of your own. Without going through this stage in the writing process, you may respond to a writing topic using only summary and paraphrase. In other words, you may only be able to repeat the ideas of the reading selection's writer rather than develop your own ideas. The ability to summarize or paraphrase another's ideas will be important when you are asked to demonstrate that you understand what you have read. But when you are asked to write an argument, mere summary or paraphrase will not be enough. You will have to bring your own voice and ideas to develop an argument of your own.

Study carefully the following pages on summary, paraphrase, and analysis. Practice these techniques so that you can distinguish each from the others and can use them with confidence when reading and responding to the reading selections in Part III.

Summary and Paraphrase

A **summary** presents a short version of another writer's ideas. Its purpose is to convey a sense of the main points of the other writer's argument. A summary might condenses a few paragraphs into one or two sentences, or several pages into one or two paragraphs.

When you summarize:

1. use *only* your own words and cite the source

Example:

Original

> "London, one of the world's greatest cities, is the center of the thriving English mystery world. Beginning with Charles Dickens and Wilkie Collins, who lived and worked in London, and including Edgar Allan Poe, who attended school there, nearly every mystery writer worth his or her salt has set at least one tale against a London backdrop. Even so American a writer as Robert Parker, in his *The Judas Goat*, took Spenser across the Atlantic to pursue his quarry in London. Because of the richness of its mystery associations, modern London is a mystery reader's mecca, filled with the real sights and sounds that give the stories their authentic atmosphere."
>
> Barbara Hendershott, *Mystery Reader's Walking Guide: London*

Summary

> Because London is the perfect setting for many well-known mystery novels, people who enjoy reading mysteries will find it an exciting and interesting city to visit (Hendershott 13).

Unacceptable Summary or Plagiarism:

> London is the center of the English mystery world and therefore it is a mecca for all mystery readers (Hendershott 13).

Use your own words: notice that none of the words and phrases that are copied from the original are in quotation marks, but they should be because they are lifted directly from the original source. When summarizing, avoid lifting language from the original.

2. do not give background information

Example:

Original

> "Work through each exercise carefully and methodically, and the result will be an insightful and well-written essay."
>
> Linda Strahan and Kathleen Moore, *Write It Review*

Summary

> According to Strahan and Moore, doing the exercises helps students write good essays (32).

3. do not give details

Example:

Original

> "It does not signify that man is a sparse, inhuman thing at his center. He is all right. It only says what we've always known and never had enough time to worry about, that we haven't yet learned to stay human when assembled in masses."
>
> Lewis Thomas, "The Iks"

Summary

Individuals, though basically good, behave badly in groups (Thomas page 33).

4. do not give examples

Example:

Original

"The time has come for a respect, a reverence, not just for all human beings, but for all life forms—as we would have respect for a masterpiece of sculpture or an exquisitely tooled machine."

Carl Sagan, *The Cosmic Connection*

Summary

Sagan believes that, today, all life should be valued (Sagan page 33).

Follow-Up Activity

Look at the following passage. Read it carefully, and then write your summary of it on the lines below. Don't forget to locate the essay in this book so that, along with the author's last name, you can give the page number where the quotation appears.

Original

"Sykes explains to me that a bit of DNA called mtDNA is key to his investigations. A circular band of genes residing separately from twenty-three chromosomes of the double helix, mtDNA is passed down solely through the maternal line. Sykes used mtDNA to discover something astounding."

David Ewing Duncan, *"DNA as Destiny"*

Summary

_____

_____

_____

_____

A **paraphrase** puts someone else's ideas into your own words. Writers use paraphrase when another writer's ideas are important to help support or explain a concept or argument, but the exact words of the other writer need simplification for the audience or are not particularly noteworthy. A **paraphrase** is a restatement of something you have read.

When you paraphrase:

1. you cite the source

Example:

Original

> "Work through each exercise carefully and methodically, and the result will be an insightful and well-written essay."
>
> Linda Strahan and Kathleen Moore, *Write It Review*

Paraphrase

> Do all the prewriting activities to the best of your abilities, and your final essay will be thoughtful and have good sentences and paragraphs (Strahan and Moore 32).

2. you choose your own words and sentence structure

Example:

Original

> "It does not signify that man is a sparse, inhuman thing at his center. He is all right. It only says what we've always known and never had enough time to worry about, that we haven't yet learned to stay human when assembled in masses."
>
> Lewis Thomas, "The Iks"

Paraphrase

> It doesn't mean that people are unfeeling and heartless. They are basically fine. It just reminds us of something that we so far ignored. When people are in groups, they do things they wouldn't do on their own (Thomas page 33).

3. you do not change the length of the material being paraphrased

Example:

Original

> "The time has come for a respect, a reverence, not just for all human beings, but for all life forms—as we would have respect for a masterpiece of sculpture or an exquisitely tooled machine."
>
> Carl Sagan, *The Cosmic Connection*

Paraphrase

> Now is the time for us to begin to show appreciation for all living things. We should admire them the same way we would a work of art or value them just as we do technologies (Sagan page 33).

4. you are truthful to the meaning of the original

Example:

Original

> "People who have developed a firm faith, grounded in understanding and rooted in daily practice, are in general, much better at coping with adversity than those who have not."
>
> Dalai Lama, "The Role of Religion in Modern Society"

Paraphrase

> Those who have religious beliefs that they practice every day can handle life's challenges and setbacks better than those who have no faith (Dalai Lama 113).

Follow-Up Activity

Look at the following passage. Read it carefully, and then paraphrase it on the lines below. Share and compare your version of the passage with that of a classmate. The two versions should say that same thing, but they will not be identical in word choices or sentence structure. Don't forget to locate the essay in this book so that, along with the author's last name, you can give the page number where the quotation appears.

Original
"Sykes explains to me that a bit of DNA called mtDNA is key to his investigations. A circular band of genes residing separately from twenty-three chromosomes of the double helix, mtDNA is passed down solely through the maternal line. Sykes used mtDNA to discover something astounding"

David Ewing Duncan *"DNA as Destiny"*

Paraphrase

_____

_____

_____

_____

_____

_____

Analysis

Once you have worked with a reading to the point where you understand *what* the author is saying and can represent the author's ideas by explaining them in a short summary or by paraphrasing them in your own words, you are ready to look more closely at *how* the author presents his or her ideas to the reader. This stage of the reading process is called **analysis**. To analyze a text, you must break it down into its parts and see how these parts fit together. When you understand the way the parts relate to each other and to the author's argument as a whole, you are able to *interpret* the text and will have an in-depth understanding of what you have read.

Here are some characteristics of the writing you will want to examine to help gain this deep understanding of the text. You will want to ask yourself questions about the following areas:

Attitude

- How does the author feel about the subject?
- Are the author's feelings personal or objective?

Voice

- What role (friend? teacher? judge?) is the author taking in terms of the relationship to his or her audience?
- Does the author seem to expect the audience to agree or to disagree with his or her argument, and how does the author modify the presentation of the argument to adapt to the readers' position?

Development

- What kinds of evidence (facts? examples? definitions? reasons?) does the author use to support his or her argument?
- How is the type of evidence relevant to the argument?

Purpose

- If the essay appears to be an objective presentation of findings, why does the author think it is important to share the findings?
- If the author appears to be arguing his or her opinion, what change would he or she like to have take place?

Follow-Up Activity

1. Write definitions for summary, paraphrase, and analysis. Read your definitions to a classmate and revise them so that they are clear and complete.
2. Review what you have learned so far in Part II. Make notes about the main ideas and explain all key terms. Then tell why you think they are important to successful writing. Share your notes with the class.

So far in Part II, you have practiced some strategies for careful reading and have learned some ways to develop your ideas when you are asked to respond to a writing topic. Now you will learn how to present your ideas in a way that will help readers to understand your argument and follow your logic so that they will be convinced by what you write.

Study the diagram of an academic essay found on the next page. Notice that each part has a specific job to do in an essay.

A Suggested Structure for an Essay
That Responds to Another Writer's Essay

The structure of a thesis-centered essay is established by convention. That is, the thesis essay format has an introduction that contains the thesis statement, followed by body paragraphs that support it, and ending with a conclusion that gives closure to the essay.

An Introduction That Contains

an introductory sentence
   that gives the reading selection's
   title, author, and subject

-a summary of the reading selection
   that includes an answer
   to the writing topic question

-your **THESIS STATEMENT**

Body Paragraphs That Include

-a topic sentence that gives
   the paragraph's central
   point, one that supports the thesis

- sentences that tell more about the
   topic

-evidence that supports the topic
   sentence

-a discussion of how and why the
   evidence ties to the thesis

A Conclusion That

-in a few sentences, reinforces
   your thesis and gives a sense
   of closure to your essay

Follow-Up Activity

Questions for Discussion

1. Tell, in your own words, what things are usually included in an introduction.
2. From studying the above diagram, what do you see as the goal of the body of an essay?
3. What are some of the ways a concluding paragraph can differ from other paragraphs in an essay?

Read the following selection and notice the bracketed annotations. These annotations identify Allan Von Niks's thesis statement, and they track a few of the elements that he includes in his body paragraphs to support his thesis. Pay careful attention to the connections between the diagram above and the annotations in Von Nik's essay, including his use of examples and other evidence to support his argument.

Use the six steps you learned for a thoughtful reading, and add your annotations to those already given.

Television: The Great Unifier

Essay

ALLAN VON NIKS

American critics love to blame technology for all of our social, economic, and familial problems; the technology that is the favorite scapegoat today is television. If you believe these critics, television is responsible for every American problem from illiteracy to juvenile delinquency, from our national economic decline to voter apathy, from obesity to violence. According to these television pundits, TV is like a national drug, a narcotic, a vast mindless wasteland, an evil disease infecting Americans. For example, Walter Shapiro, media critic for Time magazine, criticizes "the insidious ways in which prime-time TV distorts America's sense of itself." Michael Ventura goes even further in his attack, arguing that TV is at the heart of what he sees as an escapist American people's growing alienation from reality: "Media is not experience. In its most common form, media substitutes a fantasy of experience [. . .] for the living fact. But in our culture the absorption of media has become a substitute for experience."

Pundits such as Shapiro and Ventura, in addition to absurdly overstating their case, fail to realize that they are blaming the messenger for the sins of the message writers. What I mean by this is that television is only a tool like any other tool. It is not an evil force any more than fire, the wheel, or the lever. Tools are good or bad depending on how we make use of them. The question with TV is whether or not we are using this powerful tool positively and productively. While many critics want us to believe that we are a society of TV junkies, needing our daily fix of a destructive drug, we are in fact using television in a largely positive way in our society. While much of what is on TV is obviously either empty-headed or pure rubbish, what the critics ignore is that TV, with all of its faults, serves an essential function for our culturally and ethnically diverse society; television is the great unifier. **(THESIS STATEMENT)**

America is a unique spot with unique needs; our revolutionary experiment in diversity demands some sort of balancing force of unification. **(TOPIC SENTENCE)** We,

(Continued)

as a nation, are made up of people who have come here speaking different languages, thinking different thoughts, holding different beliefs, and possessing different cultural values. **[MORE ABOUT THE TOPIC]** In America's early history, the majority of immigrants, excluding African slaves, came from Europe. Today, most of our new immigrants come from Asia and Latin America. **[EVIDENCE THAT SUPPORTS THE TOPIC]** With this change, America's diversity is now growing at a greater pace than ever before. **[MORE ABOUT THE TOPIC]** Few other countries have ever attempted this experiment in national diversity, and none of those that made the attempt have succeeded. How then can we keep so many different people from so many different cultures together as one harmonious people? How can we prevent racial violence and social anarchy from occurring as the natural results of our ethnic, cultural, and religious diversity? The answer t5o these questions may just lie with television. **[PARAGRAPH AS A WHOLE GIVES BACKGROUND INFORMATION THAT EXPLAINS MORE ABOUT AMERICA'S DIVERSITY]**

The primary way that TV unifies us is by acting as the first teacher and social unifier for almost all American children and new immigrants. **[TOPIC SENTENCE]** Because of our extreme cultural diversity, we cannot expect the US to stay united without the cohesive force of a common language, namely English. **[MORE ABOUT THE TOPIC]** TV teaches English to non-native speakers in a fairly easy, painless, and inexpensive way, thereby beginning their process of "Americanization." TV also teaches the essential liberal difference that allows for peaceful coexistence in our nation. A good example of a TV program that teaches this essential value is *Sesame Street*, a staple in the life of the typical pre-school age child. **[EVIDENCE THAT SUPPORTS THE TOPIC]** *Sesame Street*'s primary didactic lesson to children is to accept difference and cooperate with others. In *Sesame Street*'s ideal world, Africans, Asians, Latinos, Caucasians, Birds, Monsters, and even Grouches all tolerate, respect, and even like each other. This kind of positive social message is not only found in a quality show like *Sesame Street*, even the average sitcom or TV talk show, such as *Home Improvement* or *Oprah*, tries to teach moral lessons essential to maintaining a harmonious multicultural society. **[EXPLANATION OF HOW THE EVIDENCE SUPPORTS THE THESIS STATEMENT]**

TV not only teaches essential skills and values needed to unite our society, but it also provides our society with common stories and myths. TV truly has become the common moral "book" of our time, replacing the Bible, which served this purpose earlier in our history. I don't mean to say that it is better or more moral than the Bible; I simply mean that more people watch TV today than read the Bible. Today, the stories that we all know and can discuss come not from the Bible—they come from television. If you were to ask strangers on the street about Jonah or Kind David, they would probably think you were insane or some kind of religious fanatic. But if you were to ask strangers what they thought of the Super Bowl, what happened on the last episode of *Friends*, who killed Jon Benet Ramsey, whether O.J. Simpson was innocent or guilty, or whether they preferred *The Brady Bunch* or *I Love Lucy*, then you might just start up a conversation. All cultures need common stories to bind their people into a nation; our common stories now come from TV.

So, the next time you hear some critic blaming television for all of America's problems, remember all of the positive things that TV does for us. Television may have its flaws, but it still remains an essential unifying force, and perhaps the essential unifying force, for American Society.

"Television: The Great Unifier" by Allan Von Niks. Reprinted by permission.

Writing Topic

According to Von Niks, in what ways does television unify American society? Do you think he is correct? Relying on your own experience, observations, or readings, support your view.

Follow-Up Activity

1. Why does Von Niks call television a tool? Explain why he labels TV in this way.

2. How does television encourage person-to-person interaction in our society, according to Von Niks? Give any examples you can think of from your own experience that demonstrate television's role in shaping the way we talk to each other.

3. Explain how Von Niks uses a well-known television show to demonstrate TV's ability to unite very different groups of people. Choose a TV show that you and your peers watch. Do you think it functions in the way that Von Niks claims *Sesame Street* or *Oprah* function? Explain.

4. Why does Von Niks claim that, in some important ways, TV has replaced the Bible? Why does he claim that "all cultures need common stories to bind their people into a nation"?

5. Prepare and then give a three-minute presentation to the class or a partner on the future use of television, *if you were put in charge.*

Writing an Introduction to an Argument Essay

The introduction is often the hardest part of an essay to draft, but if you carefully consider the requirements of an introduction in an argument essay, especially in response to the writing topic, an introduction can also help you focus the rest of your essay.

The paper's opening creates a first impression for the readers. In addition to answering the question, it needs to do three things:

- capture readers' attention
- set the context for the paper's argument
- present the thesis statement of the essay

The first two of these things can be done in the context of answering the question, but the thesis, which is customarily but not always the last sentence of the introduction, has to follow the *directed summary* organically. That is, it must be an extension of the argument already presented. It must be the direct response of your own to that argument and show that you fully understand the author's argument. By including the thesis statement at the end of the introduction, you will ensure that readers understand the paper's purpose from the outset.

When you write your introduction, follow these steps:

- Introduce the reading selection by giving its title and the name of its author.
- Include a directed summary of the reading selection (see next section).
- Present the thesis statement.

Be careful to avoid these missteps:

- a flat, uninteresting explanation of your plan for the essay (e.g., "*This essay will discuss. . . .*")
- use of a cliché to open or close the introduction (e.g., "*It is true that love is blind.*")
- use of meaningless platitudes (e.g., "*Tomorrow will be a brighter day.*")
- use of sweeping or overly broad statements (e.g., "*Since the beginning of time, people have wanted peace.*")

Guidelines for Writing a Directed Summary

Often when students are asked to answer a question about something they have read, their answer will require a brief summary of a particular part of the reading's argument. This kind of question, known as an interrogative sentence, is easy to identify because it will usually begin with one of the interrogative pronouns, *who, which, whom, whose,* or *what,* or another question word, such as *how, where, when,* or *why.* Students' first prewriting task is to identify the particular question or questions being asked and to isolate within the text all the material that answers that particular question or questions. While using *Write It .5,* you might find it helpful to circle all of the question words in the writing topic, and then go back to the reading selection and highlight sentences that respond directly to the question or questions being asked.

For example: Imagine that you had just read the story "Goldilocks and the Three Bears" and were asked the question "*Why* did Goldilocks go into the cabin in the woods and use things that belonged to the bears?" You would have to go back to the story to find out *why* she sat on the bears' furniture, ate their food, and slept in their beds. It would not be enough to isolate her actions and tell *what* she did because the question does not ask *what*; it asks *why.* You would need to explain the reasons for her actions in order to answer the question *why.* The story describes Goldilocks's physical state before each action; she was *tired, hungry, and sleepy.* In order to write a *directed summary* that responds to a specific question, it is necessary to answer the proper question. In your summary of "Goldilocks," you would write primarily about her physical state of being because her fatigue, hunger, and sleepiness cause her to use the bears' chairs, eat their food, and sleep in their beds.

Once you have read the writing topic, underlined the question word or words, and examined the reading selection to locate the answer to the specific question or questions, draft your answer using certain guidelines:

1. In or near the opening sentence, include the title of the essay in quotation marks.

2. Early in your summary paragraph, identify the author of the essay. The first time the author is mentioned, use his or her full name. In subsequent referrals to the author, use only the last name.

You should also avoid including any of the following in a *directed summary*:

1. minor details or points that are irrelevant to the question

2. your own opinion or ideas

3. examples of your own, and unless particularly helpful, those of the author

Advice on Writing a Thesis Statement

The thesis statement is an important part of an argument essay because it gives the writer's point of view or opinion on the subject of an essay. The paragraphs that follow the thesis statement serve to develop and support the thesis statement's point of view, so the thesis statement also unifies the essay. Any writer usually does extensive thinking and prewriting before he or she is ready to draft a thesis statement.

When writing in response to a particular writing assignment, you must be careful to follow the requirements of the assignment. All of the lead unit essays in Part III of this book are followed by a writing assignment, called a "writing topic." These writing topics have a similar structure. You will see that each of them has, in some form, three parts. The first part asks you to summarize the reading selection's point of view on an aspect covered in the reading; the second part asks, usually using different terms, whether you agree with that point of view; and the third part asks you to support your point of view, that is, whether you agree or not, with specific evidence. To respond successfully to any of these writing topics, you will have to determine:

- the subject of the reading selection that is the focus of the writing topic
- the point of view on that subject taken by the author of the reading selection
- your point of view on that subject

Before you begin to construct your thesis, answer the following questions:

- What is the subject asked about in the writing topic?
- What is the opinion of the reading selection's writer about the subject?
- What is my opinion about the subject, and does it agree or disagree with the reading selection writer's opinion?

The writing topics in Part III are challenging because they ask you to deal with several elements in order to write a strong essay that responds to all of the parts of these writing topics. The thesis statements you write as you respond to these various writing topics will be complex but very important because they will have two jobs: one, to satisfy the requirements of the writing topics, and two, to unify your essays using statements that give your overarching point of view or opinion about particular subjects. Here are some guidelines:

- Sometimes students feel a bit overwhelmed by the challenge of writing a strong thesis statement, and they are led to write a thesis statement that merely says "I agree with her views," or "I disagree with him." This will not be enough for a strong thesis. A thesis statement will have to respond fully to the second part of the writing topic. In other words, it will have to state the reading selection writer's opinion about a specific subject, state whether you agree with that opinion, and present a clear opinion of your own on the subject.
- Remember that, even when you want to agree with the reading selection author's opinion, it is best to state your opinion *in your own words*. You can write a thesis statement that responds to the writing topic but avoids simply saying that you agree or disagree if you let your point of view suggest, by the way you phrase it, whether or not you agree with the selection's author.
- Here are some sample sentence patterns that show you how to write a thesis statement that shows whether you agree or disagree without actually using those terms.

Sample Patterns Signaling Agreement:

- As author X correctly states,. . . .
- It is true that. . . .
- I'm convinced that. . . .
- Like author X, I think. . . .
- X's message is important because. . . .

- X's argument that . . . is true/correct.
- My point of view on subjectY, like author X's, is. . . .

Sample Patterns Signaling Disagreement:

- Unlike author X, who claims. . . . , I think. . . ."
- Although author X argues that . . . , actually. . . ."
- Author X's opinion is. . . , but actually. . . ."
- My point of view on subject Y is rather. . . ."
- Author X says that . . . ,but I think. . . ."

Follow-Up Activity

Draft an introductory paragraph that responds to one of the writing topics for the two essays that you read earlier in Part II, "Sibling Rivalry" or "The Flight from Conversation." To do this, follow these steps:

1. Look back at the work you have already done in earlier pages to analyze the essay and develop your ideas about its subject.

2. Study the writing topic and underline the question words.

3. Look for the answer to the first part of the writing topic, the question that asks for a summary of the author's opinion on a specific subject.

4. Draft your summary of that opinion.

5. Decide what your opinion on the subject is and determine whether it agrees with the reading selection author's opinion.

6. Draft Your thesis statement using the guidelines just above this follow-up activity.

7. Now put it all together to create an introductory paragraph: introduce the title and author of the reading selection; follow that opening with the summary you wrote in response to the first part of the writing topic; and, finally, present your thesis statement.

8. Exchange your paragraph with a classmate. Read one another's paragraphs and discuss the strengths and weaknesses of each. If there is time, rewrite your paragraph so that it is stronger.

Developing Body Paragraphs for an Essay That Presents a Thesis

Body paragraphs make up the largest part of an essay. The job of each body paragraph is to develop one point that supports the thesis statement. Taken together, these points constitute the argument of the essay. Writing a good body paragraph can be easy once you understand the criteria that the body paragraph must fulfill. Here are the three most important criteria for paragraphs in an argumentative essay:

1. an appropriate or suitable topic
2. evidence (fact, example, and/or idea)
3. a link to the thesis

Appropriate or Suitable Topic

First, write a topic sentence that states the point you wish to make in this paragraph. The point must be on topic; that is, it must introduce an argument that is relevant to the claim you make in your thesis.

Evidence

The major part of the paragraph will be devoted to evidence. Most often in your essays, that evidence will be an example, but specific facts, quotations, and ideas can also help support the topic sentence of your paragraph. You must be careful to choose a clear example, one that clearly demonstrates the point of the paragraph. Then you must explain the example with details.

Link to the Thesis

After you have given all the evidence and supplied all the details that support the topic sentence of the paragraph, you must show the way this evidence links back to the thesis of your essay. It is not enough to just provide an example. You have to tell the reader the reason this particular example connects to the main argument of your essay.

Here is an example:
Thesis:

Speaking a language at home that differs from standard spoken English can be a valuable resource for members of a family.

Appropriate Topic:
Write a sentence stating the point you wish to make in this paragraph:

The feeling of intimacy given by the use of a "family" language can be a source of comfort in times of stress.

Evidence:
Write an example that provides support for the point being made in the paragraph:

Last year my grandmother back in Vietnam was very ill. The doctors said she needed an operation, so she went to the hospital. There was nothing my family could do to help her from so far away. We just had to wait to hear news. My mother told me to go to school. It would be a while until the phone call came telling us whether my grandmother was alive or not. My friends and teachers at school gave me their well wishes all day, but their voices were like sandpaper rubbing my heart. When I got home, there was still no word from overseas. My mother spoke to me in the dialect of her village, grandmother's home, telling me not to worry. The sound of these words calmed me, and I felt comforted.

Link to Thesis:
Write a sentence or more that explains the way this example connects to the thesis of your essay:

Her use of our family language was important to me at this time. It told me that she shared and understood my worries the way no one outside the family could. Hearing Vietnamese spoken when I was stressed gave me comfort and made me feel connected to my grandmother. Our special language is a resource my family is lucky to have.

Follow-Up Activity

1. Study the thesis statement below. Then fill in the outline form for a possible body paragraph using the three parts of a well-developed paragraph presented above.

   Thesis Statement:

   Life on a college campus offers many opportunities for personal growth.

   A Body Paragraph

   Appropriate topic

   _____

   _____

   Evidence

   _____

   _____

   _____

   _____

   Link to thesis statement

   _____

   _____

   _____

   _____

2. Discuss with the class some other topic ideas and supporting evidence you could use if you were asked to write this essay.

A Basic Outline Form for an Essay That Presents a Thesis

Strong writers always create a basic plan of their essay to ensure that all its parts are complete and that they make logical sense. There are several ways to create a working plan for an essay.

Here is an outline form that you can use; it will work effectively for the kinds of essays assigned in *Write It .5.*

I. Introductory Paragraph:

A. Draft one or two opening sentences that give the reading selection's title, author, and main topic:

_____

_____

B. To plan your response to the first part of the writing topic, list the main points that will be included in your directed summary:

1.

2.

3.

4.

C. Write out your thesis statement. Be sure that it presents a clear position on the subject asked about in the writing topic State your thesis in your own words.

_____

II. Body Paragraphs: For each body paragraph, plan the following parts:

A. Write down the main idea for the paragraph.

B. List the evidence you will use to support your topic idea (fact, example, etc.).

C. Tell how the evidence and your ideas link to the thesis statement.

(Repeat this part of the outline as often as necessary to plan all of your body paragraphs.)

III. Conclusion: Draft some general remarks you can make to close your essay. Perhaps you will remind your readers of the main argument of your paper—your opinion or point of view on the subject of your essay.

Drafting Your Essay

Once you have an outline or basic plan for your essay, including its specific and essential parts, you are ready to begin drafting it. Here are some helpful guidelines:

- Most people begin by drafting the introductory paragraph, but you may decide instead to begin with one of the body paragraphs.

- Remember that your thinking may develop as you draft your essay and you may decide at some point to change or modify your thesis statement. Writers almost never keep the identical thesis statement they initially drafted because it is almost certain that drafting leads them to think even more deeply about their topic. Extended thinking usually brings new insights that a writer will want to include in his or her argument.

- Be sure that the evidence you use to support your topic idea and thesis statement is clear and specific.

- When you link the evidence to the thesis statement, be sure to explain fully and clearly how the evidence proves the thesis. The evidence parts of the argument are places where readers pay close attention to see if they understand you and to see if they find your ideas valid.

- Most important: do not feel bound to the outline plan you began with at the draft stage of the writing process. Allow your thoughts to develop and then capture those ideas in your essay—but do so in a systematic way. Always use the academic essay diagram to help you decide how to add new material to your essay.

A Rubric for Evaluating Student Essays

A rubric is a scoring tool that identifies the expectations for an assignment. A rubric divides the assignment into parts and gives descriptions of each part at varying levels of mastery. Rubrics are often used by instructors as grading guides that help ensure that their grading standards do not change over time or from student to student.

Rubrics also help students by giving them a clear set of guides to use as they complete assignments, and to give them valuable feedback on their graded work. Rubrics are an important part of academic culture, especially in courses that require a significant amount of writing. These rubrics identify the conventional standards of successful and effective writing in an academic setting. Here is the rubric that will be used in this course:

Grading Rubric

High Pass: (Highly satisfactory for BW3 students)
A paper in this range commands attention because of an insightful, cogent response to the text and contains few (or no) markers that indicate a student not fluent with English.

1. The paper has an impressive thesis or point of focus, elaborating that response with interesting ideas and well-chosen, persuasive supporting evidence.
2. The paper demonstrates the student's reading comprehension and analytical ability.
3. The paper's paragraphs are generally well-organized and clearly pertinent to the point of focus.
4. A "High Pass" paper shows that the writer can use a variety of sentence patterns with relative ease, usually choose words precisely and aptly, and observe the conventions of written English with few errors.
5. Although rare instances of non-standard English errors might be found in the paper's sentences and word choice, the sentences and diction are usually impressive, and the errors at this level can be corrected as the student takes English 4.

Pass: (Clearly satisfactory for BW 3 students)
A paper in this range provides a clearly acceptable response to the text, and ESL errors that occur are not the defining characteristic of the essay.

1. The paper has a strong thesis or point of focus, elaborating that response with appropriate examples and sensible reasoning.
2. The paper clearly and thoughtfully responds to the writing topic's demands, demonstrating the student's understanding of the reading selection and of essay writing in general.
3. The paper's paragraphs are usually organized and appropriate to the point of focus.
4. Although limited ESL-type errors might be evident in the paper's sentences and word choice, the sentences and diction are usually clearly proficient, and the errors at this level are able to be corrected in English 4.

Low Pass: (Marginally satisfactory for BW 3 students)
A paper in this range provides an adequate response to the text (sometimes marginally so), and ESL errors do not impede understanding or occur so frequently as to be distracting.

1. The content of the paper is appropriate to the writing topic and demonstrates that the student can identify and write about the main ideas in the reading selection.

2. The paper has a point of focus (some sort of thesis), and a structure that includes support for that focus, but it may lack adequate development of ideas or of supporting evidence.

3. The paper shows evidence in most paragraphs that the writer understands how paragraphs should be organized.

4. Although a variety of non-standard English errors may be evident in the construction of sentences or in word choice, these errors do not markedly impede understanding. Most sentences and diction are at least marginally acceptable. A pattern of mixed constructions, repeated errors in basic tense formation and agreement, and/or multiple serious errors in word choice and word formation are NOT acceptable at this level. Likewise, overly short essays that demonstrate comfort only with simplistic sentence patterns and limited vocabulary are not acceptable (these are often marked by stilted language).

High Fail: (Not satisfactory for BW3 students)

A paper in this range may provide an adequate response in terms of content; however, its dominant feature is the use of non-standard English errors—though certainly not in the majority of the paper's sentences.
This grade range indicates a major problem in one or more of the following areas:

1. It may demonstrate some lack of understanding of the reading selection.

2. It may lack acceptable support, though there should be a clear attempt at producing a focused response.

3. It may contain an unacceptable number or variety of errors associated with ESL students. However, these errors will not be so pervasive as to appear in a majority of sentences. These papers are often characterized by an unevenness of sentence-level control or a limited ability to produce sentences beyond a particular style.

4. The paper's sentence-level errors are often part of a pattern: mixed constructions, basic errors in tense formation and agreement, and/or incorrect or inappropriate diction and word forms.

Fail: (Indicates major language difficulties for BW3 students)

A paper in this range may provide a basic (though perhaps limited) response in terms of content; however, its defining feature is the consistent use of ESL errors of several varieties and in the majority of the sentences. Where a paper fits in this range should be determined by the density of errors.
This grade range indicates a major problem in one or more of the following areas:

1. The paper often demonstrates a misreading of the reading selection.

2. It typically lacks support and/or a clear thesis.

3. It almost always contains an unacceptable number of serious sentence-level errors associated with ESL students: mixed constructions, basic errors in tense formation and agreement, and/or significant problems with word choice and word forms. The density, variety, seriousness, or frequency of these errors makes a higher grade inappropriate.

4. Often, there are instances when a student's phrasing and word order will seem like direct translation from the student's native language, instead of indicating an understanding of how to construct sentences in English.

Low Fail: (Indicates profound language deficiencies for BW3 students)
A paper in this range will often fail to provide any understandable response to the writing topic, and standard English language deficiencies may make the essay almost unreadable.
This grade range indicates a major problem in one or more of the following areas:

1. Almost no understanding of the reading selection.
2. Usually no significant support.
3. A pattern of ESL errors so pervasive that it blocks coherence and meaning.

Follow-Up Activity

1. Share with the class your ideas about how you could use the scoring rubric to help you write your essays. How might the rubric be helpful after you draft your paper? How might it be helpful after you receive your graded essay back from your instructor?

2. Read the following essay written by a college student. Then, working with a partner, with a small group, or with the class as a whole, use the scoring rubric to decide how the paper should be graded. Be sure that you can point to places in the essay to justify the grade you gave. Discuss your assessment of the essay with the class, and, if there is significant disagreement, offer your views.

Rejecting or Accepting Technology

Each an everyday we come up with new inventions, new technology that help make the world easier and more convenient place. In the essay "Accepting or rejecting innovation" by Jared Diamond, we see how people accept or reject certain inventions on the market. One technology we all use is a phone. We see how the newest phones come out and we automatically want the newest phone on stores. For example the iPhone they keep creating with different versions of the phone the iPhone 1, 2, 3, 4, and now 5 and sometimes there is not much difference between the versions. Like the iPhone 4 and the 4s they are exactly the same the only difference is that the 4s has SARI already integrated. But what helps customers accept or reject a new invention? Economy, prestige, vested interest are factors that help a consumer reject or accept a new invention. This essay helps you understand how a customer takes these three factors in to place well trying out a new invention. In this essay, we see how people look at the price before they buy it; that's when economy takes in to place. They see what brand it is and sometimes how good the product is doesn't count. What counts is the companies name, that's where the prestige comes in. Also, people see what they are used to and if the majority doesn't want to change some to a new invention they won't accept a new one that's where vested interest comes in to place. All of these come to a person's head before deciding how they feel towards a new invention out in the market.

Economy is a big factor that help a consumer decide if to accept or reject a new invention. The price and economical standing of a person matters when a new product is on the market. For example, if the price is extremely high, the consumer would double think itself to figure out in the product is really worth buying, if the price is really low the consumer might think the invention is not good enough if it's so cheap. So in other words the product has to be worth its value when it is brand new to the market. In other cases some people might not have a very good economic standing, the product and its price is fair and good but the consumer might not have enough money to purchase the product. Sometimes the idea is good, but money stands in the way of you trying it.

However economy isn't the only factor that takes in to place will purchasing a new product, prestige also takes in to place. In most cases the brand matters. For example, if we have two pairs of running shoes that have the work exactly the same they help your foot function and feel comfortable. Then you put the name Nike on one of them and increase the price. Most people will go on and buy the more expensive one simply because it has the name Nike on it. That is because people are used to brand names most people judge and care about what brand name you are wearing, not what the product functions for. In some rear cases it works the opposite. For example in the essay "the highs of low technology" by Johanne Mednick. In this essay we see how mednick explains that people start to admire her old bike because it's vintage. It's not a common bike, it not like any other because it's so old they don't make models like that anymore, as contrast to all the new models that there are tons of. The brand and the name matters to the consumer more than the product.

Last but not least, we also have a factor that takes in to place vested interest. For example, we have had the same keyboard for years and we don't manage to change it. Why? It will make our lives easier. Right? Yes, indeed it will make our live easier in the long run but it also means that people will have to get accustomed to a new thing professional writers will slow down because they would have to learn a whole new concept. New computers will have to be made to replace the old keyboards and lots of money would have to be invested on these acts. Therefore it cost too much money to do so and it's not that important for people to learn a new keyboard if they have already gotten use to one. The money and time invested matters to keep the usual going on rather than the new.

In conclusion all these factors take in to place when we want to buy a new product in the market. Let's face it we think of all of these things before purchasing a brand new product. Most of us try to save our money but still have the latest brands and products out there.

WRITING ASSIGNMENTS

Composition studies have identified four basic stages of the writing process—prewriting, drafting, revising, and editing. Research has taught us that writers who use these stages consciously and deliberately write more thoughtful and successful papers. Initially, you will find that using the writing process demands time and effort, but *Write It .5* will support that effort by giving you structured activities that help you to engage in systematic prewriting, drafting, and revising exercises. As you work through *Write It .5*, you will develop your own methods for using the writing process strategies you will learn in Part III. Once you learn how to make these strategies work for you, you can and should rely on them whenever you are given a writing assignment. Soon you will be able to use them more efficiently and productively to critically read, think, and write in an academic setting.

Assignment 1

Gloria Watkins's "Keeping Close to Home"

Read the following essay by Gloria Watkins and study the essay topic that follows it. Then fill in the sections that follow to help you understand and evaluate Watkins's argument, and develop your own thesis statement and supporting evidence in preparation for writing your own essay.

Fill in all sections carefully and thoroughly. Students sometimes think that they need not bother with some of these sections, but we have noticed a direct correlation between student essays that use these sections and those that do not. Use the ideas you developed in these sections to write an essay that responds to the writing topic that follows Watkins's essay.

Keeping Close to Home

GLORIA WATKINS

Gloria Watkins, known also by her pen name bell hooks, is an American author, feminist, and social activist. She has published many books, mainstream essays, and scholarly articles to present her views on and interest in race, class, and gender. She earned a Ph.D. from the University of California, Santa Cruz. In 2004 she became a Distinguished Professor in Residence at Berea College in Kentucky.

In the distance the bus approaches. Just before I board the bus I turn, staring into my mother's face. I am momentarily back in time, seeing myself eighteen years ago, at this same bus stop, staring into my mother's face, continually turning back, waving farewell as I returned to college—that experience which first took me away from our town, from family. Departing was as painful then as it is now. Each movement away makes return harder. Each separation intensifies distance, both physical and emotional.

To a southern black girl from a working-class background who had never been on a city bus, who had never stepped on an escalator, who had never traveled by plane, leaving the comfortable confines of a small town Kentucky life to attend Stanford University was not just frightening; it was utterly painful. My parents had not been delighted that I had been accepted and adamantly opposed my going so far from home. At the time, I did not see their opposition as an expression of their fear that they would lose me forever. Like many working-class folks, they feared what college education might do to their children's minds even as they unenthusiastically acknowledged its importance. They did not understand why I could not attend a college nearby, an all-black college. To them, any college would do. I would graduate, become a school teacher, make a decent living and a good marriage. And even though they reluctantly and skeptically supported my educational endeavors, they also subjected them to constant harsh and bitter critique.

It is difficult for me to talk about my parents and their impact on me because they have always felt wary, ambivalent, mistrusting of my intellectual aspirations even as they have been caring and supportive. I want to speak about these contradictions because sorting through them, seeking resolution and reconciliation, has been important to me both as it affects my development as a writer, my effort to be fully self-realized, and my longing to remain close to the family and community that provided the groundwork for much of my thinking, writing, and being. My parents' ambivalence about my love for reading led to intense conflict. They (especially my mother) would work to ensure that I had access to books, but they would threaten to burn the books or throw them away if I did not conform to other expectations. Or they would insist that reading too much would drive me insane. Their ambivalence nurtured in me a like uncertainty about the value and significance of intellectual endeavor that took years for me to unlearn. While this aspect of our class reality was one that wounded and diminished, their vigilant insistence that being smart did not make me a "better" or "superior" person (which often got on my nerves because I think I wanted to have that sense that it did indeed set me apart, make me better) made a profound impression. From them I learned to value and respect various skills and talents folks might have, not just to value people who read books and talk about ideas. They and my grandparents might say about somebody, "Now he don't read nor write a lick, but he can tell a story," or as my grandmother would say, "call out the hell in words."

(Continued)

Open honest communication is the most important way we can maintain relationships with kin and community as our class experience and background change. It is as vital as the sharing of resources. I do not know that my mother's mother ever acknowledged my college education except to ask me once, "How can you live so far away from your people?" Yet she gave me sources of admiration and nourishment, sharing the legacy of her quilt-making, of family history, of her incredible way with words. Recently, when our father retired after more than thirty years of work as a janitor, I wanted to pay tribute to this experience, to identify links between his work and my own as writer and teacher. Reflecting on our family past, I recalled ways he had been an impressive example of diligence and hard work, approaching tasks with a seriousness of concentration I work to mirror and develop, with a discipline I struggle to maintain. Sharing these thoughts with him keeps us connected, nurtures our respect for each other, maintaining a space, however large or small, where we can talk.

Writing Topic

In Watkins's essay, how are her values and identity formed from different, and sometimes conflicting, sources? Do you think this is true for most people? Be sure to support your opinion with specific examples. These examples can be taken from your own experience and observations or from anything you have read.

Vocabulary and Dictionary Practice

Part I. Look up the following words used in "Keeping Close to Home." For each, write the two most common definitions on the lines provided and include what part of speech each definition is (noun, verb, adjective, etc). Then, under each of the two definitions, write a sentence that uses the word in a way that reflects that particular definition and part of speech.

1. confines
2. adamant
3. skeptical
4. subjected
5. critique
6. ambivalent
7. aspirations
8. endeavor
9. vigilant
10. diminished

1. **confines**

first definition: _____

_____

part of speech: _____

sentence: _____

_____

second definition: _____

_____

part of speech: _____

sentence: _____

_____

2. **adamant**

first definition: _____

_____

part of speech: _____

sentence: _____

_____

second definition: _____

_____

part of speech: _____

sentence: _____

_____

3. **skeptical**

first definition: _____

_____

part of speech: _____

sentence: _____

_____

second definition: _____

_____

part of speech: _____

sentence: _____

_____

4. **subjected**

first definition: _____

_____

part of speech: _____

sentence: _____

_____

second definition: _____

_____

part of speech: _____

sentence: _____

_____

5. **critique**

first definition: _____

_____

part of speech: _____

sentence: _____

_____

second definition: _____

_____

part of speech: _____

sentence: _____

_____

6. **ambivalent**

first definition: _____

_____

part of speech: _____

sentence: _____

_____

second definition: _____

_____

part of speech: _____

sentence: _____

_____

7. **aspirations**

first definition: _____

_____

part of speech: _____

sentence: _____

_____

second definition: _____

_____

part of speech: _____

sentence: _____

_____

8. **endeavor**

first definition: _____

_____

part of speech: _____

sentence: _____

_____

second definition: _____

_____

part of speech: _____

sentence: _____

_____

9. **vigilant**

first definition: _____

_____

part of speech: _____

sentence: _____

_____

second definition: _____

_____

part of speech: _____

sentence: _____

_____

10. **diminished**

first definition: _____

_____

part of speech: _____

sentence: _____

_____

second definition: _____

_____

part of speech: _____

sentence: _____

_____

Part II.
  A. Write down each sentence from Watkins's essay that contains the following words.
  B. Tell which of the word's various definitions best fits the sentence.
  C. Paraphrase the sentence without using the vocabulary word; in other words, write the sentence using your own words.

1. **confines**

    A. _____

    _____

    B. _____

    _____

    C. _____

    _____

2. **adamant**

    A. _____

    _____

    B. _____

    _____

    C. _____

    _____

3. **skeptical**

    A. _____

    _____

    B. _____

    _____

    C. _____

    _____

4. **subjected**

    A. _____

    _____

    B. _____

    _____

    C. _____

    _____

5. **critique**

    A. _____

    _____

B. _____

_____

C. _____

_____

6. **ambivalent**

A. _____

_____

B. _____

_____

C. _____

_____

7. **aspirations**

A. _____

_____

B. _____

_____

C. _____

_____

8. **endeavor**

A. _____

_____

B. _____

_____

C. _____

_____

9. **vigilant**

A. _____

_____

B. _____

_____

C. _____

_____

10. **diminished**

    A. _____

    _____

    B. _____

    _____

    C. _____

    _____

Part III. For each of these words from "Keeping Close to Home," tell something new and interesting you learned about the word from the dictionary. For example, you might have found the correct way to pronounce a word you were already familiar with from reading but not from speaking, or you might have learned that a word you thought of as entirely English came from a foreign language.

1. **confines**

    _____

    _____

2. **adamant**

    _____

    _____

3. **skeptical**

    _____

    _____

4. **subjected**

    _____

    _____

5. **critique**

    _____

    _____

6. **ambivalent**

    _____

    _____

7. **aspirations**

    _____

    _____

8. **endeavor**

_____

_____

9. **vigilant**

_____

_____

10. **diminished**

_____

_____

Follow-Up Activity

Look over the sentences that you created using the vocabulary words. Choose your favorite and read it out loud to the class. Explain your reason for choosing this sentence, and tell why you think this vocabulary word will help you to write and communicate effectively in English.

Doing a Careful Reading of "Keeping Close to Home"

First, if time permits, begin by reading "Keeping Close to Home" aloud with the class. Take turns reading paragraphs. This exercise will allow you to listen to the essay as someone else speaks it, giving you a unique experience in absorbing the essay's ideas.

Now that you have familiarized yourself with the definitions of some of the more difficult terms in "Keeping Close to Home," use the "Steps for a Thoughtful Reading of an Essay" that you learned in Part II to help you study it more carefully and come to understand it better. Here are the steps:

1. **Read the title again.**
   - The title will tell you something about the reading's main topic.
   - It may also tell you something about Watkins's opinion on the topic.
   - Think about what you already know about the topic and what more you want to know.

2. **Learn about the author.**
   - Sometimes a reading selection presents biographical information about the author at the top of the selection. For "Keeping Close to Home," information about Watkins's life is also part of her essay.
   - As you go through the remaining steps below, take note of how Watkins's life or work might connect with her topic.

3. **Read through the selection once quickly.**
   - Read quickly through the reading again so that you get a general fresh impression of what it is about and what Watkins's attitude is toward the topic.
   - Notice the things—people, places, experiences, concepts, for example—she brings up to develop and support her opinion about the topic.

4. **Read again to identify the thesis.**
   - Now read the selection a second time, but more slowly and carefully, and *with a pen or highlighter in your hand.*
   - Find the thesis and underline it or write it in the margin. Remember, the thesis states Watkins's overall opinion on the topic of the reading. Often the thesis is contained in a single sentence, but, in some cases, it takes several sentences to make the main argument of the reading selection clear. There are times, too, when the author does not state his or her thesis explicitly, but, if you read the selection carefully, you should be able to state it and then write it in the margin.
   - To help, ask yourself, "What does Watkins seem to want readers to think about her topic?"

5. **Read slowly and methodically through the rest of the reading.**
   - Examine each body paragraph one at a time and list or underline the kinds of evidence that Watkins uses to support her thesis.
   - Look in each body paragraph for a *topic sentence*—a sentence that both presents an idea and tells how it gives support to the reading's overall opinion.

- As you read and study the selection, *be sure to write down any thoughts you have* about the writer's opinion and supporting evidence.
- It is your job to evaluate this evidence for its logic and validity, so be sure to *make notes in the margins* as you read.
- *Mark the points* that you found interesting or convincing and write a few words explaining your thoughts.
- Note, too, any weaknesses you find.
- When you look back at the notes you made in the margins, you should have a general idea of how convincing you found the reading and what you found to be its strengths and weaknesses.

6. **Read again for review.**
   - Once you have thought through the reading selection, read it once more, looking for places where you don't quite understand what is being said.
   - Underline any terms that you aren't familiar with and look them up in a dictionary.
   - Mark any places in the reading that don't fit with your understanding of the reading as a whole. Decide whether this is something that Watkins should have revised, or whether it is something that you need to read again because you don't understand it. You may find that you need to go back to Step 4 and begin working through the reading again.
   - Once you are certain that you understand the entire reading, you are prepared to discuss, summarize, and/or respond to the reading with your own essay.

Questions to Review Your Understanding of "Keeping Close to Home"

Answer the following questions to check your complete understanding of Watkins's argument as a whole.

Paragraph 1

Explain the two kinds of distance that Gloria Watkins experienced as a result of leaving home. In what ways can you relate to her experience?

Paragraph 2

Where did Watkins grow up?

What is her ethnicity?

What was her socioeconomic status?

Why didn't her parents want her to go to Stanford?

Describe the future her parents imagined for her.

Why is it important for Watkins to understand the mixed messages her parents gave her about her intellectual goals?

Paragraph 3

How did Watkins's parents show their ambivalence about "book learning"? What were the other things that her parents taught her to respect?

Paragraph 4

What does Watkins feel is the best way to stay close to family? Can you suggest other means that you think might work as well?

What specific things that contributed to Watkins's growth and development did she learn from her mother's mother?

What connections does Watkins see between her father's work as a janitor and her profession as a writer?

Responding to the Writing Topic

You have spent time with "Keeping Close to Home" and should now have a good understanding of its ideas and overall message. It is important now to look at the writing topic at the bottom of the selection because the essay you write must directly answer the questions in the writing topic. Here it is again, but this time formatted so that each part is on its own line:

Writing Topic

In Watkins's essay, how are her values and identity formed from different, and sometimes conflicting, sources?

Do you think this is true for most people?

Be sure to support your opinion with specific examples. These examples can be taken from your own experience and observations or from anything you have read.

Pay careful attention to all parts of the writing topic.

- You are first asked a question about a specific aspect of "Keeping Close to Home," a question that asks you to consider what the essay tells us about **how** a person's values and identity are formed. Your essay will have to answer this question. When examining a writing topic, always underline the question words (who, what, why, how, when, where).

- The second question in the writing topic asks you to state whether you think that Watkins's views on identity formation hold true for most people. Are most of us a mixture of values and goals built on things we learn from our parents, or are our values and goals shaped only partially by what we learn from our parents? Your answer to this question will become the thesis of your essay because it will state your overarching view on the topic.

- The third part of the writing topic tells you to support your opinion—your thesis—with clear examples taken from your own experiences. The following activity will help you begin to find some of those examples. Be sure to keep notes on your ideas so that you can turn back to them later.

Follow-Up Activity

1. Tell your classmates the best five adjectives that describe your own point of view on "home." Explain why you chose them, and then give a brief memory that shows the significance of at least one of your adjectives.

2. Tell your classmates the best five adjectives that describe your first weeks as a college student. Explain why you chose them and then give a brief memory that shows the significance of at least one of your adjectives.

3. Compare the list of adjectives you made for #1 to the list you made for #2. Describe any similarities or differences you see.

4. Working in small groups, identify for your group the person in your early home life who most influenced you. Describe your relationship with this person and characterize the values or ideals he or she gave you that have stayed with you into adulthood.

5. Briefly tell your classmates why you want to earn a college degree, and describe any challenges you had to overcome to be able to go to college.

Strategies to Help You Analyze a Reading Selection and Develop Your Ideas for Writing a Response

Now you are ready to build on the annotations you made in the reading selection and develop a more systematic analysis of it and of your ideas. Use the prewriting guides that you were introduced to in Part II. They will help to guide your thinking about Watkins's essay, but they will also help you to clarify and put into words your own views on how our values and identity are formed.

Questioning

- Questions about the highlighting you did:
  - Why did I underline this part of the reading?
  - How is this information important to the author's point?
  - What is the relationship between this information and the question I am being asked to write about?
- Questions about Watkins's ideas:
  - What things in this essay do not make sense to me?
  - Where do I think the author should have explained further?
  - How do the examples in the essay relate to the author's point?
- Questions about "Keeping Close to Home" that seem important:
  - What are some of the things that the author says that I am happy to hear someone say?
  - What things that the author says seem true to me?
  - What things that the author says seem wrong to me?
  - What thing that the author says is most important to me?
  - What idea in this essay is completely new to me?

Freewriting

If you still feel that you have little to say to respond to Watkins's essay and topic, try some freewriting.

- Pick one or more of your answers to the questions you have already answered, and just begin to write about it.
- While you are doing this writing, do not stop or censor yourself; just let the words come.
- Do this for about five or ten minutes without thinking about spelling, grammar, word choice, or even the sense of what you are saying.
- When you have completed this activity, you will want to take a break.
- After your brief break, come back and read what you have written. Most of what you now have down on paper will not end up in your essay, but, as you read through your freewriting, you will find one or more sentences or ideas that seem interesting, important, or even compelling to you. Highlight these points and ideas.

Listing

With this strategy, you simply list all of the thoughts and reactions you have noted so far. By looking down your list, you may see a pattern of ideas develop, one that you can use to develop an essay of your own.

- List all of the annotations you made for "Keeping Close to Home."
- List the main ideas you can see in your answers to the questioning phase above.
- List any main ideas that developed from your responses to the follow-up activity above.

- Be sure to list all the items from your freewriting that you thought were interesting. As you make this list, other ideas may come into your head. Put them on your list as well.

Study your list. Connect with some kind of mark all the ideas that seem related to each other. When you are done, one related group of ideas will probably be longer than the others. This group should give you a good start on what you want to say in your own essay in response to Watkins's essay.

Shaping Your Ideas into a Rough Draft

At this stage of the writing process, you are ready to begin planning your essay draft. It is important to understand the conventional structure of an academic essay because it will guide you when you are ready to put your ideas in writing. Turn back to Part II and examine "A Suggested Structure for an Essay That Responds to Another Writer's Essay."

As you review the writing topic for this assignment, notice that it asks you to do three things:

1. **Summarize** a topic idea that Watkins develops in her essay.
2. **Present** your position on this topic idea.
3. **Support and develop** your position using specific evidence taken from your own experiences and readings.

Here is the first question in the writing topic:

In Watkins's essay, how are her values and identity formed from different, and sometimes conflicting, sources?

Notice the important action word *how*. This tells you that you will have to explain a process where certain things *cause* a certain result. Your job will be to summarize *how* that process works. The writing topic does *not* ask you to summarize all of the ideas in "Close to Home," but only Watkins's idea of *how* our values and identity *are the result of* different, even conflicting, sources. To help focus your thinking, answer the following questions. You will use your answers to begin drafting your *directed summary* in response to the first writing topic question.

1. What was the precise moment in time when Watkins separated from her family?

2. Why did she leave them?

3. How did Watkins's parents feel about her acceptance to Stanford?

4. Why did they oppose her decision to attend Stanford?

5. As Watkins was growing up, did her parents provide her with educational materials?

6. What did Watkins's parents do to keep her from putting too much value on education?

7. What other things did Watkins's parents teach her to value and respect?

8. What does Watkins remember and value about her childhood experiences?

9. In what ways does she seem proud of herself as an adult?

Follow-Up Activity

Working with a partner or a small group, take turns reading your answers to the above questions and getting feedback from your partner or group members. For each answer, ask your partner or group:

How clearly written was your answer?

Did it thoroughly answer the question, or could more have been added to make it clear?

What suggestions can you make to help me improve my work?

Give everyone a chance to give and to receive feedback.

Drafting Your Directed Summary

- Begin drafting the directed summary by reviewing the writing topic for "Keeping Close to Home," paying particular attention to the first question asked. The answer you give to this question is called a *directed summary* because it summarizes only the parts of Watkins's essay that answer this first question.

- As you learned in Part II, the question that calls for a directed summary often opens with a question word such as *what, how,* or *why*. In Watkins's essay, the first question asks, "*How* are her values and identity formed from different, and sometimes conflicting, sources?" You will have to go back to her essay to find the information that tells *how* her identity formed from different sources. It will not be enough simply to tell what those sources were; you will also have to summarize *how* they shaped Watkins's development into an adult.

- You might find it helpful to turn back to "Keeping Close to Home" and mark the sentences that respond directly to the directed summary question. When writing your directed summary, be very careful to use your own words to *paraphrase* her ideas, as you learned to do in Part II.

- You should avoid including any of the following in a *directed summary*:

  1. a summary of the entire essay rather than a summary that pays attention only to what is asked for in the first question of the writing topic

  2. minor details or points that are irrelevant to the question

  3. your own opinion or ideas

  4. examples of your own, and, unless particularly helpful, those of the author

Once you have written a directed summary, you will be ready to draft your essay's introductory paragraph. These steps will help guide you:

- Introduce Watkins's essay by giving its title and the full name of its author.

- Follow these opening sentences with the directed summary.

- Last, present your thesis statement, or the answer to the second question in the writing topic. To develop your thesis statement, use the guides in the following section.

Follow-Up Activity

1. After the class as a whole has discussed the important points from "Keeping Close to Home" that need to be included in the directed summary, form small groups. Have each member of the group read his or her summary aloud; then discuss the correctness and completeness of each summary.

2. Cut up your directed summary so that each strip of paper contains only one sentence. Exchange sentence strips with a partner. See if you can reassemble the directed summary so that it matches your partner's original version.

Developing Your Thesis Statement

The second question in the writing topic asks you to evaluate Watkins's point of view on self-identity and then decide whether you agree with her assessment of how the majority of people form their values and identities. The question asks:

"Do you think this is true for most people?"

Your answer to this question will be the *thesis* of your essay. The rest of your essay will be built around your answer to this question, so you want to make sure your answer is clear, concise, and relevant. Begin by taking special notice of the important words. Before you decide on your response, you will have to determine what the word *this* refers to, and you should also notice the word *most*, "for most people." You will have to look back to your directed summary to understand the referent for *this*, and it is important that you understand what Watkins's essay says about how her values and her identity were formed because the second question is asking if you think *most* people are shaped by different and sometimes conflicting influences.

Before you begin to construct your thesis, ask yourself the following questions;

- What is the subject of Watkins's argument?
  Notice that, although we can say that "home" is the topic idea of Watkins's essay, in fact it is the formation of one's identity that is the actual subject of her argument.

- Based on her own experiences, what is her opinion about the subject?
  Although Watkins doesn't directly state her thesis, we can determine her argument by reading the entire essay. She claims that identity is formed from a mixture of influences: the values we learn at home as children, and the values we develop for ourselves based on our experiences or on our own character. Sometimes, these influences contradict one another. She explains this by her love of her father and the values he gave her, even though he did not support or understand her desire to leave home and get a good education. As an adult, she values both of these influences.

- Do I think that her understanding of how we form our identities is true for most people?
  Do you think this is a shared experience for most people, or do you think most people form their identities from the values given them by their parents, or perhaps by values outside the home, say from peers or other authority figures?

The second question in the writing topic asks you to think about Watkins's position on the subject of identity and the evidence she uses to support her point of view. You must evaluate her point of view and decide whether or not you think it is right.

You must also be careful to provide an exact answer to the writing topic, and your answer should be clear, concise, and relevant.

Look back to Part II and review the sentence types for signaling agreement or disagreement when writing a thesis statement. You may choose to use one of the sample types to shape your own thesis statement.

Before you begin to construct your thesis, answer the following questions:

- What is the subject of Watkins's essay?

_____

- What is her opinion about the subject?

_____

- Do I agree or disagree with her opinion?

_____

Now, use these answers to help write your own thesis. Your thesis will need to include:
- the subject being considered
- the author's claim about the subject
- your opinion about the subject

Now use your answers to write out your thesis statement on the lines below.

subject/author's idea about the subject   your opinion about the subject

_____

_____

_____

_____

_____

_____

After you have finished writing your sentence, review your statement to see that it contains the following elements:
- Watkins's point of view on the subject
- your point of view on the subject

If either of these elements is missing, rewrite your thesis statement so that both are included.

Developing Body Paragraphs for an Essay That Presents a Thesis

Body paragraphs make up the largest part of an essay.

- The job of each body paragraph is to develop one point that supports the thesis statement.
- These points taken together build the argument of the essay.
- Writing an effective body paragraph can be easy once you understand the elements that the body paragraph must contain.

Here are the three most important elements for paragraphs in an argumentative essay:

Body Paragraphs Need:
1. an appropriate or suitable topic
2. evidence (fact, example, and/or idea)
3. a link to the thesis

Appropriate or suitable topic

First write a topic sentence that states the point you wish to make in this paragraph. The point must be on topic; that is, it must state an idea that is relevant to the claim you make in your thesis.

Evidence

The major part of the paragraph will be devoted to evidence. Most often in your essays, that evidence will be an example, but specific facts, quotations, and ideas can also help support the topic sentence of your paragraph. You must be careful to choose a clear example, one that clearly demonstrates the point of the paragraph. Then you must explain the example with details.

Link to the thesis

After you have given all the evidence and supplied all the details that support the topic sentence of the paragraph, you must show the way this evidence links back to the thesis of your essay. It is not enough to just provide an example. You have to tell the reader the reason this particular example connects to the main argument of your essay.

A Basic Outline Form for an Essay That Presents a Thesis

All of the work you have done so far—reading and carefully annotating "Keeping Close to Home," analyzing its ideas, writing a directed summary in response to the first question in the writing topic, thinking about your own experiences and deciding on your thesis statement, and drafting your essay's introduction—should be gathered together now into a shape that will become your essay, your response to the writing topic at the bottom of "Keeping Close to Home."

- Remember that you should follow the basic structure of an academic essay.
- To refresh your memory, turn back to Part II and review the diagram of the academic essay format.
- As you begin filling in this diagram form, you should be able to turn back to material you have already drafted as you worked through the exercises in this unit.
- Fill in the diagram form as fully as you can. A good plan will help you draft an essay that is clear and coherent.

I. **Introductory Paragraph:**

A. one or two opening sentences that give the reading selection's title, author, and main topic:

_____

_____

_____

B. the main points that will be included in the directed summary:

1.

2.

3.

4.

C. your thesis statement: Be sure that it presents a clear position in response to the writing topic. State your thesis in your own words.

_____

_____

_____

II. Body Paragraphs: For each body paragraph you will include in your essay, plan the following parts:

Write down the topic idea for the paragraph.

_____

_____

_____

List the evidence you will use to support your topic idea (fact, example, etc.).

_____

_____

_____

_____

_____

Tell how the evidence and your ideas link to the thesis statement.

_____

_____

_____

_____

_____

(Repeat this part of the outline as often as necessary to plan all of your body paragraphs.)

III. Conclusion: What are some general remarks you can make to close your essay? Perhaps you will remind your readers of the main argument of your paper, for example.

_____

_____

_____

A Review of the Parts of an Academic Essay

Now that you are ready to draft your essay, be sure to rely on the parts that you have already developed as you completed the exercises in this unit. If you completed these exercises carefully and thoroughly, it should be relatively easy for you to use them as a strong basis for building your draft.

Here is a visual guide that will help you to organize your draft:

INTRODUCTORY PARAGRAPH

1. Write an opening sentence or two that introduce the reading selection's title and author.
2. Using the exercises you have already completed as a guide, draft a directed summary that answers the first question in the writing topic.
   vocabulary pages
   comprehension questions
   annotating, listing, freewriting, and questioning activities
3. Look back at the thesis statement you drafted on the "Developing a Thesis" page. If necessary, revise it, and then put it at the end of the introductory paragraph so that it follows your directed summary.

BODY PARAGRAPHS

Use the outline you completed in "Developing Body Paragraphs" as a guide for drafting your essay's body paragraphs.

1. Be sure that your body paragraphs have the three essential components:
   an appropriate or suitable topic
   evidence (fact, example, and/or idea)
   a link to the thesis
2. To find suitable topics and evidence, turn back to:
   your responses to some of the follow-up activities
   annotating, questioning, freewriting, and listing activities

CONCLUSION

Bring closure to your essay by restating your thesis statement using different words. Add a brief summary of your significant evidence that supports it.

Drafting Your Essay

Now that you have a basic plan for the structure of your essay and a map of its various parts, you are ready to begin drafting.

- Turn back to the helpful guidelines in Part II before you begin. These guidelines will help you to evaluate the parts of your draft and your essay as a whole.
- If your thinking changes as you draft, return to your outline and make necessary adjustments. Every time you decide to revise your outline and essay, remember that this is a good sign, a sign that your thinking is developing and becoming more thoughtful and convincing.
- Keep turning back to all of the activities in this unit as you draft your essay. Try to recall some of your reactions, thoughts, and ideas as you worked on these activities. This may help you to strengthen, expand on, or more fully develop your essay's argument.

Follow-Up Activity

Your draft will always benefit from careful rereadings. Even better is to let others hear or read your draft and give you their feedback. Sometimes, a classmate or family member can spot places in your draft where you aren't clear, or where you have neglected to fix a grammar error.

1. Working with a partner or small group, read your draft out loud slowly. Ask your partner or group to stop you whenever he, she, or they hear a problem or an error. As you listen to their feedback, make notes on the changes you want to make. Then discuss the draft with your partner or group. Give everyone a chance to hear his or her draft read out loud.

2. Read a classmate's rough draft silently. Then choose the paragraph or group of sentences that, in your opinion, are the strongest part of the essay. Read the sentences out loud to the writer of the draft and explain why you chose them.

Supplemental Reading

Read the following short story by Alice Walker. See if you can determine the story's message. What do you think the author wants readers to think when they finish reading? In other words, why do you think she wrote this story? As you think, try to imagine what Gloria Watkins would think of this story.

If time permits, consider reading the story aloud, taking turns so that everyone gets a chance to read. Some of the names may be difficult to pronounce; see if you can sound them out a couple of times until you are comfortable saying them.

Everyday Use

Essay

ALICE WALKER

Alice Walker is an African American, Pulitzer Prize-winning novelist and poet, perhaps best known for her novel The Color Purple *(1982). Her parents were sharecroppers in Georgia, and Walker began writing in secret as a young girl. She won a scholarship to college and graduated from Sarah Lawrence College. She became very involved in the Civil Rights Movement and is a civil rights activist and a feminist. She continues to write novels, essays, and poetry.*

I will wait for her in the yard that Maggie and I made so clean and wavy yesterday afternoon. A yard like this is more comfortable than most people know. It is not just a yard. It is like an extended living room. When the hard clay is swept clean as a floor and the fine sand around the edges lined with tiny, irregular grooves, anyone can come and sit and look up into the elm tree and wait for the breezes that never come inside the house.

Maggie will be nervous until after her sister goes: she will stand hopelessly in corners, homely and ashamed of the burn scars down her arms and legs, eying her sister with a mixture of envy and awe. She thinks her sister has held life always in the palm of one hand, that "no" is a word the world never learned to say to her.

You've no doubt seen those TV shows where the child who has "made it" is confronted, as a surprise, by her own mother and father, tottering in weakly from backstage. (A pleasant surprise, of course: What would they do if parent and child came on the show only to curse out and insult each other?) On TV, mother and child embrace and smile into each other's faces. Sometimes the mother and father weep, the child wraps them in her arms and leans across the table to tell how she would not have made it without their help. I have seen these programs.

Sometimes I dream a dream in which Dee and I are suddenly brought together on a TV program of this sort. Out of a dark and soft-seated limousine I am ushered into a bright room filled with many people. There I meet a smiling, gray, sporty man like Johnny Carson who shakes my hand and tells me what a fine girl I have. Then we are on the stage and Dee is embracing me with tears in her eyes. She pins on my dress a large orchid, even though she has told me once that she thinks orchids are tacky flowers.

In real life I am a large, big-boned woman with rough, man-working hands. In the winter I wear flannel nightgowns to bed and overalls during the day. I can kill and clean a hog as mercilessly as a man. My fat keeps me hot in zero weather. I can work outside all day, breaking ice to get water for washing; I can eat pork liver cooked over the open fire minutes after it comes steaming from the hog. One winter I knocked a bull calf straight in the brain between the eyes with a sledge hammer and had the meat hung up to chill before nightfall. But of course all this does not show on television. I am the way my daughter would want me to be: a hundred pounds lighter, my skin like an uncooked barley pancake. My hair glistens in the hot bright lights. Johnny Carson has much to do to keep up with my quick and witty tongue.

But that is a mistake. I know even before I wake up. Who ever knew a Johnson with a quick tongue? Who can even imagine me looking a strange white man in the eye? It seems to me I have talked to them always with one foot raised in flight, with my head turned in whichever way is farthest from them. Dee, though. She would always look anyone in the eye. Hesitation was no part of her nature.

"How do I look, Mama?" Maggie says, showing just enough of her thin body enveloped in pink skirt and red blouse for me to know she's there, almost hidden by the door.

"Come out into the yard," I say.

Have you ever seen a lame animal, perhaps a dog run over by some careless person rich enough to own a car, sidle up to someone who is ignorant enough to be kind to him? That is the way my Maggie walks. She has been like this, chin on chest, eyes on ground, feet in shuffle, ever since the fire that burned the other house to the ground.

Dee is lighter than Maggie, with nicer hair and a fuller figure. She's a woman now, though sometimes I forget. How long ago was it that the other house burned? Ten, twelve years? Sometimes I can still hear the flames and feel Maggie's arms sticking to me, her hair smoking and her dress falling off her in little black papery flakes. Her eyes seemed stretched open, blazed open by the flames reflected in them. And Dee. I see her standing off under the sweet gum tree she used to dig gum out of; a look of concentration on her face as she watched the last dingy gray board of the house fall in toward the red-hot brick chimney. Why don't you do a dance around the ashes? I'd wanted to ask her. She had hated the house that much.

I used to think she hated Maggie, too. But that was before we raised money, the church and me, to send her to Augusta to school. She used to read to us without pity; forcing words, lies, other folks' habits, whole lives upon us two, sitting trapped and ignorant underneath her voice. She washed us in a river of make-believe, burned us with a lot of knowledge we didn't necessarily need to know. Pressed us to her with the serious way she read, to shove us away at just the moment, like dimwits, we seemed about to understand.

Dee wanted nice things. A yellow organdy dress to wear to her graduation from high school; black pumps to match a green suit she'd made from an old suit somebody gave me. She was determined to stare down any disaster in her efforts. Her eyelids would not flicker for minutes at a time. Often I fought off the temptation to shake her. At sixteen she had a style of her own: and knew what style was.

I never had an education myself. After second grade the school was closed down. Don't ask me why: in 1927 colored asked fewer questions than they do now. Sometimes Maggie reads to me. She stumbles along good-naturedly but can't see well. She knows she is not bright. Like good looks and money, quickness passed her by. She will marry John Thomas (who has mossy teeth in an earnest face) and then I'll be free to sit here and I guess just sing church songs to myself. Although I never was a good singer. Never could carry a tune. I was always better at a man's job. I used to love to milk till I was hooked in the side in 49'. Cows are soothing and slow and don't bother you, unless you try to milk them the wrong way.

I have deliberately turned my back on the house. It is three rooms, just like the one that burned, except the roof is tin; they don't make shingle roofs any more. There are no real windows, just some holes cut in the sides, like the portholes in a ship, but not round and not square, with rawhide holding the shutters up on the outside. This house is in a pasture, too, like the other one. No doubt when Dee sees it she will want to tear it down. She wrote me once that no matter where we "choose" to live, she will manage to come see us. But she will never bring her friends. Maggie and I thought about this and Maggie asked me, "Mama, when did Dee ever *have* any friends?"

She had a few. Furtive boys in pink shirts hanging about on washday after school. Nervous girls who never laughed. Impressed with her they worshiped the well-turned phrase, the cute shape, the scalding humor that erupted like bubbles in lye. She read to them.

When she was courting Jimmy T she didn't have much time to pay to us, but turned all her faultfinding power on him. He *flew* to marry a cheap city girl from a family of ignorant flashy people. She hardly had time to recompose herself.

When she comes I will meet—but there they are!

Maggie attempts to make a dash for the house, in her shuffling way, but I stay her with my hand. "Come back here," I say. And she stops and tries to dig a well in the sand with her toe.

It is hard to see them clearly through the strong sun. But even the first glimpse of leg out of the car tells me it is Dee. Her feet were always neat-looking, as if God himself had shaped them with a certain style. From the other side of the car comes a short, stocky man. Hair is all over his head a foot long and hanging from his chin like a kinky mule tail. I hear Maggie suck in her breath. "Uhnnnh," is what it sounds like. Like when you see the wriggling end of a snake just in front of your foot on the road. "Uhnnnh."

Dee next. A dress down to the ground, in this hot weather. A dress so loud it hurts my eyes. There are yellows and oranges enough to throw back the light of the sun. I feel my whole face warming from the heat waves it throws out. Earrings gold, too, and hanging down to her shoulders. Bracelets dangling and making noises when she moves her arm up to shake the folds of the dress out of her armpits. The dress is loose and flows, and as she walks closer, I like it. I hear Maggie go "Uhnnnh" again. It is her sister's hair. It stands straight up like the wool on a sheep. It is black as night and around the edges are two long pigtails that rope about like small lizards disappearing behind her ears.

"Wa-su-zo-Tean-o!" she says, coming on in that gliding way the dress makes her move. The short stocky fellow with the hair to his navel is all grinning and he follows up with "Asalamalakim, my mother and sister!" He moves to hug Maggie but she falls back, right up against the back of my chair. I feel her trembling there and when I look up I see the perspiration falling off her chin.

"Don't get up," says Dee. Since I am stout it takes something of a push. You can see me trying to move a second or two before I make it. She turns, showing white heels through her sandals, and goes back to the car. Out she peeks next with a Polaroid. She stoops down quickly and lines up picture after picture of me sitting there in front of the house with Maggie cowering behind me. She never takes a shot without making sure the house is included. When a cow comes nibbling around the edge of the yard she snaps it and me and Maggie and the house. Then she puts the Polaroid in the back seat of the car, and comes up and kisses me on the forehead.

Meanwhile Asalamalakim is going through motions with Maggie's hand. Maggie's hand is as limp as a fish, and probably as cold, despite the sweat, and she keeps trying to pull it back. It looks like Asalamalakim wants to shake hands but wants to do it fancy. Or maybe he don't know how people shake hands. Anyhow, he soon gives up on Maggie.

"Well," I say. "Dee."

"No, Mama," she says. "Not 'Dee,' Wangero Leewanika Kemanjo!"

"What happened to 'Dee'?" I wanted to know.

"She's dead," Wangero said. "I couldn't bear it any longer, being named after the people who oppress me."

"You know as well as me you was named after your aunt Dicie," I said. Dicie is my sister. She named Dee. We called her "Big Dee" after Dee was born.

"But who was she named after?" asked Wangero.

"I guess after Grandma Dee," I said.

"And who was she named after?" asked Wangero.

(Continued)

"Her mother," I said, and saw Wangero was getting tired. "That's about as far back as I can trace it," I said. Though, in fact, I probably could have carried it back beyond the Civil War through the branches.

"Well," said Asalamalakim, "there you are."

"Uhnnnh," I heard Maggie say.

"There I was not," I said, "before 'Dicie' cropped up in our family, so why should I try to trace it that far back?"

He just stood there grinning, looking down on me like somebody inspecting a Model A car. Every once in a while he and Wangero sent eye signals over my head.

"How do you pronounce this name?" I asked.

"You don't have to call me by it if you don't want to," said Wangero.

"Why shouldn't I?" I asked. "If that's what you want us to call you, we'll call you."

"I know it might sound awkward at first," said Wangero.

"I'll get used to it," I said. "Ream it out again."

Well, soon we got the name out of the way. Asalamalakim had a name twice as long and three times as hard. After I tripped over it two or three times he told me to just call him Hakim-a-barber. I wanted to ask him was he a barber, but I didn't really think he was, so I didn't ask.

"You must belong to those beef-cattle peoples down the road," I said. They said "Asalamalakim" when they met you, too, but they didn't shake hands. Always too busy: feeding the cattle, fixing the fences, putting up salt-lick shelters, throwing down hay. When the white folks poisoned some of the herd the men stayed up all night with rifles in their hands. I walked a mile and a half just to see the sight.

Hakim-a-barber said, "I accept some of their doctrines, but farming and raising cattle is not my style." (They didn't tell me, and I didn't ask, whether Wangero (Dee) had really gone and married him.)

We sat down to eat and right away he said he didn't eat collards and pork was unclean. Wangero, though, went on through the chitlins and corn bread, the greens and everything else. She talked a blue streak over the sweet potatoes. Everything delighted her. Even the fact that we still used the benches her daddy made for the table when we couldn't effort to buy chairs.

"Oh, Mama!" she cried. Then turned to Hakim-a-barber. "I never knew how lovely these benches are. You can feel the rump prints," she said, running her hands underneath her and along the bench. Then she gave a sigh and her hand closed over Grandma Dee's butter dish. "That's it!" she said. "I knew there was something I wanted to ask you if I could have." She jumped up from the table and went over in the corner where the churn stood, the milk in it clabber by now. She looked at the churn and looked at it.

"This churn top is what I need," she said. "Didn't Uncle Buddy whittle it out of a tree you all used to have?"

"Yes," I said.

"Uh huh," she said happily. "And I want the dasher, too."

"Uncle Buddy whittle that, too?" asked the barber.

Dee (Wangero) looked up at me.

"Aunt Dee's first husband whittled the dash," said Maggie so low you almost couldn't hear her. "His name was Henry, but they called him Stash."

"Maggie's brain is like an elephant's," Wangero said, laughing. "I can use the churn top as a centerpiece for the alcove table," she said, sliding a plate over the churn, "and I'll think of something artistic to do with the dasher."

When she finished wrapping the dasher the handle stuck out. I took it for a moment in my hands. You didn't even have to look close to see where hands pushing the dasher up and down to make butter had left a kind of sink in the wood. In fact, there were a lot of small sinks; you could see where thumbs and fingers had sunk into the wood. It was beautiful light yellow wood, from a tree that grew in the yard where Big Dee and Stash had lived.

After dinner Dee (Wangero) went to the trunk at the foot of my bed and started rifling through it. Maggie hung back in the kitchen over the dishpan. Out came Wangero with two quilts. They had been pieced by Grandma Dee and then Big Dee and me had hung them on the quilt frames on the front porch and quilted them. One was in the Lone Star pattern. The other was Walk Around the Mountain. In both of them were scraps of dresses Grandma Dee had worn fifty and more years ago, bits and pieces of Grandpa Jarrell's paisley shirts, and one teeny faded blue piece, about the size of a penny matchbox, that was from Great Grandpa Ezra's uniform that he wore in the Civil War.

"Mama," Wangero said sweet as a bird. "Can I have these old quilts?"

I heard something fall in the kitchen, and a minute later the kitchen door slammed.

"Why don't you take one or two of the others?" I asked. "These old things was just done by me and Big Dee from some tops your grandma pieced before she died."

"No," said Wangero. "I don't want those. They are stitched around the borders by machine."

"That'll make them last better," I said.

"That's not the point," said Wangero. "These are all pieces of dresses Grandma used to wear. She did all this stitching by hand. Imagine!" She held the quilts securely in her arms, stroking them.

"Some of the pieces, like those lavender ones, come from old clothes her mother handed down to her," I said, moving up to touch the quilts. Dee (Wangero) moved back just enough so that I couldn't reach the quilts. They already belonged to her.

"Imagine!" she breathed again, clutching them closely to her bosom.

"The truth is," I said, "I promised to give them quilts to Maggie, for when she marries John Thomas."

She gasped like a bee had stung her.

"Maggie can't appreciate these quilts!" she said. "She'd probably be backward enough to put them to everyday use."

"I reckon she would," I said. "God knows I been saving em' for long enough with nobody using em'. I hope she will!" I didn't want to bring up how I had offered Dee (Wangero) a quilt when she went away to college. Then she had told me they were old-fashioned, out of style.

"But they're *priceless*!" she was saying now, furiously; for she has a temper. "Maggie would put them on the bed and in five years they'd be in rags. Less than that!"

"She can always make some more," I said. "Maggie knows how to quilt."

Dee (Wangero) looked at me with hatred. "You just will not understand. The point is these quilts, *these* quilts!"

"Well," I said, stumped. "What would *you* do with them"

"Hang them," she said. As if that was the only thing you *could* do with quilts.

Maggie by now was standing in the door. I could almost hear the sound her feet made as they scraped over each other.

"She can have them, Mama," she said, like somebody used to never winning anything, or having anything reserved for her. "I can member' Grandma Dee without the quilts."

I looked at her hard. She had filled her bottom lip with checkerberry snuff and gave her face a kind of dopey, hangdog look. It was Grandma Dee and Big Dee who taught her how to quilt herself. She stood there with her scarred hands hidden in the folds of her skirt. She looked at her sister with something like fear but she wasn't mad at her. This was Maggie's portion. This was the way she knew God to work.

(*Continued*)

When I looked at her like that something hit me in the top of my head and ran down to the soles of my feet. Just like when I'm in church and the spirit of God touches me and I get happy and shout. I did something I never had done before: hugged Maggie to me, then dragged her on into the room, snatched the quilts out of Miss Wangero's hands and dumped them into Maggie's lap. Maggie just sat there on my bed with her mouth open.

"Take one or two of the others," I said to Dee.

But she turned without a word and went out to Hakim-a-barber.

"You just don't understand," she said, as Maggie and I came out to the car.

"What don't I understand?" I wanted to know.

"Your heritage," she said. And then she turned to Maggie, kissed her, and said, "You ought to try to make something of yourself, too, Maggie. It's really a new day for us. But from the way you and Mama still live you'd never know it."

She put on some sunglasses that hid everything above the tip of her nose and chin.

Maggie smiled; maybe at the sunglasses. But a real smile, not scared. After we watched the car dust settle I asked Maggie to bring me a dip of snuff. And then the two of us sat there just enjoying, until it was time to go in the house and go to bed.

Follow-Up Activity

Questions for Discussion

1. How is the narrator related to Maggie and Dee?

2. In what ways were Maggie and Dee alike and different when they were growing up?

3. Why does Maggie want the quilts? For what reason does Dee (Wangero) want the quilts? Explain which of the sisters you think deserves to keep them.

4. Compare Dee's motivations for leaving and visiting home to those of Gloria Watkins's. In what ways do you think each author regards the life and values of her own background?

Assignment 2

Lewis Thomas's "The Iks"

As in the previous unit on "Keeping Close to Home," this unit takes you through the writing process, helping you analyze Lewis Thomas's ideas and write an essay of your own in response to his ideas. This unit will take you through the writing process using the strategies that you were introduced to in Part II and that you practiced in Assignment #1. As you work through these strategies again in Assignment #2, see if you can use them more deliberately this time. In other words, personalize these strategies and make them yours. For each activity, ask yourself what the goal of the lesson is and how you can best use each activity or exercise to maximize its benefits for you. Remember that, ultimately, you are working through each page in this unit in order to produce the best, most successful essay that you can. Try to determine how each page can help you to accomplish that goal.

The Iks

Essay

LEWIS THOMAS

"The Iks," by physician-scientist Lewis Thomas, was originally published in the New England Journal of Medicine *in the early 1970s. It is part of a collection of 29 essays that center on science, but that range in focus from molecules, to organisms, to organisms' organization in societies, and even to the search for life forms not of the Earth. Thomas's consistent idea throughout the collection is that there are many replications between the enclosed unit of a cell and the complex interactions of a society. Thomas's belief, one that comes out of his life of study in the sciences, is that we humans are a very young species and just beginning to learn about how to get along with one another to ensure our survival. His optimism about our future is based on his belief that, like other much older species have done, we will continue our social development and learn better ways to get along.*

The small tribe of Iks, formerly nomadic hunters and gatherers in the mountain valleys of northern Uganda, have become celebrities, literary symbols for the ultimate fate of disheartened, heartless mankind at large. Two disastrously conclusive things happened to them: the government decided to have a national park, so they were compelled by law to give up hunting in the valleys and become farmers on poor hillside soil, and then they were visited for two years by an anthropologist who detested them and wrote a book about them.

The message of the book is that the Iks have transformed themselves into an irreversibly disagreeable collection of unattached, brutish creatures, totally selfish and loveless, in response to the dismantling of their traditional culture. Moreover, this is what the rest of us are like in our inner selves, and we will all turn into Iks when the structure of our society comes all unhinged.

The argument rests, of course, on certain assumptions about the core of human beings, and is necessarily speculative. You have to agree in advance that man is fundamentally a bad lot, out for himself alone, displaying such graces as affection and compassion only as learned habits. If you take this view, the story of the Iks can be used to confirm it. These people seem to be living together, clustered in small, dense villages, but they are really solitary, unrelated individuals with no evident use for each other. They talk, but only to make ill-tempered demands and cold refusals. They share nothing. They never sing. They turn the children out to forage as soon as they can walk, and desert the elders to starve whenever they can, and the foraging children snatch food from the mouths of the helpless elders. It is a mean society.

They breed without love or even casual regard. They defecate on each other's doorsteps. They watch their neighbors for signs of misfortune, and only then do they laugh. In the book they do a lot of laughing, having so much bad luck. Several times they even laughed at the anthropologist, who found this especially repellent (one senses, between the lines, that the scholar is not himself the world's luckiest man). Worse, they took him into the family, snatched his food, defecated on his doorstep, and hooted dislike at him. They gave him two bad years.

It is a depressing book. If, as he suggests, there is only Ikness at the center of each of us, our sole hope for hanging onto the name of humanity will be in endlessly mending the structure of our society, and it is changing so quickly and completely that we may never find the threads in time. Meanwhile, left to ourselves alone, solitary, we will become the same joyless, zestless, untouching lone animals.

But this may be too narrow a view. For one thing, the Iks are extraordinary. They are absolutely astonishing, in fact. The anthropologist has never seen people like them anywhere, nor have I. You'd think, if they were simply examples of the common essence of mankind, they'd seem more recognizable. Instead, they are bizarre, anomalous. I have known my share of peculiar, difficult, nervous, grabby people, but I've never encountered any genuinely, consistently detestable human beings in all my life. The Iks sound more like abnormalities, maladies.

I cannot accept it. I do not believe that the Iks are representative of isolated, revealed man, unobscured by social habits. I believe their behavior is something extra, something laid on. This unremitting, compulsive repellence is a kind of complicated ritual. They must have learned to act this way; they copied it, somehow. I have a theory, then. The Iks have gone crazy. The solitary Ik, isolated in the ruins of an exploded culture, has built a new defense for himself. If you live in an unworkable society you can make up one of your own, and this is what the Iks have done. Each Ik has become a group, a one-man tribe on its own, a constituency. → body of supporter

Now everything falls into place. This is why they do seem, after all, vaguely familiar to all of us. We've seen them before. This is precisely the way groups of one size or another, ranging from committees to nations, behave. It is, of course, this aspect of humanity that has lagged behind the rest of evolution, and this is why the Ik seems so primitive. In his absolute selfishness, his incapacity to give anything away, no matter what, he is a successful committee. When he stands at the door of his hut, shouting insults at his neighbors in a loud harangue, he is a city addressing another city. Cities have all the Ik characteristics. They defecate on doorsteps, in rivers and lakes, their own or anyone else's. They leave rubbish. They detest all neighboring cities, give nothing away. They even build institutions for deserting elders out of sight.

 Nations are the most Ik-like of all. No wonder the Iks seem familiar. For total greed, rapacity, heartlessness, and irresponsibility there is nothing to match a nation. Nations, by law, are solitary, self-centered, withdrawn into themselves. There is no such thing as affection between nations, and certainly no nation ever loved another. They bawl insults from their doorsteps, defecate into whole oceans, snatch all the food, survive by detestation, take joy in the bad luck of others, celebrate the death of others, live for the death of others.

That's it, and I shall stop worrying about the book. It does not signify that man is a sparse, inhuman thing at his center. He's all right. It only says what we've always known and never had enough time to worry about, that we haven't yet learned how to stay human when assembled in masses. The Ik, in his despair, is acting out this failure, and perhaps we should pay closer attention. Nations have themselves become too frightening to think about, but we might learn some things by watching these people.

Writing Topic

According to Thomas, why can the behavior of individual Iks be compared to the behavior of "groups of one size or another, ranging from committees to nations"? What do you think of his argument? Support your answer with examples from your own experience, your observation of others, or your readings.

Vocabulary and Dictionary Practice

Part I. "The Iks" uses several words that may be new for you. Here are ten that you should familiarize yourself with in order to fully understand Thomas's ideas. Add to this list any other words in the reading selection that you do not know.

For each word on the list, write the two most common definitions on the lines provided and include what part of speech each definition is (noun, verb, adjective, etc). Then, under each of the two definitions, write a sentence that uses the word in a way that reflects that particular definition and part of speech.

1. dismantle
2. speculative
3. zest
4. anomalous
5. malady
6. obscured
7. unremitting
8. constituency
9. harangue
10. rapacity

1. dismantle

first definition: _____

_____

part of speech: _____

sentence: _____

_____

second definition: _____

_____

part of speech: _____

sentence: _____

_____

2. speculative

first definition: _____

_____

part of speech: _____

sentence: _____

_____

second definition: _____

_____

part of speech: _____

sentence: _____

_____

3. zest

first definition: _____

_____

part of speech: _____

sentence: _____

_____

second definition: _____

_____

part of speech: _____

sentence: _____

_____

4. anomalous

first definition: _____

_____

part of speech: _____

sentence: _____

_____

second definition: _____

_____

part of speech: _____

sentence: _____

_____

5. malady

first definition: _____

_____

part of speech: _____

sentence: _____

_____

second definition: _____

_____

part of speech: _____

sentence: _____

_____

6. obscured

first definition: _____

_____

part of speech: _____

sentence: _____

_____

second definition: _____

_____

part of speech: _____

sentence: _____

_____

7. unremitting

first definition: _____

_____

part of speech: _____

sentence: _____

_____

second definition: _____

_____

part of speech: _____

sentence: _____

_____

8. constituency

first definition: _____

_____

part of speech: _____

sentence: _____

_____

second definition: _____

_____

part of speech: _____

sentence: _____

_____

9. harangue

first definition: _____

_____

part of speech: _____

sentence: _____

_____

second definition: _____

_____

part of speech: _____

sentence: _____

_____

10. rapacity

first definition: _____

_____

part of speech: _____

sentence: _____

_____

second definition: _____

_____

part of speech: _____

sentence: _____

_____

Part II.
A. Write down each sentence from Thomas's essay that contains the following words.
B. Tell which of the word's various definitions best fits the sentence.
C. Paraphrase the sentence without using the vocabulary word; in other words, write the sentence using your own words.

1. dismantle

A. _____

_____

B. _____

_____

C. _____

_____

2. speculative

A. _____

_____

B. _____

_____

C. _____

_____

3. zest

A. _____

_____

B. _____

_____

C. _____

_____

4. anomalous

A. _____

_____

B. _____

_____

C. _____

_____

5. malady

A. _____

_____

B. _____

_____

C. _____

_____

6. obscured

A. _____

_____

B. _____

_____

C. _____

_____

7. unremitting

A. _____

_____

B. _____

_____

C. _____

_____

8. constituency

A. _____

_____

B. _____

_____

C. _____

_____

9. harangue

A. _____

_____

B. _____

_____

C. _____

_____

10. rapacity

A. _____

_____

B. _____

_____

C. _____

_____

Part III. For each of these words from "The Iks," tell something new and interesting you learned about the word from the dictionary. For example, you might have found the correct way to pronounce a word you were already familiar with from reading but not from speaking, or you might have learned that a word you thought of as entirely English came from a foreign language.

1. dismantle

_____

_____

2. speculative

_____

_____

3. zest

_____

_____

4. anomalous

_____

_____

5. malady

_____

_____

6. obscured

_____

_____

7. unremitting

_____

_____

8. constituency

_____

_____

9. harangue

_____

_____

10. rapacity

_____

_____

Follow-Up Activity

Write two sentences and use at least two of the vocabulary words in each sentence. Be sure that they make sense. Read your sentences to the class.

Doing a Careful Reading of "The Iks"

Now that you know the meaning of all of the words in "The Iks," you should spend more time with the essay, focusing this time on the essay's ideas so that you not only get a better understanding of it, but you also begin forming judgments about its ideas. Use the "Steps for a Thoughtful Reading of an Essay" (introduced in Part II) to help you with this part of the writing process. Here are the steps:

1. **Read the title again.**
   - The title will tell you something about the reading's main topic.
   - It may also tell you something about Thomas's opinion on the topic.
   - Think about what you already know about the topic and what more you want to know.

2. **Learn about the author.**
   - Read the biographical information about Lewis Thomas at the top of the selection.
   - As you go through the remaining steps below, take note of how Thomas's life or work might connect with his topic.

3. **Read through the selection once quickly.**
   - Read quickly through "The Iks" again so that you get a general fresh impression of what it is about and what Thomas's attitude is toward the topic.
   - Find and mark the things—people, places, experiences, concepts, for example—that he brings up to develop and support his opinion about the topic.

4. **Read again to identify the thesis.**
   - Now read Thomas's essay a second time, but more slowly and carefully, and *with a pen or highlighter in your hand.*
   - Find the thesis and underline it or write it in the margin. Remember, the thesis states the author's overall opinion on the topic of the reading. Often the thesis is contained in a single sentence, but, in some cases, it takes several sentences to make the main argument of the reading selection clear. There are times, too, when the author does not state his or her thesis explicitly, but, if you read the selection carefully, you should be able to state it and then write it in the margin.
   - To help, ask yourself, "What does Thomas seem to want readers to think about his topic?"

5. **Read slowly and methodically through the rest of the reading.**
   - Examine each body paragraph one at a time and list or underline the kinds of evidence that Thomas uses to support his thesis
   - Look in each body paragraph for a *topic sentence*—a sentence that both presents an idea and tells how it gives support to the author's overall opinion.
   - As you read and study the selection, *be sure to write down any thoughts you have* about the author's opinion and his supporting evidence.
   - It is your job to evaluate this evidence for its logic and validity, so be sure to *make notes in the margins* as you read.
   - *Mark the points* that you found interesting or convincing and write a few words explaining your thoughts.

- Note, too, any weaknesses you find.
- When you look back at the notes you made in the margins, you should have a general idea of how convincing you found "The Iks" and what you found to be its strengths and weaknesses.

6. Read again for review.

- Once you have completed steps 1-5 and have thought carefully about Thomas's ideas, read it once more, looking for places where you don't quite understand what is being said.
- Underline any terms that you aren't familiar with and look them up in a dictionary.
- Mark any places that don't fit with your understanding of "The Iks" as a whole. Decide whether this is something that Thomas should have revised, or whether it is something that you need to read again because you don't understand it. You may find that you need to go back to Step 4 and begin working through the reading selection again.
- Once you are certain that you understand the entire reading, you are prepared to discuss, summarize, and/or respond to the writing topic that follows "The Iks."

Follow-Up Activity

Before taking this class, how many times did you usually read an essay such as "The Iks" before you felt you understood it entirely? Go back over the six steps for a careful reading listed above and count how many times you are directed to read through "The Iks." Compare the two numbers and, if they do not match, evaluate your reading strategy before taking this class against the one you are using now. Explain your conclusions to the class.

Questions to Review Your Understanding of "The Iks"

Working with a partner, write your answers to the following questions. Then share your answers with the class.

Paragraph 1

What two bad things does the author say happened to the Iks? Do you agree that these things should both be called "bad"? Explain.

Paragraph 2

What kind of people did the Iks turn into as a result of the bad things that happened to them? When the rest of us have similarly bad experiences, what, according to the anthropologist, will happen to us?

Paragraphs 3–5

To agree that we all have the potential to turn into Iks, what assumptions about human nature must we make?

Paragraphs 6–7

Why does Thomas say the Iks are not representative of ordinary human nature?

Paragraphs 7–8

What is Thomas's theory about the Iks? Does his explanation seem plausible to you? Why or why not?

Paragraph 9

In what ways are cities and nations like the Iks?

Paragraph 10

What do you think Thomas means when he concludes that we must "learn to stay human when assembled in masses"? Do you agree?

Responding to the Writing Topic

You should now have a good understanding of the ideas and overall message of "The Iks." Now is a good time in the writing process to look again at the writing topic and begin to think about how you will respond. Remember that the essay you write must respond to all parts of the writing topic. Here is the topic again:

Writing Topic

According to Thomas, why can the behavior of individual Iks be compared to the behavior of "groups of one size or another, ranging from committees to nations"? What do you think of his argument? Support your answer with examples from your own experience, your observation of others, or your readings.

Examine all parts of the writing topic:

- You are first asked a question about a specific aspect of "The Iks," a question that uses the word **"why."** It asks you to explain **why** Thomas believes that the behavior of the Iks is similar to the behavior of groups, including political ones. Why does he make that claim, and how does he support his argument? Your essay will have to answer this first part of the writing topic.

  As you learned in Assignment #1, your response to this part of the writing topic can be called the *directed summary*, and you will present it in the introductory paragraph of your essay.

- The second question in the writing topic asks you to state whether you think that Thomas's claim that these two things—Iks and various kinds of groups—holds true. If you annotated "The Iks" carefully, you should have identified the characteristics of the Iks. Think about the various kinds of groups you have belonged to or observed. Do most of them act in ways similar to the Iks, as Thomas claims? Your answer to this question will become the thesis of your essay because it will state your overarching view on the topic.

  As you learned in Assignment #1, your *thesis statement* will follow your directed summary and will close your introductory paragraph.

- The third part of the writing topic tells you to support your opinion—your thesis—with clear examples taken from your own experiences. The following activity will help you begin to find some of those examples. Be sure to keep notes on your ideas so that you can turn back to them later.

Follow-Up Activity

1. List ten groups that you have been a part of or have observed—for example, college or professional football teams, Republicans and Democrats during an election year, sororities and fraternities, or perhaps groups formed as part of a church or religious institution.

2. Under each of the ten groups you listed, give five words or phrases that describe the group's actions. Try to choose five words or phrases that capture how each group behaves or what they try to accomplish.

3. From your list of ten and based on each group's actions and accomplishments, choose the group you would most want to be a part of, and tell why.

4. From your list of ten and based on each group's actions and accomplishments, choose the group you would least want to be a part of, and tell why.

5. Partner with a classmate and both of you discuss your lists and opinions.

Strategies to Help You Analyze a Reading Selection and Develop Your Ideas for Writing a Response

All of the activities you have done so far will contribute to the essay you ultimately write, but a deeper analysis of Thomas's ideas is an important part of the process. You want to be sure to avoid misrepresenting any author's ideas or views.

It is especially important that you begin with an open mind and fully explore all of the aspects of an author's ideas. If you do not spend time with them, you might represent them unfairly or less seriously than the ideas deserve. To avoid these mistakes, use the strategies for analysis that you learned in Assignment #1. Take your time with them and, keeping an open mind, use them to look more deeply at Thomas's argument and evidence.

Remember the strategies for analyzing a reading selection: *questioning, freewriting,* and *listing.* This time, as you use the various subparts under each, see if you can commit them to memory so that you can use them any time you engage with reading material. Each time you use them, you will notice that one strategy may work better for a particular reading selection than the others. If you memorize them, you will be able to decide which strategy or strategies might work best for the writing assignment you are completing. For now, though, because they are new to you, go through them all to analyze "The Iks."

Questioning

- questions about the highlighting you did:
  Why did I underline this part of the reading?

  How is this information important to Thomas's point?

  What is the relationship between this information and the question I am being asked to write about?

- questions about Thomas's ideas:
  What things in this essay do not make sense to me?

  Where do I think the author should have explained further?

  How do the examples in the essay relate to the author's point?

- questions about "The Iks" that seem important:
  What are some of the things that Thomas says that I am happy to hear someone say?

  What things that the author says seem true to me?

  What things that the author says seem wrong to me?

  What thing that the author says is most important to me?

  What idea in this essay is completely new to me?

Freewriting

If you still feel that you have little to say to respond to Thomas's essay and topic, try some freewriting.

- Pick one or more of your answers to the questions you have already answered, and just begin to write about it.
- While you are doing this writing, do not stop; do not censor yourself; just let the words come.
- Do this for about five or ten minutes without thinking about spelling, grammar, word choice, or even the sense of what you are saying.
- When you have completed this activity, you will want to take a break.
- After your brief break, come back and read what you have written. Most of what you now have down on paper will not end up in your essay, but, as you read through your freewriting, you will find one or more sentences or ideas that seem interesting, important, or even compelling to you. Highlight these points and ideas.

Listing

With this strategy, you simply list all of the thoughts and reactions you have noted so far. By looking down your list, you may see a pattern of ideas develop, one that you can use to develop an essay of your own.

- List all of the annotations you made for "The Iks."
- List the main ideas you can see in your answers to the questioning phase above.
- List any main ideas that developed from your responses to the follow-up activities above.
- Be sure to list all the items from your freewriting that you thought were interesting. As you make this list, other ideas may come into your head. Put them on your list as well.

Study your list. Connect with some kind of mark all the ideas that seem related to each other. When you are done, one related group of ideas will probably be longer than the others. This group should give you a good start on what you want to say in your own essay in response to Thomas's ideas.

Shaping Your Ideas into a Rough Draft

Now that you have done extensive prewriting, you are prepared to plan the rough draft of your essay. Although you may already have written out parts of your draft as you worked on some of the activities above, it is time now to think about each part of your essay and how you will compose it. Turn back to Part II and examine "A Suggested Structure for an Essay That Responds to Another Writer's Essay." Also, look again at the writing topic for "The Iks." Notice that it asks you to do three things:

1) Write a summary that tells **why** Thomas believes that the behavior of individual Iks can be compared to the behavior of people in groups.

Remember that you have already worked on this in earlier activities. Look back now to the work you did. You may be able to use some of it below, when you write your essay's *directed summary*.

2) Take a position on this idea; do you agree with Thomas?

This is your thesis statement, and it will unify your essay, so it's important that you write it out clearly. Turn back to the review questions and follow-up activities you answered. What were your thoughts and ideas? You will use them below when you write a thesis statement. Remember that you can always revise it as you work on your rough draft.

3) Support and develop your position using specific evidence taken from your own experiences and readings.

Your response to this part of the writing topic will make up nearly your entire essay. The explanations and support you offer will make up your essay's body paragraphs. Remember some of the thinking you did about groups you've belonged to or observed. You will be able to use some of this as evidence to support your thesis. Remember it when you begin working on body paragraphs.

Drafting Your Directed Summary

Here are some questions that will help you answer the first part of the writing topic. Answer each one as thoroughly and carefully as you can; then use your answers and those you wrote in earlier activities to draft a directed summary that answers the first question:

> According to Thomas, **why** can the behavior of individual Iks **be compared to** the behavior of "groups of one size or another, ranging from committees to nations"?

Notice that this question does *not* ask you to summarize the entire essay. Rather, it asks you to explain one aspect of Thomas's essay. The important action words are bolded. Notice that the first question asks you to **explain why** Thomas finds similarities between the Iks and groups of various sizes. How do Iks behave, and why does Thomas find the same kind of behavior when people are in groups, including large groups such as committees and nations?

Here are some questions that will help you plan your directed summary in response to the first question.

1. Why does Thomas say the Iks have a "mean society"?

2. Why does he think the Iks act in the way that they do?

3. In what ways do groups exhibit behavior similar to the Iks, according to Thomas?

4. Why does he think groups act the way they do?

Follow-Up Activity

1. After completing the questions above, share your answers with the class. Discuss the important points from "The Iks" that should be included in the directed summary.
2. Draft your directed summary.
3. Form small groups and take turns in each group reading your summaries aloud. Discuss the strengths and weaknesses of each.

Developing Your Thesis Statement

The second question in the writing topic asks you to evaluate Thomas's point of view regarding the behavior patterns shared by the Iks and groups of various sizes. Do groups frequently exhibit the kinds of behavior shown by the Iks? You are asked: "What do you think of his argument?" How will you respond to this question? Your answer will be the *thesis* of your essay.

As you learned in Assignment #1, think of your thesis as composed of three parts:

- the subject being considered
- Thomas's claim about the subject
- your opinion about the subject

Fill in your answers on the line below to form your thesis statement.

The subject/Thomas's idea about the subject AND your opinion about the subject

_____

_____

_____

_____

_____

_____

After you have finished writing your sentence, review your statement to see that it contains the following elements:

- Thomas's point of view on the subject
- your point of view on the subject

If either of these elements is missing, rewrite your thesis statement so that both are included.

Up to this point, you have been planning the draft of your introductory paragraph. Now that you have drafted your thesis statement, you can begin planning your body paragraphs. They will have to explain your ideas and give support to your thesis statement.

Developing Body Paragraphs for an Essay That Presents a Thesis

Reminders:

Body paragraphs make up the largest part of an essay.

- The job of each body paragraph is to develop one point that supports the thesis statement.
- These points taken together constitute the argument of the essay.
- Writing a good body paragraph can be easy once you understand the criteria that the body paragraph must fulfill.

Here is a review of the three most important criteria for paragraphs in an argumentative essay:

1. **an appropriate or suitable topic**—one that supports the thesis statement

2. **evidence**—for instance, a concrete fact, example, or quotation—that demonstrates the point of the paragraph

3. **a link to the thesis**—sentences that show how and why the paragraph, including the evidence, relates to the thesis

A Basic Outline Form for an Essay That Presents a Thesis

All of the work you have done so far—reading and carefully annotating "The Iks," analyzing its ideas, writing a directed summary in response to the first question in the writing topic, thinking about your own experiences and deciding on your thesis statement, and drafting your essay's introduction—should be gathered together now into a shape that will become your essay, your response to the writing topic for "The Iks."

- Remember that you should follow the basic structure of an academic essay.
- To refresh your memory, turn back to Part II and review the diagram of the academic essay format.
- As you begin filling in this diagram form, you should be able to turn back to material you have already drafted as you worked through the exercises in this unit.
- Fill in the diagram form as fully as you can. A good plan will help you draft an essay that is clear and coherent.

I. **Introductory Paragraph:**

   A. one or two opening sentences that give the reading selection's title, author, and main topic:

   _____

   _____

   _____

   B. the main points that will be included in the directed summary:

   1.

   2.

   3.

   4.

   C. your thesis statement: Be sure that it presents a clear position in response to the writing topic. State your thesis in your own words.

   _____

   _____

   _____

II. Body Paragraphs: For each body paragraph you will include in your essay, plan the following parts:

Write down the topic idea for the paragraph.

_____

_____

_____

List the evidence you will use to support your topic idea (fact, example, etc.).

_____

_____

_____

_____

Tell how the evidence and your ideas link to the thesis statement.

_____

_____

_____

_____

(Repeat this part of the outline as often as necessary to plan all of your body paragraphs.)

III. Conclusion: What are some general remarks you can make to close your essay? Perhaps you will remind your readers of the main argument of your paper, for example.

_____

_____

_____

Drafting Your Essay

Now that you have a basic plan for the structure of your essay and a map of its various parts, you are ready to begin drafting.

- Look back to Part II and review the diagram of the thesis-centered essay. It will help you to keep a coherent structure in mind as you put together the sections of your outline.

- If your thinking changes as you draft, return to your outline and make necessary adjustments. Every time you decide to revise your outline and essay, remember that this is a good sign, a sign that your thinking is developing and becoming more thoughtful and convincing.

- Don't stop thinking. Allow yourself to pursue lines of thought that sometimes develop during the drafting stage. Keep turning back to all of the activities in this unit as you draft your essay. Try to recall some of your reactions, thoughts, and ideas as you worked on these activities. This may help you to strengthen, expand on, or more fully develop your essay's argument.

Follow-Up Activity

Your draft will always benefit from careful rereadings. Even better is to let others hear or read your draft and give you their feedback. Sometimes, a classmate or family member can spot places in your draft where you aren't clear, or where you have neglected to fix a grammar error.

1. Working with a partner or small group, have a classmate read your draft out loud slowly. Stop the person whenever anyone hears a problem or an error. As you listen, make notes on the changes you want to make. Then discuss the draft with your partner or group. Give everyone a chance to hear his or her draft read out loud.

2. Read a classmate's rough draft. Then choose the paragraph or group of sentences that, in your opinion, are the strongest part of the essay. Read the sentences out loud to the writer of the draft and explain why you chose them.

3. Working with a partner, each of you read aloud one of the two student essays below. As one person reads it, the second one should mark places where revision is necessary or where it would help improve the essay. After you finish reading, discuss your suggestions for revising the essay.

Student Essay 1

Essay

THE IKS

In the essay the "Iks" by Lewis Thomas, the author describes a society that had got their homes taken away by the government. The Iks were a tribe of selfish people, who didn't care for anybody but for themselves. They left the elderly to starve and die, in the middle of nowhere, and they did not care about their children. Anthropologists were sent to observe the Iks behavior after they were removed from their home. Knowing they were being watched, it caused them to act differently. Thomas believed that nations behave like the Iks quoting, "groups of one size or another, ranging from committees to nations," meaning that cities and nations all over the world act like Iks because of the selfish ways they obtain. If people were to look the way each nation treats each other is the same way, the Iks treat one another. Thomas implies that many nations' and cities' behavior can be compared to the Iks; this is true due to all the discrimination, racism, and cruelty people present to each other in various ways.

Discrimination is an act or instance, when distinctions are made between 'two groups. Thomas suggests that cities and nations behave like the Iks because of all the selfish things nations do to each other. In the United States there is major historical events of discrimination, showing how the United States behaved like the !ks. The trail of tears was one of America's worst examples of discrimination. In the 1800's, President Andrew Jackson passed the Indian removal act of 1830, making all Indian nations move out to the city of Oklahoma, where all Indian tribes were kept. This example is very accurate to Thomas' essay because it proves how nations discriminate against others even if they live on the same land.

Racism to this day continues to be a major act of discrimination all over the world. Edward Said's Essay "Clashing Civilizations" explains how racial discrimination is expressed. Since the air plane crash of 9111, Americans come together in memory of the tragical event that took place. Said quotes, "What has persisted, often insidiously and implicitly, in discussion since the terrible events of September 11." Said's meaning to this quote is that since the United States knows that Osama Binladin was responsible for this horrible event, and just because his ethnicity is Muslim, U.S. citizens believe that all Muslim nations are bad just because of one man's actions. Not all Muslims are bad as there are innocent men, women and children just like in every other country. Even in the United States, many ethnic groups discriminate each other based on the color of their skin. White men come together and formed the KKK, discriminating against African Americans because of their skin color.

In all these Major events, evidence of cruelty is the reason why people feel depressed and makes nations behave differently. When Anthropologist were observing the !ks, the tribe acted differently, and became angry towards the outsiders. In my opinion that would be known as cruelty. In World War 2, Adolf Hitler wanted to abolish the Jewish nation by sending them to concentration camps where they were tortured, burned, and shot. All these cruel horrific crimes were very shocking to many, but the Nazis didn't care about anybody but for Germans. The whole point ofa World War, is the battle of nations fighting for territory, land, or supplies for their country.

In conclusion, Thomas's argument about nations and cities behaving like the !ks is correct. The discrimination, racism, and cruelty happening around the world prove his point. Historical events in the United States prove that nations are selfish and only care about what benefits them and people only come together, to battle other nations and prove whose better than the other. In addition, internal discrimination takes place when citizens form ethnic groups and discriminate against each other, and cause racism in the nation. All these events are very cruel and still persist today, as if nothing has really changed.

Student Essay 2

THE "IKS"

In "The Iks", Lewis Thomas compares the behavior of the Iks with nations and committees. The behaviors ofIks are demeaning and are known as " brutish creatures" (Lewis Thomas "The Iks"). The Iks are known to defecate on "each other's doorstep." Thomas uses cities and nation as his examples for comparing the Iks. Thomas compares them to nations because the individual Iks are their own country. Fending off for themself and telling others that he is their own man. Thomas' explanation of the Iks being their own group is because

(Continued)

they "built a new defense for himself" (Lewis Thomas "The Iks"). Since the govermnent of Uganda took away their land and life as nomads. With their main resource gone, Iks started to behave irregularly. An anthropologist, who had stayed and studied the Iks was treated in a ill-mannered fashion. For two years, he was constantly harassed and shamed by the Iks, in the end he wrote a book on how he despised the Iks. According to Thomas, nations resemble the Iks since they usually help themselves and do not bother to help others. He believes that Iks are like this because of their own egoism. I do not agree with Thomas' conclusion of nations and cities becoming like the Iks, because the country of Taiwan, United States of America, and Thomas' example do not resemble the Iks at all.

The government and cities of Taiwan has always helped their own people and tried do their very best when the inhabitants were in dire need. Taiwan was in deep trouble when the ex-president, Chen Shui-bian, was in presidency. He was well known for scandals that caused Taiwan's system to be in chaos. He and his wife, Wu Shu-chen, have been stealing money from the government spending. Also, stealing money that was to be given to the needy. Each city in Taiwan detested the president, because he had claim he did take the money. These two people were very corrupted and the citizens had to do something about them. During the year 2008, many citizens and some of the government officials who despised Chen, voted for the other president, Ma Ying-jeou. Most citizens admired Ma because he was true to his country. Also, he campaigned his own opinions to help Taiwan's economy and government. While, Chen tried to sabotage Ma's rating of the votes. The behaviors of the citizens has redefined Taiwan's system. Since the inauguration of Ma, the economy of Taiwan has been growing rapidly. The citizens has acted in unification to rid the illness causing Taiwan's problems. Taiwan as a nation has proven Thomas's conclusion to be incorrect. Like Taiwan, United States of America has been helpful to other nations.

Their is no relation between the Iks and America, because America helps other nation's problems while trying to fix their own problems. United States has been known for helping other nations who can not defend for themselves. America has also forgiven the debts of other countries and lent aid to nations that are in need of military support and funding: America's troops are spread out in different countries to take care and help out. Thomas believes that "their is no such thing as affection between nations" (Lewis Thomas "The Iks"). America has shown affection towards nations, such as Iraq, Japan, and third world countries. Each city in America are unique in their own ways. All cities has their own governor. The citizens of each city, voices their own opinions to the governor in order to get an idea across. America will never come close to becoming like the Iks. The information Thomas gives, reveal that the Iks does not have a base system anymore.

The Iks has been cornered off by the government of Uganda. Their hunting rights has been revoked in front of their very own eyes. Also, they are made to convert to farming with an area to poor to grow crops. Thomas's theory of "the Iks have gone crazy" (Lewis Thomas "The Iks") is completely true. Which tribe would not have gone crazy, if their main export is hunting and it has been taking right out of their hands. Also, to be given farming supplies to farm, where the idea of farming is new to them. The Iles should not be distinguished between nations because the Iks are just not adapting to what they have right now. The tribe is showing survival of the fittest instead of staying as a group and trying to figure out things to benefit each other. If the Iks had put their heads together and think, they would not be known as "brutish creatures who are heartless" (Lewis Thomas "The Iks").

The whole idea of Thomas's statement of Iks being just like nations, should be revoked. The Iks are not nations nor cities, they are a tribe that does not know what to do when things are taken away from them. The example of Taiwan has proven cities to be helpful towards their citizens and not to be greedy. Nations, such as America, are helpful towards other nations and are not irresponsible. I believe Iks are their own group and should not be compared to committees, cities, nor nations. People try to help each other out unlike the Iks, who only help themselves.

Supplemental Reading

A World Not Neatly Divided

AMARTYA SEN

Amartya Sen is an economist presently teaching at Harvard. Many of his books and articles focus on globalization and gender inequality.

When people talk about clashing civilizations, as so many politicians and academics do now, they can sometimes miss the central issue. The inadequacy of this thesis begins well before we get to the question of whether civilizations must clash. The basic weakness of the theory lies in its program of categorizing people of the world according to a unique, allegedly commanding system of classification. This is problematic because civilizational categories are crude and inconsistent and also because there are other ways of seeing people (linked to politics, language, literature, class, occupation, or other affiliations).

The befuddling influence of a singular classification also traps those who dispute the thesis of a clash: To talk about "the Islamic world" or "the Western world" is already to adopt an impoverished vision of humanity as unalterably divided. In fact, civilizations are hard to partition in this way, given the diversities within each society as well as the linkages among different countries and cultures. For example, describing India as a "Hindu civilization" misses the fact that India has more Muslims than any other country except Indonesia and possibly Pakistan. It is futile to try to understand Indian art, literature, music, food, or politics without seeing the extensive interactions across barriers of religious communities. These include Hindus and Muslims, Buddhists, Jains, Sikhs, Parsees, Christians (who have been in India since at least the fourth century, well before England's conversion to Christianity), Jews (present since the fall of Jerusalem), and even atheists and agnostics. Sanskrit has a larger atheistic literature than exists in any other classical language. Speaking of India as a Hindu civilization may be comforting to the Hindu fundamentalist, but it is an odd reading of India.

A similar coarseness can be seen in other categories invoked, like "the Islamic world." Consider Akbar and Aurangzeb, two Muslim emperors of the Mogul dynasty in India. Aurangzeb tried hard to convert Hindus into Muslims and instituted various policies in that direction, of which taxing the non-Muslims was only one example. In contrast, Akbar reveled in his multiethnic court and pluralist laws, and issued official proclamations insisting that no one "should be interfered with on account of religion" and that "anyone is to be allowed to go over to a religion that pleases him."

If a homogeneous view of Islam were to be taken, then only one of these emperors could count as a true Muslim. The Islamic fundamentalist would have no time for Akbar; Prime Minister Tony Blair, given his insistence that tolerance is a defining characteristic of Islam, would have to consider excommunicating Aurangzeb. I expect both Akbar and Aurangzeb would protest, and so would I. A similar crudity is present in the characterization of what is called "Western civilization." Tolerance and individual freedom have certainly been present in European history. But there is no dearth of diversity here, either. When Akbar was making his pronouncements on religious tolerance in Agra, in the 1590s, the Inquisitions were still going on; in 1600, Giordano Bruno was burned at the stake, for heresy, in Campo dei Fiori in Rome.

Dividing the world into discrete civilizations is not just crude. It propels us into the absurd belief that this partitioning is natural and necessary and must overwhelm all other ways of identifying people. That imperious view goes not only against the sentiment that "we human beings are all much the same," but also against the more plausible

(Continued)

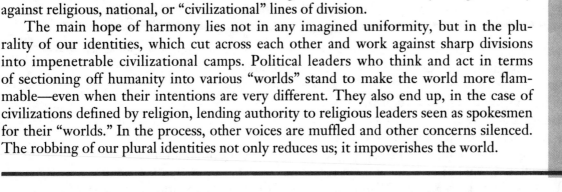

understanding that we are diversely different. For example, Bangladesh's split from Pakistan was not connected with religion, but with language and politics.

Each of us has many features in our self-conception. Our religion, important as it may be, cannot be an all-engulfing identity. Even a shared poverty can be a source of solidarity across the borders. The kind of division highlighted by, say, the so-called "antiglobalization" protesters—whose movement is, incidentally, one of the most globalized in the world—tries to unite the underdogs of the world economy and goes firmly against religious, national, or "civilizational" lines of division.

The main hope of harmony lies not in any imagined uniformity, but in the plurality of our identities, which cut across each other and work against sharp divisions into impenetrable civilizational camps. Political leaders who think and act in terms of sectioning off humanity into various "worlds" stand to make the world more flammable—even when their intentions are very different. They also end up, in the case of civilizations defined by religion, lending authority to religious leaders seen as spokesmen for their "worlds." In the process, other voices are muffled and other concerns silenced. The robbing of our plural identities not only reduces us; it impoverishes the world.

Follow-Up Activity

Questions for Discussion

1. Why, according to Sen, is it wrong to classify the people of the world into clashing civilizations?

2. How does his example of Akbar and Aurangzeb illustrate his point about the failure of civilization categories?

3. What change in conception about the world and its people does Sen propose?

from *The Cosmic Connection*

CARL SAGAN

Carl Sagan (1934–1996) was an American astronomer, an astrochemist, and a successful writer. He popularized astronomy and astrophysics, and promoted the search for Extra-Terrestrial Intelligence. He was a professor at Cornell University and a leading promoter of the space program. Sagan contributed to most of the unmanned space missions that explored the solar system, and he conceived the idea of adding a universal message on spacecraft charted to leave the solar system that might be understood by any extraterrestrial intelligence.

In our earliest history, so far as we can tell, individuals held an allegiance toward their immediate tribal group, which may have numbered no more than ten or twenty individuals, all of whom were related by blood. As time went on, the need for cooperative behavior—in the hunting of large animals or large herds, in agriculture, and in the development of cities—forced human beings into larger and larger groups. The group that was identified with, the tribal unit, enlarged at each stage of this evolution. Today, a particular instant in the 4.5-billion-year history of Earth and in the several-million-year history of mankind, most human beings owe their primary allegiance to the nation-state (although some of the most dangerous political problems still arise from tribal conflicts involving smaller population units).

Many visionary leaders have imagined a time when the allegiance of an individual human being is not to his or her particular nation-state, religion, race, or economic group, but to mankind as a whole; when the benefit to a human being of another sex, race, religion, or political persuasion ten thousand miles away is as precious to us as to our neighbor or our brother. The trend is in this direction, but it is agonizingly slow. There is a serious question whether such a global self-identification of mankind can be achieved before we destroy ourselves with the technological forces our intelligence has unleashed.

There is no doubt that our instinctual apparatus has changed little from the hunter-gatherer days of several hundred thousand years ago. Our society has changed enormously from those times, and the greatest problems of survival in the contemporary world can be understood in terms of this conflict—between what we feel we must do because of our primeval instincts and what we know we must do because of our learned knowledge.

If we survive these perilous times, it is clear that even an identification with all of mankind is not the ultimate desirable identification. If we have a profound respect for other human beings as co-equal recipients of this precious patrimony of 4.5 billion years of evolution, why should the identification not apply also to all the other organisms on Earth, which are equally the product of 4.5 billion years of evolution? We care for a small fraction of the organisms on Earth—dogs, cats, and cows, for example—because they are useful or because they flatter us. But spiders and salamanders, salmon and sunflowers are equally our brothers and sisters.

I believe that the difficulty we all experience in extending our identification horizons in this way is itself genetic. Ants of one tribe will fight to the death intrusions by ants of another. Human history is filled with monstrous cases of small differences—in skin pigmentation, in religious beliefs, or even manner of dress and hair style—being the cause of harassment, enslavement, and murder.

A being quite like us, but with a small physiological difference—a third eye, say, or blue hair covering the nose and forehead—somehow evokes feelings of revulsion. Such

(Continued)

feelings may have had adaptive value at one time in defending our small tribe against the beasts and neighbors. But in our times, such feelings are obsolete and dangerous.

The time has come for a respect, a reverence, not just for all human beings, but for all life forms—as we would have respect for a masterpiece of sculpture or an exquisitely tooled machine. This, of course, does not mean that we should abandon the imperatives for our own survival. Respect for the tetanus bacillus does not extend to volunteering our body as a culture medium. But at the same time we can recall that here is an organism with a biochemistry that tracks back deep into our planet's past. The tetanus bacillus is poisoned by molecular oxygen, which we breathe so freeely. The tetanus bacillus, but not we, would be at home in the hydrogen-rich oxygen-free atmosphere of primitive Earth.

A reverence for all life is implemented in a few of the religions of the planet Earth—for example, among the Jains of India. And something like this idea is responsible for vegetarianism, at least in the minds of many practitioners of the dietary constraint. But why is it better to kill plants than animals?

Human beings can survive only by killing other organisms. But we can make ecological compensation by also growing other organisms; by encouraging the forest; by preventing the wholesale slaughter of organisms such as seals and whales, imagined to have industrial or commercial value; by outlawing gratuitous hunting; and by making the environment of Earth more livable—for all its inhabitants.

There may be a time when contact will be made with another intelligence on a planet of some far-distant star, beings with billions of years of quite independent evolution, beings with no prospect of looking very much like us—although they may think very much like us. It is important that we extend our identification horizons, not just down to the simplest and most humble forms of life on our own planet, but also up to the exotic and advanced forms of life that may inhabit, with us, our vast galaxy of stars.

Follow-Up Activity

Questions for Discussion

1. Explain the evolutionary trend that Sagan sees toward global self-identification. Do you think we will ever reach this state? Why or why not?

2. What does Sagan believe to be the greatest threat to the survival of our world? What do you think is the biggest danger facing the world as we know it?

3. Give an example of an organism Sagan would believe it is necessary to kill. How does he justify killing such a life form? Do you support his position? What does Sagan think humans must do to compensate for killing these organisms? What other compensatory actions can you suggest?

4. Compare Sagan ideas to Thomas's. Considering such anomalies as the Iks and the examples of political situations pointed out by Sen, whose exploration of group-think makes the most sense to you? Explain your choice.

Assignment 3

Just as you did in Assignments #1 and #2, read the following essay and the writing topic that follows it. Then use the exercises and activities that follow to move through the writing process and develop your own essay in response to the argument Tan presents in "Mother Tongue."

Mother Tongue

Essay

AMY TAN

Amy Tan is an American writer whose novels examine family relationships, especially those of mothers and daughters. She has written several bestselling novels, such as The Joy Luck Club *and* The Kitchen God's Wife. *Tan has a B.A. and M.A. from San Jose State University.*

I am not a scholar of English or literature. I cannot give you much more than personal opinions on the English language and its variations in this country or others. I am a writer. And by that definition, I am someone who has always loved language. I am fascinated by language in daily life. I spend a great deal of time thinking about the power of language—the way it can evoke an emotion, a visual image, a complex idea, or a simple truth. Language is the tool of my trade. And I use them all—all the Englishes I grew up with.

Recently, I was made keenly aware of the different Englishes I do use. I was giving a talk to a large group of people, the same talk I had already given to a half a dozen other groups. The nature of the talk was about my writing, my life, and my book, *The Joy Luck Club*. The talk was going along well enough, until I remembered one major difference that made the whole talk sound wrong. My mother was in the room. And it was perhaps the first time she had heard me give a lengthy speech, using the kind of English I have never used with her. I was saying things like, "The intersection of memory upon imagination" and "There is an aspect of my fiction that relates to thus-and-thus"—a speech filled with carefully wrought grammatical phrases, burdened, it suddenly seemed to me, with nominalized forms, past perfect tenses, conditional phrases, all the forms of standard English that I had learned in school and through books, the forms of English I did not use at home with my mother.

Just last week, I was walking down the street with my mother, and I again found myself conscious of the English I was using, the English I do use with her. We were talking about the price of new and used furniture and I heard myself saying this: "Not waste money that way." My husband was with us as well, and he didn't notice any switch in my English. And then I realized why. It's because over the twenty years we've been together I've often used that same kind of English with him, and sometimes he even uses it with me. It has become our language of intimacy, a different sort of English that relates to family talk, the language I grew up with.

So you'll have some idea of what this family talk I heard sounds like, I'll quote what my mother said during a recent conversation which I videotaped and then transcribed. During this conversation, my mother was talking about a political gangster in Shanghai who had the same last name as her family's, Du, and how the gangster in his early years

(Continued)

wanted to be adopted by her family, which was rich by comparison. Later, the gangster became more powerful, far richer than my mother's family, and one day showed up at my mother's wedding to pay his respects. Here's what she said in part:

"Du Yusong having business like fruit stand. Like off the street kind. He is Du like Du Zong—but not Tsung-ming Island people. The local people call putong, the river east side, he belong to that side local people. That man want to ask Du Zong father take him in like become own family. Du Zong father wasn't look down on him, but didn't take seriously, until that man big like become a Mafia. Now important person, very hard to inviting him. Chinese way, came only to show respect, don't stay for dinner. Respect for making big celebration, he shows up. Mean gives lots of respect. Chinese custom. Chinese social life that way. If too important won't have to stay too long. He come to my wedding. I didn't see, I heard it. I gone to boy's side, they have YMCA dinner. Chinese age I was nineteen."

You should know that my mother's expressive command of English belies how much she actually understands. She reads the *Forbes* report, listens to *Wall Street Week*, converses daily with her stockbroker, reads all of Shirley MacLaine's books with ease—all kinds of things I can't begin to understand. But when I was growing up, my mother's "limited" English limited *my* perception of her. I was ashamed of her English. I believed that her English reflected the quality of what she had to say. That is, because she expressed them imperfectly, her thoughts were imperfect. And I had plenty of empirical evidence to support me: the fact that people in department stores, at banks, and at restaurants did not take her seriously, did not give her good service, pretended not to understand her, or even acted as if they did not hear her. Today, some of my friends tell me they understand 50 percent of what my mother says. Some say they understand 80 to 90 percent. Some say they understand none of it, as if she were speaking pure Chinese.

But to me, my mother's English is perfectly clear, perfectly natural. It's my mother tongue. Her language, as I hear it, is vivid, direct, full of observation and imagery. That was the language that helped shape the way I saw things, expressed things, made sense of the world. It captures my mother: her intent, her passion, her imagery, the rhythms of her speech, and the nature of her thoughts.

Writing Topic

What are the "different Englishes" Tan discusses, and how does she view them? What do you think of her view? To support your position, be sure to use specific evidence taken from your own experience, observations, or reading.

Vocabulary and Dictionary Practice

Part I. Look up the following words used in "Mother Tongue." For each, write the two most common definitions on the lines provided and include what part of speech each definition is (noun, verb, adjective, etc.). Then, under each of the two definitions, write a sentence that uses the word in a way that reflects that particular definition and part of speech.

evoke
wrought
nominalize
expressive
belies
empirical
vivid

1. **evoke**

   first definition: _____

   _____

   part of speech: _____

   sentence: _____

   _____

   second definition: _____

   _____

   part of speech: _____

   sentence: _____

   _____

2. **wrought**

   first definition: _____

   _____

   part of speech: _____

   sentence: _____

   _____

   second definition: _____

   _____

   part of speech: _____

   sentence: _____

   _____

3. **nominalize**

first definition: _____

_____

part of speech: _____

sentence: _____

_____

second definition: _____

_____

part of speech: _____

sentence: _____

_____

4. **expressive**

first definition: _____

_____

part of speech: _____

sentence: _____

_____

second definition: _____

_____

part of speech: _____

sentence: _____

_____

5. **belies**

first definition: _____

_____

part of speech: _____

sentence: _____

_____

second definition: _____

_____

part of speech: _____

sentence: _____

_____

6. **empirical**

first definition: _____

_____

part of speech: _____

sentence: _____

_____

second definition: _____

_____

part of speech: _____

sentence: _____

_____

7. **vivid**

first definition: _____

_____

part of speech: _____

sentence: _____

_____

second definition: _____

_____

part of speech: _____

sentence: _____

_____

Part II.

A. Write down each sentence from Tan's essay that contains the following words.

B. Tell which of the word's various definitions best fits the sentence.

C. Paraphrase the sentence without using the vocabulary word; in other words, write the sentence using your own words.

1. **evoke**

A. _____

_____

B. _____

_____

C. _____

_____

2. wrought

A. _____

_____

B. _____

_____

C. _____

_____

3. nominalize

A. _____

_____

B. _____

_____

C. _____

_____

4. expressive

A. _____

_____

B. _____

_____

C. _____

_____

5. belies

A. _____

_____

B. _____

_____

C. _____

_____

6. **empirical**

A. _____

_____

B. _____

_____

C. _____

_____

7. **vivid**

A. _____

_____

B. _____

_____

C. _____

_____

Part III. For each of these words from the essay, tell something new and interesting you learned about the word from the dictionary. For example, you might have found the correct way to pronounce a word you were already familiar with from reading but not from speaking, or you might have learned that a word you thought of as entirely English came from a foreign language.

1. **evoke**

_____

_____

2. **wrought**

_____

_____

3. **nominalize**

_____

_____

4. **expressive**

_____

_____

5. **belies**

_____

_____

6. **empirical**

_____

_____

7. **vivid**

_____

_____

Follow-Up Activity

Write a five-sentence description of your bedroom, your pet, your car, or your good friend. Your description must include at least three of the vocabulary words above. Read your description aloud to the class.

Doing a Careful Reading of "Mother Tongue"

By now you should be aware of the importance of working systematically with a reading selection to make sure that you understand its purpose and ideas. In Assignments #1 and #2, you practiced some helpful techniques to help you do a thoughtful reading of an essay; use them again now to better understand "Mother Tongue."

The steps are reproduced here, but your goal should be to memorize them so that they become a normal part of the writing process for you.

1. **Read the title again.**
   - The title will tell you something about the reading's main topic.
   - It may also tell you something about Tan's opinion on the topic.
   - Think about what you already know about the topic and what more you want to know.

2. **Learn about the author.**
   - Read the biographical information about Tan at the top of the selection.
   - As you go through the remaining steps below, take note of how Tans's life or work might connect with her topic.

3. **Read through the selection once quickly.**
   - Read quickly through the reading again so that you get a general fresh impression of what it is about and what Tan's attitude is toward the topic.
   - Notice the things—people, places, experiences, concepts, for example—she brings up to develop and support her opinion about the topic.

4. **Read again to identify the thesis.**
   - Now read the selection a second time, but more slowly and carefully, and *with a pen or highlighter in your hand.*
   - Find the thesis and underline it or write it in the margin. Remember, the thesis states Tan's overall opinion on the topic of the reading. Often the thesis is contained in a single sentence, but, in some cases, it takes several sentences to make the main argument of the reading selection clear. There are times, too, when the author does not state his or her thesis explicitly, but, if you read the selection carefully, you should be able to state it and then write it in the margin.
   - Ask yourself, "What does Tan seem to want readers to think about her topic?"

5. **Read slowly and methodically through the rest of the reading.**
   - Examine each body paragraph one at a time and list or underline the kinds of evidence that Tan uses to support her thesis.
   - Look in each body paragraph for a *topic sentence*—a sentence that both presents an idea and tells how it gives support to the reading's overall opinion.
   - As you read and study the selection, *be sure to write down any thoughts you have* about Tan's opinion and supporting evidence.
   - It is your job to evaluate this evidence for its logic and validity, so be sure to *make notes in the margins* as you read.

- *Mark the points* that you found interesting or convincing and write a few words explaining your thoughts.
- Note, too, any weaknesses you find.
- When you look back at the notes you made in the margins, you should have a general idea of how convincing you found "Mother Tongue" and what you found to be its strengths and weaknesses.

6. Read again for review.
- Once you have thought through the reading selection, read it once more, looking for places where you don't quite understand what is being said.
- Underline any terms that you aren't familiar with and look them up in a dictionary.
- Mark any places in the reading that don't fit with your understanding of the reading as a whole. Decide whether this is something that Tan should have revised, or whether it is something that you need to read again because you don't understand it. You may find that you need to go back to Step 4 and begin working through the reading again.
- Once you are certain that you understand the entire reading, you are prepared to discuss, summarize, and/or respond to the reading with your own essay.

Follow-Up Activity

Close this book. Then, on a sheet of paper, try writing down the six steps for a careful reading using your memory and your own words.

- Think back and remember the strategies you used to help you examine both Watkins's and Tan's essays more carefully.
- When you are finished, open the book to this page and see how you did.
- Take careful note of any steps you omitted.
- Looking over your list, put a star next to the steps that are most helpful to you and briefly explain why.
- Consider more carefully the steps that you did not star and think about how you might alter them so that they would be more helpful.

Discuss the results of this activity with the class. Compare your results and conclusions.

Questions to Review Your Understanding of "Mother Tongue"

Answer the following questions to make sure that you have a clear understanding of Tan's argument as a whole. Be sure to respond to each as thoroughly as you can.

Paragraph 1

Explain Amy Tan's use and feelings about the English language.

Paragraph 2

Why did having her mother in the audience help Tan recognize that there are different forms of English? Explain the difference between standard English and these other forms.

Paragraph 3

In what situations and with what people would Tan use a non-standard form of English? What meaning does the use of this non-standard form have for her?

Paragraph 4

Rewrite Tan's mother's contribution to their conversation in standard English.

Paragraphs 5–6

Explain the difference between the way the young Amy felt about her mother's use of non-standard English and the way she feels about it now.

Responding to the Writing Topic

You should now have a good understanding of the ideas and overall message of "Mother Tongue." You are ready to look again at the writing topic and begin thinking about how you will respond to it. Here it is again, this time with each of three requirements on its own line:

Writing Topic

What are the "different Englishes" Tan discusses, and how does she view them?

What do you think of her view?

To support your position, be sure to use specific evidence taken from your own experience, observations, or reading.

_____

_____

Here is a closer look at the writing topic's three parts:

- The first question asks you to summarize a specific aspect of "Mother Tongue." As you read it carefully, you will notice that it has two question words, **what** and **how**. Keep them in mind because they should shape your response to this question. In other words, your directed summary should tell both "what" and "how."

- The second question asks you to take a stand. You may not be ready to do so, but as you continue working through the activities and exercises here, you will clarify your thoughts and decide what argument you want to make.

- The last part of the writing topic is a directive that requires you to provide evidence in support of the stand you have taken.
  Remember that you will have to respond carefully to all three parts of the writing topic.

Follow-Up Activity

How would you describe your day today if you were talking with a friend? How would you describe your day if you were talking with one of your professors? How would you describe your day to your mother, father, or grandfather? Explain any differences you noticed. Think about both the kind of information you would provide to each of the three and the language you would use.

Strategies to Help You Analyze a Reading Selection and Develop Your Ideas for Writing a Response

Now you are ready to build on the annotations you made earlier when you did a careful reading of "Mother Tongue." Remember the strategies of *questioning*, *freewriting*, and *listing* that you used in writing about "Keeping Close to Home" and "The Iks." By now we hope you realize that these forms of prewriting are an important and productive part of the writing process. If you use them in a focused and sustained way, they lead you to a more systematic analysis of any reading selection. Use these strategies now on "Mother Tongue" as you begin to form your own opinions and ideas. They will guide and clarify your thinking about Tan's essay. They will also help you to put into words your own views on the topic she writes about—that standard and non-standard forms of language have equally expressive power to foster understanding and connection.

Questioning

- questions about the highlighting you did:
  Why did I underline this part of the reading?

  How is this information important to Tan's point?

  What is the relationship between this information and the question I am being asked to write about?

- questions about Tan's ideas:
  What things in this essay do not make sense to me?

  Where do I think Tan should have explained further?

  How do the examples in the essay relate to her point?

- questions about "Mother Tongue" that seem important:
  What are some of the things that Tan says that I am happy to hear someone say?

  What things that she says seem true to me?

  What things that she says seem wrong to me?

  What thing that she says is most important to me?

  What idea in this essay is completely new to me?

Freewriting

Use freewriting now to explore your responses to the questions above:
- Pick one or more of your answers to the questions you have already answered, and just begin to write about it.
- While you are doing this writing, do not stop or censor yourself; just let the words come.

- Do this for about five or ten minutes without thinking about spelling, grammar, word choice, or even the sense of what you are saying.
- When you have completed this activity, you will want to take a break.
- After your brief break, come back and read what you have written. Most of what you now have down on paper will not end up in your essay, but, as you read through your freewriting, you will find one or more sentences or ideas that seem interesting, important, or even compelling to you. Highlight these points and ideas. Are you beginning to develop your thoughts in a way that will shape your essay?

Listing

With this strategy, you simply list all of the thoughts and reactions you have noted so far. By looking down your list, you may see a pattern of ideas develop, one that you can use to develop an essay of your own.

- List all of the annotations you made for "Mother Tongue."
- List the main ideas you can see in your answers to the questioning phase above.
- List any main ideas that developed from your responses to the follow-up activities above.
- Be sure to list all the items from your freewriting that you thought were interesting. As you make this list, other ideas may come into your head. Put them on your list as well.

Look over your list and group all the ideas that seem related to each other. See if you can find one related group of ideas that is longer than the others. These ideas may suggest what you want to say in response to Tan's essay.

Shaping Your Ideas into a Rough Draft

By now you should feel prepared to begin planning your rough draft. If you aren't, go back through some of the activities above and talk with classmates to see what they are thinking. Sometimes it takes a while before your ideas are formed enough; take as much time as you need to clarify your thoughts.

When you are ready to focus on your rough draft, you will have to think about each part of your essay and how you will compose it. Turn back to Part II and examine "A Suggested Structure for an Essay That Responds to Another Writer's Essay." Also, look again at the writing topic for "Mother Tongue." Remind yourself that it asks you to do three things:

1) **Write a summary** that identifies the "different Englishes" that Tan discusses and explains how she views them.

Remember that you have already worked on this in earlier activities. Look back now to the work you did. You may be able to use some of it below, when you write your essay's *directed summary*.

2) **Take a position** on this idea; do you agree with Tan's view?

This is your thesis statement, and it will unify your essay, so it's important that you write it out clearly. Turn back to the review questions and follow-up activities you answered. What were your thoughts and ideas? You will use them below when you write a thesis statement. Remember that you can always revise it as you work on your rough draft.

3) **Support and develop your position using specific evidence** taken from your own experiences and readings. In other words, explain your thinking and why you have the view you present—and don't forget to include the specific "proof" that convinced you to take the position you take.

The explanation of your thoughts and the evidence that led you to draw those conclusions will make up nearly your entire essay. Look back to earlier exercises in this unit to remind yourself of some of the thinking you did about the different forms of English you have used or experienced. You will be able to use some of this as evidence to support your thesis. Remember it when you begin working on body paragraphs.

Drafting Your Directed Summary

Here are some questions that will help you answer the first part of the writing topic. Answer each one as thoroughly and carefully as you can; then use your answers and those you wrote in earlier activities to draft a directed summary that answers the first question:

What are the "different Englishes" Tan discusses, and **how** does she view them?

Notice that this question does *not* ask you to summarize the entire essay. Rather, it asks you to explain one aspect of Tan's essay. There are two important action words in this question, "what" and "how." You will have to identify the "different Englishes" Tan talks about in "Mother Tongue," and you will have to explain her point of view on them.

Here are some steps that will help you plan your directed summary in response to the first question.

1. List the "Englishes" that Tan identifies in her essay.

2. After each one, write down where she uses it.

3. Now find and list the descriptive words that she uses as she talks about each form of English.

4. Look over Tan's descriptions and see if you can identify the associations she makes for each form. What do you think she is trying to show readers?

Follow-Up Activity

1. Write the lists you developed above on the board. Compare your lists with your classmates' and discuss.
2. Draft your directed summary.
3. Working in small groups or with a partner, take turns reading your directed summary aloud. Discuss the strengths and weaknesses of each summary.

Developing Your Thesis Statement

The second question in the writing topic asks "What do you think of her view?" In other words, it asks you to *evaluate* Tan's point of view on non-standard forms of English and *weigh the evidence* she uses to support her position. Do you agree with her view of non-standard forms of English? Your answer to this will be your essay's thesis statement.

Think of your thesis as needing three parts:

- the subject being considered
- Tan's claim about the subject
- your opinion about the subject

Fill in your answers on the line below to form your thesis statement.

The subject/Tan's idea about the subject AND your opinion about the subject

_____

_____

_____

_____

_____

_____

After you have finished writing your sentence, review your statement to see that it contains the following elements:

- Tan's point of view on the subject
- your point of view on the subject

If either of these elements is missing, rewrite your thesis statement so that both are included.

Up to this point, you have been planning the draft of your introductory paragraph. Now that you have drafted your thesis statement, you can begin planning your body paragraphs. They will have to explain your ideas and give support to your thesis statement.

Developing Body Paragraphs for an Essay That Presents a Thesis

Reminders:

Body paragraphs make up the largest part of an essay.

- The job of each body paragraph is to develop one point that supports the thesis statement.
- These points taken together constitute the argument of the essay.
- Writing a good body paragraph can be easy once you understand the elements that the body paragraph must contain.

Here is a review of the three most important elements for paragraphs in an argumentative essay:

Parts of a Body Paragraph

an appropriate or suitable topic—one that supports the thesis statement

evidence—for instance, a concrete fact, example, or quotation—that demonstrates the point of the paragraph

a link to the thesis—sentences that show how and why the paragraph, including the evidence, relates to the thesis

A Basic Outline Form for an Essay That Presents a Thesis

Let's look back at all of the work you have done so far:

You have read and carefully annotated "Mother Tongue."

You have analyzed its ideas.

You have written a directed summary in response to the first question in the writing topic.

You have thought about your own experiences and decided on your thesis statement.

You have drafted your essay's introduction.

All of that work should be gathered together now into a shape that will become your essay, your response to the writing topic for "Mother Tongue."

- Remember that you should follow the basic structure of an academic essay.

- To refresh your memory, turn back to Part II and review the diagram of the academic essay format.

- As you begin filling in this diagram form, you should be able to turn back to material you have already drafted as you worked through the exercises in this unit.

- Fill in the diagram form as fully as you can. A good plan will help you draft an essay that is clear and coherent.

I. Introductory Paragraph:

A. one or two opening sentences that give the reading selection's title, author, and main topic:

_____

_____

_____

B. the main points that will be included in the directed summary:

1.

2.

3.

4.

C. your thesis statement. Be sure that it presents a clear position in response to the writing topic. State your thesis in your own words.

_____

_____

_____

II. Body Paragraphs: For each body paragraph you will include in your essay, plan the following parts:

Write down the topic idea for the paragraph.

_____

_____

_____

List the evidence you will use to support your topic idea (fact, example, etc.).

_____

_____

_____

_____

_____

Tell how the evidence and your ideas link to the thesis statement.

_____

_____

_____

_____

_____

_____

_____

(Repeat this part of the outline as often as necessary to plan all of your body paragraphs.)

III. Conclusion: What are some general remarks you can make to close your essay? Perhaps you will remind your readers of the main argument of your paper, for example.

_____

_____

_____

Drafting Your Essay

Now that you have a basic plan for the structure of your essay and a map of its various parts, you are ready to begin drafting.

- If your thinking changes as you write your draft, return to your outline and make necessary adjustments. Every time you decide to revise your outline and essay, remember that this is a good sign, a sign that your thinking is developing and becoming more thoughtful and convincing.

- Keep turning back to all of the activities in this unit as you draft your essay. Try to recall some of your reactions, thoughts, and ideas as you worked on these activities. This may help you to strengthen, expand on, or more fully develop your essay's argument.

Follow-Up Activity

1. Read the following student essay. Then, using a pen or pencil, do the following:

   a. underline the thesis statement. If you cannot find it, or if you think it needs more work, say so and make any revisions you can to improve it;

   b. mark two places in the essay that aren't clear or that need more development, and explain why you marked them;

   c. mark two places in the essay that are good and tell why you marked them.

2. Now, working with a partner,

   a. compare your ideas about the essay;

   b. use the scoring rubric on page 51 and decide together what score you think the essay deserves.

Student Essay #1

Essay

In the essay "Mother Tongue," Amy Tan discusses the "different English" she uses to communicate with her family. "Different English" is a kind of English that relates to family talk that family members use to communicate with each other. Besides, the other trait of "different English" is that outsiders may have a hard time to understand it. Therefore, "different English" is a kind of language to show intimacy. Tan feels comfortable with "different English." The author believes her mother's "different English is perfect and clear, and this is the natural way her mother expresses herself. In the essay, the author correctly explains the advantages of speaking a language at home that is different from standard English.

Speaking a family language that differs from standard English can be valuable for family members. For example, it is a source of calmness when there is so much stress. For example, one of my friend's grandfather was very sick at home in another country. She cannot do anything to help but wait to hear news. In that period of waiting for a call about her grandfather's condition, she told me that she was so worried about her grandfather because she grew up with him. In that time, I thought she felt so stressed and worried. She was crying a lot and eating less. About three days later, she talked to her mother who spoke in the dialect of her village. To be honest, I did not understand. However, one thing I can be sure of was she told me those words made her feel calmer.

(Continued)

She felt comforted when she heard her mother's tongue. I think this is the power of family language; my friend and her mother can share and understand each other's worries that someone outside of the family cannot. The way family language expresses things gives people a feeling of intimacy. The feeling of intimacy can be a source of comfort in times of stress. Therefore, family language is valuable.

Another advantage of family language is that it makes communication vivid and lively. For instance, my family language is a kind of dialect. My mother uses it a lot because she believes it is the best language to describe things. Some of the things she says cannot even be written down as real words, but they make sense clearly to those who can speak the dialect. According to the author, although most of the people think her mother's "different English" is a poor in expression, Tan still believes that her family language, or "different English," is perfect and natural. When she hears it, it is vivid and full of observation and imagery. Family languages have their unique charms, and they cannot be replaced by other official languages. Therefore, the valuable part of family language is this language is vivid for those who understand it.

All in all, family languages make people feel comfortable in time of stress by showing intimacy between family members. Also, they are clear, natural, and vivid for family members. Therefore, we should always keep our family language.

Follow-Up Activity

Working with a partner, read the following essay aloud. Then mark three grammar or sentence changes you would make. Rewrite or correct the sentences you marked.

Student Essay #2

In the essay "Mother Tongue," Amy Tan is aware of two different Englishes she uses. The first one is standard English that Tan learned in school. She uses it to write books and to give lectures in a club. She uses complex sentences to clarify things for people. The second one is the family talk, the language she grew up with. Tan uses this kind of English with her family all the time. Even though there are not even complete sentences in this English sometimes, Tan and her mother can clearly understand each other. I really agree with Tan's idea of this kind of "family talk" or "Mother Tongue." It always has meaning deep inside; it contains the love from family. It is lovely English.

The family talk connects the members by special memories they shared. It can be anything from a New Year's Eve to someone's birthday party, or even a hike in spring. These memories prove families had fun; it's totally different from the other things of people in society. They have no pressure here, and they don't really need to care about every single word they say. So when families talk about the things in the past, they can always remember the people with them. They will always be there for them at the important times. Tan was walking down the street with her mother and husband. They used family talk and had a great time. They didn't care about the proper way of saying English; they cared about shared memories and the happiness they shared. I thin family talk signals the connection which binds them together.

Family talk is really not about the words themselves; its about the meaning behind those words. I remember a boy from a rich family. His dream was becoming a professional game player, making money by playing games. This was such a bad idea for him and for his family, but his mother only told him these words, "you be live you dream." Those simple words not only showed her trust in her son, but also the love from parents to their kids. This is why family talk is so clear. Members know the meaning and feeling behind the words. They know each other well; they understand the family talk.

Family talk can also reflect a person's nature and thought. Look at the speech of her mother Tan gave in the essay; we can see Tan's mother is such a brave woman. Even though she knew her English is not very good, she would still speak out the thought inside. And the speech also shows her intent, her nature as Tan found out. Personality is reflected through the family, actions, and by words. The speech is simple, but it shows respect and family love. It makes families love each other more for the words they use.

For the families, they don't need so many words to make sure the others in the family understand. They just need to get the feeling that the family always is there for them, and that love explains the advantage of speaking a home language different from standard English.

Follow-Up Activity

Your draft will always benefit from careful rereadings, by you or someone else. Work with a classmate now to find areas in your draft that can be improved.

Use the following process to give and receive draft feedback.

1. Exchange a typed copy of your essay with one of your classmates.
2. Using a pen and a highlighter, mark your classmate's draft in the following manner:
   - Using your pen, underline the subject of each sentence.
   - Use two lines to underline the verb in each sentence.
   - Identify the tense by writing it above the verb.
3. Using your highlighter:
   - If the subject and verb **do not agree**, highlight the sentence.
   - If the verb tense is **not correct**, highlight only the verb.
   - If the verb is irregular and improperly formed, highlight the verb.
4. Using your pen, underline the essay's thesis.
   - If the sentence is a **fragment**, enclose it in parentheses.
   - If the sentence is a **run-on**, draw two vertical lines between the independent clauses.
5. Using your pen, mark the following:
   - If it is clear, if it identifies a topic, and if it makes a claim about it, put a check in the margin.
   - If it needs more work or if you cannot find a thesis, put a dash in the margin.
6. Return the drafts and discuss your marks and suggestions.

Supplemental Reading

Read each of the following essays carefully and use the techniques you have learned to ensure that you fully understand each essay's argument and can begin analyzing its ideas. Don't forget to annotate, freewrite, list, and ask questions as you work on each. As you work with the ideas in these essays, your own ideas regarding uses and assessment of standard and non-standard English will develop. Hence, you will have more to say when you write your own essay in response to the writing topic following "Mother Tongue."

What's Wrong with Black English

Essay

RACHEL L. JONES

Rachel L. Jones was a sophomore at Southern Illinois University when she published the following essay in Newsweek *in December of 1982.*

William Labov, a noted linguist, once said about the use of black English, "It is the goal of most black Americans to acquire full control of the standard language without giving up their own culture." He also suggested that there are certain advantages to having two ways to express one's feelings. I wonder if the good doctor might also consider the goals of those black Americans who have full control of standard English but who are every now and then troubled by that colorful, grammar-to-the-winds patois that is black English. Case in point—me.

I'm a 21-year-old black born to a family that would probably be considered lower-middle class—which in my mind is a polite way of describing a condition only slightly better than poverty. Let's just say we rarely if ever did the winter-vacation thing in the Caribbean. I've often had to defend my humble beginnings to a most unlikely group of people for an even less likely reason. Because of the way I talk, some of my black peers look at me sideways and ask, "Why do you talk like you're white?"

The first time it happened to me I was nine years old. Cornered in the school bathroom by the class bully and her sidekick, I was offered the opportunity to swallow a few of my teeth unless I satisfactorily explained why I always got good grades, why I talked "proper" or "white." I had no ready answer for her, save the fact that my mother had from the time I was old enough to talk stressed the importance of reading and learning, or that L. Frank Baum and Ray Bradbury were my closest companions. I read all my older brothers' and sisters' literature textbooks more faithfully than they did, and even lightweights like the Bobbsey Twins and Trixie Belden were allowed into my bookish inner circle. I don't remember exactly what I told those girls, but I somehow talked my way out of a beating.

I was reminded once again of my "white pipes" problem while apartment hunting in Evanston, Illinois, last winter. I doggedly made out lists of available places and called all around. I would immediately be invited over—and immediately turned down. The thinly concealed looks of shock when the front door opened clued me in, along with the flustered instances of "just getting off the phone with the girl who was ahead of you and she wants the rooms." When I finally found a place to live, my roommate stirred up old memories when she remarked a few months later, "You know, I was surprised when I first saw you. You sounded white over the phone." Tell me another one, sister. I should've asked her a question I've wanted an answer to for years: how does one "talk white"? The silly side of me pictures a rabid white foam spewing forth when I speak. I don't use Valley Girl jargon, so that's not what's meant in my case. Actually, I've pretty much deduced what people mean when they say that to me, and the implications are really frightening.

It means that I'm articulate and well-versed. It means that I can talk as freely about John Steinbeck as I can about Rick James. It means that "ain't" and "he be" are not staples of my vocabulary and are only used around family and friends. (It is almost Jekyll and Hyde-ish the way I can slip out of academic abstractions into a long, lean, double-negative-filled dialogue, but I've come to terms with that aspect of my personality.) As a child, I found it hard to believe that's what people meant by "talking proper"; that would've meant that good grades and standard English were equated with white skin, and that went against everything I'd ever been taught. Running into the same type of mentality as an adult has confirmed the depressing reality that for many blacks, standard English is not only unfamiliar, it is socially unacceptable.

James Baldwin once defended black English by saying it had added "vitality to the language," and even went so far as to label it a language in its own right, saying, "Language [i.e., black English] is a political instrument" and a "vivid crucial key to identity." But did Malcolm X urge blacks to take power in this country "any way y'all can"? Did Martin Luther King, Jr. say to blacks, "I has been to the mountaintop, and I done seed the Promised Land"? Toni Morrison, Alice Walker, and James Baldwin did not achieve their eloquence, grace and stature by using only black English in their writing. Andrew Young, Tom Bradley, and Barbara Jordan did not acquire political power by saying, "Y'all crazy if you ain't gon vote for me." They all have full command of standard English, and I don't think that knowledge takes away from their blackness or commitment to black people.

I know from experience that it's important for black people, stripped of culture and heritage, to have something they can point to and say, "This is ours, we can comprehend it, we alone can speak it with a soulful flourish." I'd be lying if I said that the rhythms of my people caught up in "some serious rap" don't sound natural and right to me sometimes. But how heartwarming is it for those same brothers when they hit the pavement searching for employment? Studies have proven that the use of ethnic dialects decreases power in the marketplace. "I be" is acceptable on the corner, but not with the boss.

Am I letting capitalistic, European-oriented thinking fog the issue? Am I selling out blacks to an ideal of assimilating, being as much like whites as possible? I have not formed a personal political ideology, but I do know this: it hurts me to hear black children use black English, knowing that they will be at yet another disadvantage in an educational system already full of stumbling blocks. It hurts me to sit in lecture halls and hear fellow black students complain that the professor "be tripping dem out using big words dey can't understand." And what hurts most is to be stripped of my own blackness simply because I know my way around the English language.

I would have to disagree with Labov in one respect. My goal is not so much to acquire full control of both standard and black English, but to one day see more black people less dependent on a dialect that excludes them from full participation in the world we live in. I don't think I talk white, I think I talk right.

Follow-Up Activity

Questions for Discussion

1. What does Rachel L. Jones mean when she says that she "talks white"? What are some of the problems the way she speaks has caused for her? Tell about a situation you have been in where the way you talk has caused you to be judged.

2. What are James Baldwin's reasons for defending "black English"? How does Jones respond to his argument? Explain your reasons for finding one position more convincing than the other.

3. What similarities and differences in their experiences with language do you notice that Jones shares with Tan and Watkins?

Why and When We Speak Spanish in Public

Essay

Myriam Marquez

When I'm shopping with my mother or standing in line with my stepdad to order fast food or anywhere else we might be together, we're going to speak to one another in Spanish. That may appear rude to those who don't understand Spanish and overhear us in public places. Those around us may get the impression that we're talking about them. They may wonder why we would insist on speaking in a foreign tongue, especially if they knew that my family has lived in the United States for forty years and that my parents do understand English and speak it, albeit with difficulty and a heavy accent.

Let me explain why we haven't adopted English as our official family language. For me and most of the bilingual people I know, it's a matter of respect for our parents and comfort in our cultural roots. It's not meant to be rude to others. It's not meant to alienate anyone or to Balkanize America. It's certainly not meant to be un-American—what constitutes an "American" being defined by English speakers from North America.

Being an American has very little to do with what language we use during our free time in a free country. From its inception, this country was careful not to promote a government-mandated official language. We understand that English is the common language of this country and the one most often heard in international business circles from Peru to Norway. We know that, to get ahead here, one must learn English.

But that ought not mean that somehow we must stop speaking in our native tongue whenever we're in a public area, as if we were ashamed of who we are, where we're from. As if talking in Spanish—or any other language, for that matter—is some sort of litmus test used to gauge American patriotism.

Throughout this nation's history, most immigrants—whether from Poland or Finland or Italy or wherever else—kept their language through the first generation and, often, the second. I suspect that they spoke among themselves in their native tongue—in public. Pennsylvania even provided voting ballots written in German during much of the 1800s for those who weren't fluent in English.

In this century, Latin American immigrants and others have fought for this country in U.S.-led wars. They have participated fully in this nation's democracy by voting, holding political office, and paying taxes. And they have watched their children and grandchildren become so "American" that they resist speaking in Spanish.

You know what's rude? When there are two or more people who are bilingual and another person who speaks only English and the bilingual folks all of a sudden start speaking Spanish, which effectively leaves out the English-only speaker. I don't tolerate that.

One thing's for sure. If I'm ever in a public place with my mom or dad and bump into an acquaintance who doesn't speak Spanish, I will switch to English and introduce that person to my parents. They will respond in English, and do so with respect.

Follow-Up Activity

Questions for Discussion

1. Why does Myriam Marquez believe bilingual people speak their native language in public? What do you think might be some other reasons for them to speak a language other than English in public settings?

2. What are some of the criticisms Marquez has heard about people who speak Spanish in public? How does she counter these criticisms? Explain why you do or do not find her counterarguments convincing.

3. Tell about a time in public when you overheard a conversation in a language you did not understand. How did that make you feel?

Assignment 4

This unit's lead essay by Jared Diamond reflects on change. As in earlier units, the activities and exercises that follow Diamond's essay are there to guide you through the writing process so that you can fully comprehend the lead essay, develop your own insights about its topic, and capture those ideas fully and clearly in an essay of your own. Remember, the more carefully and thoroughly you use the supporting exercises and readings in the unit, the more thoughtful and successful your essay will be.

Accepting or Rejecting Innovation

JARED DIAMOND

Jared Diamond is a professor of geography at the University of California, Los Angeles. He began his scientific career in physiology and expanded into evolutionary biology and biogeography. He has been elected to the National Academy of Sciences, the American Academy of Arts and Sciences, and the American Philosophical Society. He has published more than six hundred articles and several books, including the New York Times *bestseller* Guns, Germs, and Steel, *which was awarded the Pulitzer Prize.*

Once an inventor has discovered a use for a new technology, the next step is to persuade society to adopt it. Merely having a bigger, faster, more powerful device for doing something is no guarantee of ready acceptance. Innumerable such technologies were either not adopted at all or adopted only after prolonged resistance. Notorious examples include the world's continued rejection of an efficiently designed typewriter keyboard and Britain's long reluctance to adopt electric lighting. What is it that promotes an invention's acceptance by a society?

The first and most obvious factor is relative economic advantage compared with existing technology. While wheels are very useful in modern industrial societies, that has not been so in some other societies. Some advanced Native American cultures in ancient Mexico invented wheeled vehicles with axles for use as toys, but not for transport. That seems incredible to us, until we reflect that the peoples of ancient Mexico lacked domestic animals to hitch to their wheeled vehicles, which therefore offered no advantage over human porters.

A second consideration is social value and prestige, which can override economic benefit—or lack thereof. Millions of people today buy designer jeans for double the price of equally durable generic jeans because the social cachet of the designer label counts for more than the extra cost. Similarly, Japan continues to use its horrendously cumbersome kanji writing system in preference to efficient alphabets or Japan's own efficient kana syllabary because the prestige attached to kanji is so great.

Still another factor is compatibility with vested interests. This book, like probably every other typed document you have ever read, was typed with a QWERTY keyboard, named for the left-most six letters in its upper row. Unbelievable as it may now sound, that keyboard layout was designed in 1873 as a feat of anti-engineering. It employs a whole series of perverse tricks designed to force typists to type as slowly as possible, such as scattering the commonest letters over all keyboard rows and concentrating them on the left side, where right-handed people have to use their weaker hand. The reason

(Continued)

behind all of those seemingly counterproductive features is that the typewriters of 1873 jammed if adjacent keys were struck in quick succession, so that manufacturers had to slow typists down. When improvements in typewriters eliminated the problem of jamming, trials in 1932 showed that an efficiently laid-out keyboard would let us double our typing speed and reduce our typing effort by 95 percent. But QWERTY keyboards were solidly entrenched by then. The vested interest of hundreds of millions of QWERTY typists, typing teachers, typewriter and computer salespeople, and manufacturers have crushed all moves toward keyboard efficiency for over 60 years.

While the story of the QWERTY keyboard may sound funny, many similar cases of resistance to change based on financial interests or settled habits have involved much heavier economic consequences. Why does Japan now dominate the world market for transistorized electronic consumer products to a degree that damages the United States's balance of payments with Japan, even though transistors were invented and patented in the United States? Japan dominates the electronics market today because the Japanese company Sony bought transistor licensing rights from the American company Western Electric at a time when the American electronics consumer industry was churning out vacuum tube models and was therefore reluctant to compete with its own products. Why were British cities still using gas street lighting into the 1920s, long after cities in the United States and Germany had converted to more efficient electric street lighting? British municipal governments rejected electric street lighting because they had invested heavily in gas lighting; to protect those investments, they placed regulatory obstacles in the way of competing electric light companies.

Writing Topic

What factors, according to Diamond, cause people to adopt technological innovations into their lives? To what extent do you think his ideas explain why people accept or reject innovations? Be sure to support your position using examples from your own experience, your observation of others, or your readings.

Vocabulary and Dictionary Practice

Part I.

Look up the following words used in "Accepting or Rejecting Innovation." If there is more than one definition, write both definitions on the lines below. For each definition, indicate the part of speech. Then write a sentence of your own using the vocabulary word as that part of speech.

1. innovation
2. prolong
3. notorious
4. porters
5. cachet
6. syllabary
7. vested
8. perverse
9. counterproductive
10. churning

1. **innovation**:

first definition _____

_____

part of speech _____

sentence _____

_____

second definition _____

_____

part of speech _____

sentence _____

_____

2. **prolong**:

first definition _____

_____

part of speech _____

sentence _____

_____

second definition _____

_____

part of speech _____

sentence _____

_____

3. **notorious:**

first definition _____

_____

part of speech _____

sentence _____

_____

second definition _____

_____

part of speech _____

sentence _____

_____

4. **porters:**

first definition _____

_____

part of speech _____

sentence _____

_____

second definition _____

_____

part of speech _____

sentence _____

_____

5. **cachet:**

first definition _____

_____

part of speech _____

sentence _____

_____

second definition _____

_____

part of speech _____

sentence _____

_____

6. **syllabary:**

first definition _____

_____

part of speech _____

sentence _____

_____

second definition _____

_____

part of speech _____

sentence _____

_____

7. **vested:**

first definition _____

_____

part of speech _____

sentence _____

_____

second definition _____

_____

part of speech _____

sentence _____

_____

8. **perverse:**

first definition _____

_____

part of speech _____

sentence _____

_____

second definition _____

_____

part of speech _____

sentence _____

_____

9. **counterproductive:**

first definition _____

_____

part of speech _____

sentence _____

_____

second definition _____

_____

part of speech _____

sentence _____

_____

10. **churning:**

first definition _____

_____

part of speech _____

sentence _____

_____

second definition _____

_____

part of speech _____

sentence _____

_____

Part II.

A. Write down each sentence from Diamond's essay that contains the following words.

B. Tell which of the word's various definitions best fits the sentence.

C. Paraphrase the sentence without using the vocabulary word; in other words, write the sentence using your own words.

1. **innovation**

   A. _____

   _____

   B. _____

   _____

   C. _____

   _____

2. **prolong**

   A. _____

   _____

   B. _____

   _____

   C. _____

   _____

3. **notorious**

   A. _____

   _____

   B. _____

   _____

   C. _____

   _____

4. **porters**

   A. _____

   _____

   B. _____

   _____

   C. _____

   _____

5. **cachet**

A. _____

_____

B. _____

_____

C. _____

_____

6. **syllabary**

A. _____

_____

B. _____

_____

C. _____

_____

7. **vested**

A. _____

_____

B. _____

_____

C. _____

_____

8. **perverse**

A. _____

_____

B. _____

_____

C. _____

_____

9. **counterproductive**

A. _____

_____

B. _____

_____

C. _____

_____

10. **churning**

A. _____

_____

B. _____

_____

C. _____

_____

Part III.
For each of these words from "Accepting or Rejecting Innovation," tell something new and interesting you learned about the word from the dictionary. For example, you might have found the correct way to pronounce a word you were already familiar with from reading but not from speaking, or you might have learned that a word had a definition that you did not know.

1. **innovation**

_____

_____

2. **prolong**

_____

_____

3. **notorious**

_____

_____

4. **porters**

_____

_____

5. **cachet**

_____

_____

6. **syllabary**

_____

_____

7. **vested**

_____

_____

8. **perverse**

_____

_____

9. **counterproductive**

_____

_____

10. **churning**

_____

_____

Follow-Up Activity

1. Show the class a piece of technology that you have with you—for example, a cell phone or a computer. Tell them how you happen to have it, why you have it, how you use it, and how you would rate it over other models of the same kind. If you bought it yourself, explain why you chose it and whether you would make the same choice today. If it was a gift, tell the class how the giver happened to buy you that particular item.

2. After several or all of your classmates have presented, discuss the results. Do Diamond's ideas seem to be supported by the limited amount of evidence that your classmates have collected through these examples of their personal experiences?

3. Choose someone in your family and explain to the class his or her relationship with technology. Why do you think he or she feels this way?

4. If you were given enough money to buy any car you wish, tell your classmates which one you would choose and why. Try to think with an open mind before you answer so that you say more than "it's a good car." See if you can come up with at least five adjectives that describe why the car attracts you.

Doing a Careful Reading of "Accepting or Rejecting Innovation"

Use the following strategies and any others you choose to guide you through a systematic reading of Diamond's essay. For each step, write as much as you can. You don't yet know what may be of value as you work your way through Diamond's ideas, formulate your own, and ultimately respond in an essay of your own.

1. **Read the title again.**
   - The title will tell you something about the reading selection's main topic.
   - It may also tell you something about Diamond's opinion on the topic.
   - Think about what you already know about the topic and what more you want to know.

2. **Learn about the author.**
   - Read the biographical information about Diamond at the top of the selection.
   - As you go through the remaining steps below, take note of how Diamond's life or work might connect with his topic.

3. **Read through the selection once quickly.**
   - Read quickly through the reading again so that you get a general fresh impression of what it is about and what Diamond's attitude is toward the topic.
   - Notice the things—people, places, experiences, concepts, for example—he brings up to develop and support his opinion about the topic.

4. **Read again to identify the thesis.**
   - Now read the selection a second time, but more slowly and carefully, and *with a pen or highlighter in your hand.*
   - Find the thesis and underline it or write it in the margin. Remember, the thesis states Diamond's overall opinion on the topic of the reading. Often the thesis is contained in a single sentence, but, in some cases, it takes several sentences to make the main argument of the reading selection clear. There are times, too, when the author does not state his or her thesis explicitly, but, if you read the selection carefully, you should be able to state it and then write it in the margin.

- To help, ask yourself, "What does Diamond seem to want readers to think about his topic?"

5. **Read slowly and methodically through the rest of the reading.**

   - Examine each body paragraph one at a time and list or underline the kinds of evidence that Diamond uses to support his thesis.

   - Look in each body paragraph for a *topic sentence*—a sentence that both presents an idea and tells how it gives support to the reading's overall opinion.

   - As you read and study the selection, *be sure to write down any thoughts you have* about Diamond's opinion and supporting evidence.

   - It is your job to evaluate this evidence for its logic and validity, so be sure to *make notes in the margins* as you read.

   - *Mark the points* that you found interesting or convincing and write a few words explaining your thoughts.

   - Note, too, any weaknesses you find.

   - When you look back at the notes you made in the margins, you should have a general idea of how convincing you found "Accepting or Rejecting Innovation" and what you found to be its strengths and weaknesses.

6. **Read again for review.**

   - Once you have thought through the reading selection, read it once more, looking for places where you don't quite understand what is being said.

   - Underline any terms that you aren't familiar with and look them up in a dictionary.

   - Mark any places in the reading that don't fit with your understanding of the reading as a whole. Decide whether this is something that Diamond should have revised, or whether it is something that you need to read again because you don't understand it. You may find that you need to go back to Step 4 and begin working through the reading again.

   - Once you are certain that you understand the entire reading, you are prepared to discuss, summarize, and/or respond to the reading with your own essay.

Follow-Up Activity

Select two of the most important things in Diamond's essay that you marked. Tell the class why you think these two parts are important.

Questions to Review Your Understanding of "Accepting or Rejecting Innovation"

Answer the following questions as thoroughly and carefully as you can to ensure that you haven't missed any of the important aspects of Diamond's argument.

Paragraph 1

What question about society and inventions concerns Diamond?

Paragraph 2

What factor does Diamond say is most apparent?

Paragraph 3

According to Diamond, what considerations can be even more important than the financial ones?

Paragraph 4

How can "vested interests" sometimes become a factor?

Paragraph 5

What are some examples of slow change due to the above factors?

Responding to the Writing Topic

You should now have a good understanding of the ideas and overall message of "Accepting or Rejecting Innovation." Now look again at the writing topic that follows Diamond's essay, and begin thinking about how you will respond to it. For convenience, here it is with some of the important action words bolded:

Writing Topic

What factors, according to Diamond, **cause** people to adopt technological innovations into their lives? To what extent do you think his ideas **explain why** people accept or reject innovations? Be sure to **support your position** using examples from your own experience, your observation of others, or your readings.

You should always spend time taking apart a writing topic before you begin planning your essay. As with all previous essays in *Write It .5*, this writing topic has three basic parts. Rewrite them on the lines below:

1. _____

2. _____

_____

3. _____

_____

Strategies to Help You Analyze a Reading Selection and Develop Your Ideas for Writing a Response

Now you are ready to build on the annotations you made in your careful reading of "Accepting and Rejecting Innovation." To develop a more systematic analysis, one that allows you to form your own opinions and ideas about those in Diamond's essay, use the prewriting guides that you were introduced to in Part II. They will help to guide your thinking about Diamond's essay, but they will also help you to clarify and put into words your own views on the topic he writes about—what makes people accept innovation.

Questioning

- Questions about the highlighting you did:
  Why did I underline this part of the reading?

  How is this information important to Diamond's point?

  How can this information relate to the question I am being asked to write about?

- Questions about Diamond's ideas:
  What things in "Accepting and Rejecting Innovation" do not make sense to me?

  Where do I think Diamond should have given more explanation?

  How well do the examples in the essay relate to the point Diamond is making?

- Questions about "Accepting and Rejecting Innovation" that seem important:
  What are some of the things that Diamond says that I am happy to hear someone say?

  What things that he says seem true to me?

  What things that he says seem wrong to me?

  What thing that Diamond says is most important to me?

  What idea in this essay is completely new to me?

Freewriting

If you still feel that you have little to say to respond to Diamond's essay and topic, try some freewriting.

- Pick one or more of your answers to the questions you have already answered, and just begin to write about it.
- While you are doing this writing, do not stop or censor yourself; just let the words come.
- Do this for about five or ten minutes without thinking about spelling, grammar, word choice, or even the sense of what you are saying.
- When you have completed this activity, you will want to take a break.
- After your brief break, come back and read what you have written. Most of what you now have down on paper will not end up in your essay, but, as you read through your freewriting, you will find one or more sentences or ideas that seem interesting, important, or even compelling to you. Highlight these points and ideas.

Listing

With this strategy, you simply list all of the thoughts and reactions you have noted so far. By looking down your list, you may see a pattern of ideas develop, one that you can use to develop an essay of your own.

- List all of the annotations you made for "Accepting and Rejecting Innovation."
- List the main ideas you can see in your answers to the questioning phase above.
- List any main ideas that developed from your responses to the follow-up activities above.
- Be sure to list all the items from your freewriting that you thought were interesting. As you make this list, other ideas may come into your head. Put them on your list as well.

Study your list. Group all the ideas that seem related to each other. When you are done, one related group of ideas will probably be longer than the others. This group should give you a good start on what you want to say in your own essay in response to Diamond's essay.

Shaping Your Ideas into a Rough Draft

If you don't feel prepared at this point to plan your rough draft, go back through some of the activities above and talk with classmates to see what they are thinking. Continue to search for evidence because, as you do, you build a solid foundation from which to draw conclusions and formulate a thesis statement. Sometimes it takes a while before your ideas are fully formed; take as much time as you need to clarify your thoughts. Sometimes it helps to begin drafting. As you do, further insights may come to you.

When you are ready to focus on your rough draft, you will have to think about each part of your essay and how you will compose it. Turn back to Part II and examine "A Suggested Structure for an Essay That Responds to Another Writer's Essay." Also, look again at the writing topic for "Accepting and Rejecting Innovation." Remind yourself that it asks you to do three things:

1. Write a summary that identifies the issue that Diamond discusses and that explains how he views it.

Remember that you have already worked on this in earlier activities when you annotated "Accepting or Rejecting Innovation" and when you answered comprehension questions and analyzed Diamond's ideas. Look back now to the work you did. You may be able to use some of it to help you collect the main ideas for your essay's *directed summary*.

2. Take a position on this idea; do you agree with Diamond's view?

This part of the writing topic will lead you to your thesis statement, and your thesis statement will unify your essay, so it's important that you clearly express the position you want to take. Turn back to the review questions and follow-up activities you answered. What were your thoughts and ideas? Collect them now so that you can use them as the basis for your working thesis statement. Remember that you can always revise it as you work on your rough draft.

3. Support and develop your position using specific evidence taken from your own experiences and readings. In other words, explain your thinking and why you have the view you present—and don't forget to include the specific "proof" that convinced you to take the position you take.

The explanation of your thoughts and the evidence that led you to draw those conclusions will make up nearly your entire essay. Look back to earlier exercises in this unit to remind yourself of some of the thinking you did about the different forms of English you have used or experienced. You will be able to use some of this as evidence to support your thesis. Remember it when you begin working on body paragraphs.

Now that you have collected your ideas and reviewed the writing topic for "Accepting and Rejecting Innovation," you are ready to refine your ideas and analysis into a rough draft. Use the sections that follow to guide you.

Drafting Your Directed Summary

- Begin drafting the directed summary by reviewing the writing topic for "Accepting or Rejecting Innovation," paying particular attention to the first question asked. The answer you give to this question is called a *directed summary* because it summarizes only the parts of Diamond's essay that answer this first question.

  As you learned in Part II, the question that calls for a directed summary often opens with a question word such as *what, how,* or *why*. In Diamond's essay, the first question asks **"What factors,** according to Diamond, **cause** people to adopt technological innovations into their lives?" You will have to go back to his essay to find the information that tells *what factors cause* people to adopt innovations. It will not be enough to simply tell what these innovations are; you will also have to summarize *what factors cause people to adopt them,* according to Diamond.

- You might find it helpful to turn back to "Accepting or Rejecting Innovation" and mark the sentences that respond directly to the directed summary question. When writing your directed summary, be very careful to use your own words to *paraphrase* his ideas, as you learned to do in Part II.

- You should avoid including any of the following in a *directed summary*:

  1. a summary of the entire essay rather than a summary that pays attention only to what is asked for in the first question of the writing topic
  2. minor details or points that are irrelevant to the question
  3. your own opinion or ideas
  4. examples of your own, and unless particularly helpful, those of the author

Once you have written a directed summary, you will be ready to draft your essay's introductory paragraph. These steps will help guide you:

- Introduce Diamond's essay by giving its title and the full name of its author.
- Follow these opening sentences with the directed summary.
- Last, present your thesis statement, or the answer to the second question in the writing topic. To develop your thesis statement, use the guides in the following section.

Follow-Up Activity

1. Write the lists you developed in the activity above on the board. Compare your lists with your classmates' and discuss.
2. Draft your directed summary.
3. Working in small groups or with a partner, take turns reading your directed summary aloud. Discuss the strengths and weaknesses of each summary.

Developing Your Thesis Statement

The second question in the writing topic asks you to form your own opinion regarding what causes people to accept innovation. Will you agree with Diamond? The question asks:

To what extent do you think his ideas explain why people accept or reject innovations?

Think of your thesis as needing three parts:

- the subject being considered
- Diamond's claim about the subject
- your opinion about the subject

You will have to provide a clear answer to this question because it will be the statement that unifies your essay and that the rest of your essay will explain and support. Use the following exercise to help you do this:

1. List the causes for accepting innovation that Diamond identifies in his essay.
2. After each one, write down a sentence or two that explains the causal relationship (where one thing causes another thing to happen) that Diamond puts forward.
3. List all the forms of new technology you can think of that are relatively new.
4. Look over your list and determine whether or not each has been accepted by society, or whether its acceptance is undecided.
5. For each item on your list, speculate as to why society has or has not accepted the new technology.
6. Look over your work and see if you agree with Diamond or if you want to make a different argument about why, overall, people accept or reject innovation.

Now use the following frame to help draft your thesis:

The subject and Diamond's idea about the subject your opinion about the subject

_____

_____

_____

_____

After you have finished writing your sentence, review your statement to see that it contains the following elements:

- Diamond's point of view on the subject
- your point of view on the subject

If either of these elements is missing, rewrite your thesis statement so that both are included. Up to this point, you have been planning the draft of your introductory paragraph. Now that you have drafted your thesis statement, you can begin planning your body paragraphs. They will have to explain your ideas and give support to your thesis statement.

Developing Body Paragraphs for an Essay That Presents a Thesis

Reminders:

Body paragraphs make up the largest part of an essay.

- The job of each body paragraph is to develop one point that supports the thesis statement.
- These points taken together constitute the argument of the essay.
- Writing a good body paragraph can be easy once you understand the elements that the body paragraph must contain.

Here is a review of the three most important elements for paragraphs in an argumentative essay:

Parts of a Body Paragraph

an appropriate or suitable topic—one that supports the thesis statement

evidence—for instance, a concrete fact, example, or quotation—that demonstrates the point of the paragraph

a link to the thesis—sentences that show how and why the paragraph, including the evidence, relates to the thesis

A Basic Outline Form for an Essay That Presents a Thesis

Let's look back at all of the work you have done so far:

You have read and carefully annotated "Accepting or Rejecting Innovation."

You have analyzed its ideas.

You have written a directed summary in response to the first question in the writing topic.

You have thought about your own experiences and decided on your thesis statement.

You have drafted your essay's introduction.

All of that work should be gathered together now into a shape that will become your essay, your response to the writing topic for "Accepting or Rejecting Innovation."

- Remember that you should follow the basic structure of an academic essay.
- To refresh your memory, turn back to Part II and review the diagram of the academic essay format.
- As you begin filling in this diagram form, you should be able to turn back to material you have already drafted as you worked through the exercises in this unit.
- Fill in the diagram form as fully as you can. A good plan will help you draft an essay that is clear and coherent.

I. Introductory Paragraph:

A. one or two opening sentences that give the reading selection's title, author, and main topic:

_____

_____

_____

B. the main points that will be included in the directed summary:

1.

2.

3.

4.

C. your thesis statement: Be sure that it presents a clear position in response to the writing topic. State your thesis in your own words.

_____

_____

_____

II. Body Paragraphs: For each body paragraph you will include in your essay, plan the following parts:

Write down the topic idea for the paragraph.

_____

_____

_____

List the evidence you will use to support your topic idea (fact, example, etc.).

_____

_____

_____

_____

_____

Tell how the evidence and your ideas link to the thesis statement.

_____

_____

_____

_____

_____

_____

_____

_____

_____

(Repeat this part of the outline as often as necessary to plan all of your body paragraphs.)

III. Conclusion: What are some general remarks you can make to close your essay? Perhaps you will remind your readers of the main argument of your paper, for example.

_____

_____

_____

Drafting Your Essay

Now that you have a basic plan for the structure of your essay and a map of its various parts, you are ready to begin drafting.

- If your thinking changes as you write your draft, return to your outline and make necessary adjustments. Every time you decide to revise your outline and essay, remember that this is a good sign, a sign that your thinking is developing and becoming more thoughtful and convincing.
- Keep turning back to all of the activities in this unit as you draft your essay. Try to recall some of your reactions, thoughts, and ideas as you worked on these activities. This may help you to strengthen, expand on, or more fully develop your essay's argument.

Follow-Up Activity

1. A draft will always benefit from careful rereadings, by the writer or by someone else. Read the following student essay on "Accepting or Rejecting Innovation." Have someone in the class or in your group read the essay aloud, and as you listen and follow along, mark the places that need more work. Share your thoughts with your group or with the class to evaluate the essay overall. Then use the essay diagram in Part II to determine whether Student Essay 1 responds to all three parts of the writing topic and whether it contains all of the necessary elements of an essay that presents an argument.

Student Essay 1

Essay

DIAMOND ESSAY FINAL DRAFT

In the essay "Accepting or Rejecting Innovation" by Jared Diamond, the author is trying to explain the reason why people accept and reject all inventions. Inventions happen as generations develop, but what is it that makes some inventions more successful than others? Diamond says, "Once an inventor has discovered a use for a new technology, the next step is to persuade society to adopt it." Inventing technology can be challenging, but the more difficult part is to make people want your invention. People want trendy and what draws attention from other people. Sometimes inventions are not very successful because consumers don't find them useful. Diamond believes the reason why an invention promotes an acceptance by a society, are the factors of vested interest, economic advantage, and prestige. New inventions can be rejected, in an economy. Prestige, economic effect, and vested interest are the main reasons people reject new technology.

Reputation is very important when technology takes off. Prestige is one reason why consumers would reject the incoming of new technology. Apple corporations are an excellent example of how prestige works. That is, many people switch their phone companies to get the iPhones because the iPhone reputation is currently off the chart. Knowing that Apple products are good quality makes people want to purchase them. Even though the iPhone is just the same as androids, why do people leave the android software, for iPhones? Androids have come up with phone models to try and compete with iPhones. The Samsung Galaxy 3 is one of the only phones that has competed with Apple products due to its graphical features. Therefore, when big named phones sell quickly and are known nation wide, consumers tend to reject other technology just to have the one with the most prestige.

(Continued)

Economic effect is another reason why technology gets rejected. As life progresses on, people tend to invent new technology. Most of time, if the invention can't be useful for purchasers, the product loses profit. An invention has to be profitable, and more importantly, it has to be useful for people. For example Robot Vacuum is an automatic vacuum that disposes its garbage on its own. Not many people care for what a vacuum does, and they are simply happy with their original vacuums. This invention is useful, but the opinion of customers is what really makes an invention successful. This relates to Wendell Berry's essay, "Why I Will Not Buy a Computer." Berry refuses to buy a computer because he doesn't see the reason for new technology. Berry disagrees with the fact technology is taking over, and believes that is not necessary for people to have the latest invention: "I do not admire computer manufactures a great deal more than I admire the energy industries." Therefore an invention has to be useful in order to make people want to buy it; if the product is just an upgrade from similar technology, it wouldn't be as profitable.

Compatibility of vested interest is yet another factor of what promotes an invention's acceptance by a society. The car is an example of how vested interest benefits the economy. Before not many people used the car for transportation, instead they used it to show off to others what they were capable of buying. Mechanic Karl Benz invented the first car in 1886, but this first invented car was only used for design. Once the motor automobile was processed, people started purchasing them because it would save them time getting to places. This proves the point of how the invention of the first car wasn't necessarily used for transportation until someone else designed a similar model but with a motor included. Consumers recognized this change and what benefits people could get from the automobile. This created a whole new society of technology and until this day people still use the automobile. It has been a successful vested interest for many, and consumers are happy with their purchase.

In conclusion, new inventions are not always accepted by society. When new inventions are created, they must have a strong reputation. Inventions have to be profitable and beneficial for people to use them. Not having these factors, an invention won't always be successful. Many people don't see the reason for new technology; this is why as time goes by, technology needs a good review in order for people to accept it. Prestige, economic effect, and vested interest are the three main factors I preferably used to prove my point of why new technology is being denied in a society. Diamond's view of what is it that promotes an invention's acceptance is correct and the view of how technology is being used in society highly proves Diamond's thesis correct.

2. Working with a partner, go through Student Essay 2 and correct all of the errors you find in the essay's sentences.

Student Essay 2

REJECTING OR ACCEPTING TECHNOLOGY

Each an everyday we come up with new inventions, new technology that help make the world easier and more convenient place. In the essay "Accepting or rejecting innovation" by Jared Diamond, we see how people accept or reject certain inventions on the market. One technology we all use is a phone. We see how the newest phones come out and we automatically want the newest phone on stores. For example the iPhone they keep creating with different versions of the phone the iPhone 1, 2, 3, 4, and now 5 and sometimes there is not much difference between the versions. Like the iPhone 4 and the 4s they are exactly the same the only difference is that the 4s has SARI already integrated. But what helps customers accept or reject a new invention? Economy, prestige, ve3sted interest are factors that help a consumer reject or accept a new invention. This essay helps you understand how a customer takes these three factors in to place well trying out a new invention. In this essay, we see how people look at the price before they buy it; that's when economy takes in to place. They see what brand it is and sometimes how good the product is doesn't count. What counts is the companies name, that's where the prestige comes in. Also, people see what they are used to and if the majority doesn't want to change some to a new invention they won't accept a new one that's where vested interest comes in to place. All of these come to a person's head before deciding how they feel towards a new invention out in the market.

Economy is a big factor that help a consumer decide if to accept or reject a new invention. The price and economical standing of a person matters when a new product is on the market. For example, if the price is extremely high, the consumer would double think itself to figure out in the product is really worth buying, if the price is really low the consumer might think the invention is not good enough if it's so cheap. So in other words the product has to be worth its value when it is brand new to the market. In other cases some people might not have a very good economic standing, the product and its price is fair and good but the consumer might not have enough money to purchase the product. Sometimes the idea is good, but money stands in the way of you trying it.

However economy isn't the only factor that takes in to place will purchasing a new product, prestige also takes in to place. In most cases the brand matters. For example, if we have two pairs of running shoes that have the work exactly the same they help your foot function and feel comfortable. Then you put the name Nike on one of them and increase the price. Most people will go on and buy the more expensive one simply because it has the name Nike on it. That is because people are used to brand names most people judge and care about what brand name you are wearing, not what the product functions for. In some rear cases it works the opposite. For example in the essay "the highs of low technology" by Johanne Mednick. In this essay we see how mednick explains that people start to admire her old bike because it's vintage. It's not a common bike, it not like any other because it's so old they don't make models like that anymore, as contrast to all the new models that there are tons of. The brand and the name matters to the consumer more than the product.

Last but not least, we also have a factor that takes in to place vested interest. For example, we have had the same keyboard for years and we don't manage to change it. Why? It will make our lives easier. Right? Yes, indeed it will make our live easier in the long run but it also means that people will have to get accustomed to a new thing professional writers will slow down because they would have to learn a whole new concept. New computers will have to be made to replace the old keyboards and lots of money would have to be invested on these acts. Therefore it cost too much money to do so and it's not that important for people to learn a new keyboard if they have already gotten use to one. The money and time invested matters to keep the usual going on rather than the new.

In conclusion all these factors take in to place when we want to buy a new product in the market. Let's face it we think of all of these things before purchasing a brand new product. Most of us try to save our money but still have the latest brands and products out there.

3. Work with a classmate now to find areas in your own draft that can be improved. Use the following process to give and receive draft feedback.

A. Exchange a typed copy of your essay with one of your classmates.

B. Using a pen and a highlighter, mark your classmate's draft in the following manner:
   - Using your pen, underline the subject of each sentence.
   - Use two lines to underline the verb in each sentence.
   - Identify the tense by writing it above the verb.

C. Using your highlighter:
   - If the subject and verb **do not agree**, highlight the sentence.
   - If the verb tense is **not correct**, highlight only the verb.
   - If the verb is irregular and improperly formed, highlight the verb.

D. Using your pen, mark the following:
   - If the sentence is a **fragment**, enclose it in parentheses.
   - If the sentence is a **run-on**, draw two vertical lines between the independent clauses.

E. Using your pen, underline the essay's thesis.
   - If it is clear, if it identifies a topic, and if it makes a claim about it, put a check in the margin.
   - If it needs more work or if you cannot find a thesis, put a dash in the margin.

F. Return the drafts and discuss your marks and suggestions.

Supplemental Reading

Cars and Their Enemies

Essay

JAMES Q. WILSON

James Q. Wilson completed his B.A. at the University of Redlands and his Ph.D. in political science at the University of Chicago. From 1961 to 1987, he was the Shattuck Professor of Government at Harvard University. He published a number of books on America's governing institutions. His most recent book is titled American Politics, Then and Now *(2010).*

Imagine the country we now inhabit—big, urban, prosperous—with one exception: the automobile has not been invented. We have trains and bicycles, and some kind of self-powered buses and trucks, but no private cars driven by their owners for business or pleasure. Of late, let us suppose, someone has come forward with the idea of creating the personal automobile. Consider how we would react to such news.

Libertarians might support the idea, but hardly anyone else. Engineers would point out that such cars, if produced in any significant number, would zip along roads just a few feet—perhaps even a few inches—from one another; the chance of accidents would not simply be high; it would be certain. Public-health specialists would estimate that many of these accidents would lead to serious injuries and deaths. No one could say in advance how common they would be, but the best experts might guess that the number of people killed by cars would easily exceed the number killed by murderers. Psychologists would point out that if any young person were allowed to operate a car, the death rate would be even higher, as youngsters—those between the ages of sixteen and twenty-four—are much more likely than older persons to be impulsive risk-takers who find pleasure in reckless bravado. Educators would explain that, though they might try by training to reduce this youthful death rate, they could not be optimistic they would succeed.

Environmentalists would react in horror to the idea of automobiles powered by the internal combustion engine, apparently the most inexpensive method. Such devices, because they burn fuel incompletely, would eject large amounts of unpleasant gases into the air, such as carbon monoxide, nitrogen oxide, and sulfur dioxide. Other organic compounds, as well as clouds of particles, would also enter the atmosphere to produce unknown but probably harmful effects. Joining in this objection would be people who would not want their view spoiled by the creation of a network of roads.

Big-city mayors would add their own objections, though these would reflect their self-interest as much as their wisdom. If people could drive anywhere from anywhere, they would be able to live wherever they wished. This would produce a vast exodus from the large cities, led in all likelihood by the most prosperous—and thus the most tax-productive—citizens. Behind would remain people who, being poorer, were less mobile. Money would depart but problems remain.

Governors, pressed to keep taxes down and still fund costly health, welfare, educational, and criminal-justice programs, would wonder who would pay for the vast networks of roads that would be needed to carry automobiles. Their skepticism would be reinforced by the worries of police officials fearful of motorized thieves evading apprehension, and by the opposition of railroad executives foreseeing the collapse of their passenger business as people abandoned trains for cars.

Energy experts would react in horror at the prospect of supplying the gasoline stations and the vast quantities of petroleum necessary to fuel automobiles which, unlike buses and trucks, would be stored at home and not at a central depot and would burn much more fuel per person carried than some of their mass-transit alternatives.

(Continued)

In short, the automobile, the device on which most Americans rely for not only transportation but mobility, privacy, and fun, would not exist if it had to be created today. Of course, the car does exist, and has powerfully affected the living, working, and social spaces of America. But the argument against it persists. That argument dominates the thinking of academic experts on urban transportation and much of city planning. It can be found in countless books complaining of dreary suburban architecture, endless trips to and from work, the social isolation produced by solo auto trips, and the harmful effects of the car on air quality, noise levels, petroleum consumption, and road congestion.

Despite the criticisms, the use of the automobile has grown. In 1960, one-fifth of all households owned no car and only one-fifth owned two; by 1990, only one-tenth owned no car and over one-third owned two. In 1969, 80 percent of all urban trips involved a car and only one-twentieth involved public transport; by 1990, car use had risen to 84 percent and public transit had fallen to less than 3 percent. In 1990, three-fourths or more of the trips to and from work in nineteen out of our twenty largest metropolitan areas were by a single person in an automobile. The exception was the New York metropolitan region, but even there—with an elaborate mass-transit system and a residential concentration high enough to make it possible for some people to walk to work—solo car use made up over half of all trips to work.

Suppose, however, that the anti-car writers were to win over the vastly more numerous pro-car drivers. Let us imagine what life would be like in a carless nation. People would have to live very close together so they could walk or, for healthy people living in sunny climes, bicycle to mass-transit stops. Living in close quarters would mean life as it is now lived in Manhattan. There would be few freestanding homes, many row houses, and lots of apartment buildings. There would be few private gardens except for flowerpots on balconies. The streets would be congested by pedestrians, trucks, and buses, as they were at the turn of the century before automobiles became common.

Moving about outside the larger cities would be difficult. People would be able to take trains to distant sites, but when they arrived at some attractive locale it would turn out to be another city. They could visit the beach, but only (of necessity) crowded parts of it. They could go to a national park, but only the built-up section of it. They could see the countryside, but (mostly) through a train window. More isolated or remote locations would be accessible, but since public transit would provide the only way of getting there, the departures would be infrequent and the transfers frequent.

In other words, you could see the United States much as most Europeans saw their countryside before the automobile became an important means of locomotion. A train from London or Paris would take you to "the country" by way of a long journey through ugly industrial areas to those rural parts where either you had a home (and the means to ferry yourself to it) or there was a resort (that would be crowded enough to support a nearby train stop).

All this is a way of saying that the debate between car defenders and car haters is a debate between private benefits and public goods. List the characteristics of travel that impose few costs on society and, in general, walking, cycling, and some forms of public transit will be seen to be superior. Non-car methods generate less pollution, use energy a bit more efficiently, produce less noise, and (with some exceptions) are safer. But list the characteristics of travel that are desired by individuals, and (with some exceptions) the car is clearly superior. The automobile is more flexible and punctual, supplies greater comfort, provides for carrying more parcels, creates more privacy, enables one to select fellow passengers, and, for distances over a mile or more, requires less travel time.

As a practical matter, of course, the debate between those who value private benefits and those who insist on their social costs is no real debate at all, since people select modes of travel based on individual, not social, preferences. That is why in almost every country in the world, the automobile has triumphed, and much of public policy has been devoted to the somewhat inconsistent task of subsidizing individual choices while attempting to reduce the costs attached to them. In the case of the automobile, governments have attempted to reduce exhaust pollution, make roadways safer, and restrict use (by tolls, speed bumps, pedestrian-only streets, and parking restrictions) in neighborhoods that attach a high value to pedestrian passage. Yet none of these efforts can alter the central fact that people have found cars to be the best means for getting about.

Take traffic congestion. Television loves to focus on grim scenes of gridlocked highways and angry motorists, but in fact people still get to work faster by car than by public transit. And the reason is not that car drivers live close to work and transit users travel a greater distance. According to the best estimates, cars outperform public transit in getting people quickly from their front doors to their work places. This fact is sometimes lost on car critics. Jane Holtz Kay, for example, writes that "the same number of people who spend an hour driving sixteen lanes of highway can travel on a two-track train line" (56). Wrong. Train travel is efficient *over a fixed, permanent route*, but people have to find some way to get to where the train starts and get to their final destination after the train stops. The *full* cost of moving people from home to work and back to the home is lower for cars than for trains. Moreover, cars are not subject to union strikes. The Long Island railroad or the bus system may shut down when workers walk off the job; cars do not.

The transportation argument rarely seems to take cognizance of the superiority of cars with respect to individual wants. Whenever there is a discussion about how best to move people about, mass-transit supporters typically overestimate, usually by a wide margin, how many people will leave their cars and happily hop onto trains or buses. So the real debate ought not be one between car enthusiasts and mass-transit advocates, but about ways of moderating the inevitable use of cars in order to minimize their deleterious effects.

Work Cited

Kay, Jane Holtz. *Asphalt Nation: How the Automobile Took Over America and How We Can Take It Back*. Berkeley: University of California Press, 1998.

Follow-Up Activity

Questions for Discussion

1. If the automobile were a recent innovation, who are the different groups that would possibly reject it, and what might the reasons be for their unwillingness to accept it? Discuss these reasons and their validity.

2. What are some reasons, including and in addition to those mentioned by James Q. Wilson, that the car was an accepted innovation? What does he mean when he says the use of the automobile comes down to a choice between private benefits and the public good?

3. In the end, where does Wilson believe we should concentrate our efforts regarding the use of cars? What ways can you think of to help accomplish this goal?

In Touch Too Much?

Essay

Mary MacVean

The big deadline for high school seniors to choose a college has passed, and parents' thoughts are turning toward the joy of less laundry or the agony of how to pay the bills—and perhaps toward how much they'll be in touch with their sons and daughters come September. It was not so long ago that parents drove a teenager to campus, said a tearful goodbye, and returned home to wait a week or so for a phone call from the dorm. Mom or Dad, in turn, might write letters—yes, with pens, on stationery.

But going to college these days means never having to say goodbye, thanks to near-saturation of cellphones, email, instant messaging, texting, Facebook, and Skype. Researchers are looking at how new technology may be delaying the point at which college-bound students truly become independent from their parents, and how phenomena such as the introduction of unlimited calling plans have changed the nature of parent-child relationships, and not always for the better. Students walking from biology class to the gym can easily fill a few minutes with a call to Mom's office to whine about a professor's lecture. Dad can pass along family news via email. Daily text messaging is not uncommon. How nice, you might think. And you might be right. Some research suggests that today's young adults are closer to their parents than their predecessors. But it's complicated. Sherry Turkle, a professor at the Massachusetts Institute of Technology whose specialty is technology and relationships, calls this a particular sort of "Huck Finn moment," in which Huck "takes his parents with him. We all sail down the Mississippi together."

From the electronic grade monitoring many high schools offer parents, it seems a small leap to keep electronic track of their (adult) children's schedules or to set reminders about deadlines or assignments. Professors have figured out that some kids are emailing papers home for parents to edit. And Skype and Facebook might be more than just chances to see a face that's missed at home; parents can peer into their little darling's messy dorm room or his messy social life. Experts said the change dates to 9/11, which upped parents' anxiety over being out of touch with their children. And the rising cost of college can threaten parents' willingness to let children make mistakes as they learn how to be adults. Many of today's college students have had so much of their schedule programmed, they may not know what to do with time and solitude, said Barbara Hofer, a Middlebury College psychology professor and author with Abigail Sullivan Moore of the book *The iConnected Parent.*

Researchers are looking at these changing relationships, formed in the last few years after parents got smartphones and Facebook accounts too—and learned how to use them. "There's a tremendous diversity in how kids handle this. Some maintain old rules. But for many, many young people, they grow up essentially with the idea that they don't have to separate from their parents," Turkle said. "It's about having an adolescence that doesn't include the kind of separation that we used to consider part of adolescence," she added. "Something has become the norm that was considered pathological."

Hofer and colleagues surveyed students at Middlebury in Vermont and at the University of Michigan, two schools different in many ways. But at both, parents and students were in contact frequently, an average of more than thirteen times a week. "The one thing I've tried hard to do is not make this a helicopter story and not make it all negative," Hofer said in a telephone interview. "The quality of relationships that many students have with their parents is really quite remarkable. That's reported from parents and students." The complicated dance toward independence creates all sorts of tricky moments for both generations. The parents of today's college students were advised to get involved in the children's lives—to communicate, communicate, communicate. All that talk can signal a close, useful relationship, but it also can leave kids lacking what they need to fend for themselves. "The parent is on speed dial, the parent is on favorites. It's about having an adolescence that doesn't include the kind of separation that we used to consider part of adolescence," Turkle said. "It opens them up to real vulnerabilities now and later in life."

Parents are not always eager for such separation, Hofer said. "We just heard so many stories, campus after campus, of parents crossing boundaries," she said. By intervening in roommate disputes or sending daily text reminders of class work to be done, parents perpetuate a feeling that the students needn't think for themselves because someone else is perfectly willing—even gleeful—to do it for them. Have you seen the TV commercial in which two young women try to deal with an abundantly overflowing washing machine? In the end, one of them calls dad. His advice? Unplug it. A parent might laugh and cry at the thought that a young adult couldn't figure that out. Hofer cited a student who said she wasn't homesick freshman year, but sophomore year her mother learned to use Skype and placed the computer on the kitchen floor so her daughter could see the family dog when it walked by. "That brought me right back into my mom's kitchen," the daughter told Hofer, and the young woman said she was homesick for the first time.

One recent evening, eight Pomona College students gathered around a table to talk about how "connected" they were to their parents. They were in touch through email or text or Skype—technologies that some parents learned through their kids. Several said keeping in touch made the transition to college easier. Freshman Tim Kung, from San Diego, said his parents "were actually very considerate" about his desire to "unfriend" them from Facebook. Talking less frequently makes their conversations more meaningful, he said. It's tough for parents to avoid the temptation to step in when they learn from a Facebook post, as Edward Chuchla, whose daughter graduated in May from Pomona, put it in a telephone interview, "about how stressful it was writing Version 927 of a politics thesis." Sometimes, he said, he takes the bait. "If they post something provocative, we pick up the phone," he said. "We just call back to tell them we love them, and we're here if they need us."

Jamie Garcia, a freshman from Rosemead, said she's friends with her mother on Facebook, but added, "I'm not worried because she doesn't know how it works. She has like five friends." Her mother, Susan, however, is adept at texting. "I get a text from my mom every night, saying goodnight. So I text her back good night, like I'm alive; I made it through the day," Jamie said. Susan Garcia said later that she's reassured by the idea that she can reach her daughter easily. Even though Jamie moved only 35 miles and her family attends her softball games, they don't spend much time together, Susan Garcia said.

Katie Bent, a sophomore, calls home to Seattle weekly. "For me, I would love to be in contact with my parents very frequently, but I also feel like this is the time I'm supposed to be learning how to function without them," she said. "So last semester I completely destroyed my glasses at one point. That probably would have been a perfect time to deal with it, to find an optometrist in the area. What I did was call my mom, and said, 'Oh my God, Mom. What am I going to do?'" Mom found an optometrist. Katie's father, Sam, said that while he and his wife are much more in touch with Katie than he was with his own parents when he left home, he thinks it's important they not talk too often. "I know I don't call Katie unless I think it's important. She's in college; she's really busy. I don't call her up just to tell her a joke," he said. "In some sense, I'm glad she's not calling every day. She's learning to solve her own problems."

(Continued)

Caitlyn Hynes, the youngest of three children, has a lot of contact with her family in Upland—not only by phone or text, but also in person. Her father takes her to baseball lessons because she doesn't have a car. Caitlyn said her mother might call to say, "You should go to bed soon," which prompts Caitlyn to ask herself, "When am I actually going to be able to make these decisions for myself? I don't have two separate worlds, home and school. It's kind of like being in high school again. It's not like I don't want to hear from her, but more like needing a sense of independence."

Edward Chuchla wants to talk to his children, to feel close to them, to give counsel when asked. He and his wife also have tried to take the advice they got from the dean when they dropped off their daughter, Grace, at Pomona College four years ago: Back off; avoid being helicopter parents. "We're very careful to make sure communication happens on their terms," said Chuchla, whose son, Ben, is finishing his sophomore year at Dartmouth. Once, he said, he went too far. When his daughter left Pomona for a semester at Oxford, she had trouble getting permission to check books out of the library. The problem wasn't getting solved, so Chuchla emailed the foreign study office himself. When he heard from Grace, the message was, "I'll kill you if you do that again." Both generations are finding their way through the transition to adulthood as technological advances present even more new ways to connect. "We're all in this together," MIT's Turkle said. "We're all a little disoriented by these new possibilities together."

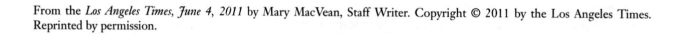

Follow-Up Activity

Questions for Discussion

1. Why does Mary MacVean say that going away to college now means "never having to say good-bye"? Discuss the amount of time you spend communicating electronically with your parents and the topics of your conversations. How are these conversations different from or the same as the ones you had with them in high school?

2. When the article quotes Sherry Turkle, who suggests that the amount of college students' parent/child contact leads to a vulnerability later in life, what types of problems do you think she anticipates? Do you think she is right to be concerned? Why or why not?

3. Discuss which of Diamond's reasons for accepting innovations best explains this use of technology by parents and their college-age children. What are some reasons that this same technology might have been rejected by the same group?

The Record Industry's Slow Fade

BRIAN HIATT AND EVAN SERPICK

Brian Hiatt and Evan Serpick are associate editors for Rolling Stone. *They wrote the following report in June 2007 in an attempt to understand the ongoing decline of the music industry and offer predictions from industry executives on the future of the music business. How has the industry fared since 2007?*

For the music industry, it was a rare bit of good news: Linkin Park's new album sold 623,000 copies in its first week this May—the strongest debut of the year. But it wasn't nearly enough. That same month, the band's record company, Warner Music Group, announced that it would lay off 400 people, and its stock price lingered at 58% of its peak from last June.

Overall CD sales have plummeted 16% for the year so far—and that's after seven years of near-constant erosion. In the face of widespread piracy, consumers' growing preference for low-profit-margin digital singles over albums, and other woes, the record business has plunged into a historic decline.

The major labels are struggling to reinvent their business models, even as some wonder whether it's too late. "The record business is over," says music attorney Peter Paterno, who represents Metallica and Dr. Dre. "The labels have wonderful assets—they just can't make any money off them." One senior music-industry source who requested anonymity went further: "Here we have a business that's dying. There won't be any major labels pretty soon."

In 2000, U.S. consumers bought 785.1 million albums; last year, they bought 588.2 million (a figure that includes both CDs and downloaded albums), according to Nielsen Sound-Scan. In 2000, the ten top-selling albums in the U.S. sold a combined 60 million copies; in 2006, the top ten sold just 25 million. Digital sales are growing—fans bought 582 million digital singles last year, up 65% from 2005, and purchased $600 million worth of ringtones—but the new revenue sources aren't making up for the shortfall.

More than 5,000 record-company employees have been laid off since 2000. The number of major labels dropped from five to four when Sony Music Entertainment and BMG Entertainment merged in 2004—and two of the remaining companies, EMI and Warner, have flirted with their own merger for years.

About 2,700 record stores have closed across the country since 2003, according to the research group Almighty Institute of Music Retail. Last year the eighty-nine-store Tower Records chain, which represented 2.5% of overall retail sales, went out of business, and Musicland, which operated more than 800 stores under the Sam Goody brand, among others, filed for bankruptcy. Around 65% of all music sales now take place in big-box stores such as Wal-Mart and Best Buy, which carry fewer titles than specialty stores and put less effort behind promoting new artists.

Just a few years ago, many industry executives thought their problems could be solved by bigger hits. "There wasn't anything a good hit couldn't fix for these guys," says a source who worked closely with top executives earlier this decade. "They felt like things were bad and getting worse, but I'm not sure they had the bandwidth to figure out how to fix it. Now, very few of those people are still heads of the companies."

More record executives now seem to understand that their problems are structural: The Internet appears to be the most consequential technological shift for the business of selling music since the 1920s, when phonograph records replaced sheet music as the industry's profit center. "We have to collectively understand that times have changed,"

(Continued)

says Lyor Cohen, CEO of Warner Music Group USA. In June, Warner announced a deal with the Website Lala.com that will allow consumers to stream much of its catalog for free, in hopes that they will then pay for downloads. It's the latest of recent major-label moves that would have been unthinkable a few years back: In May, one of the four majors, EMI, began allowing the iTunes Music Store to sell its catalog without the copy protection that labels have insisted upon for years. When YouTube started showing music videos without permission, all four of the labels made licensing deals instead of suing for copyright violations. To the dismay of some artists and managers, labels are insisting on deals for many artists in which the companies get a portion of touring, merchandising, product sponsorships, and other non-recorded-music sources of income.

So who killed the record industry as we knew it? "The record companies have created this situation themselves," says Simon Wright, CEO of Virgin Entertainment Group, which operates Virgin Megastores. While there are factors outside of the labels' control—from the rise of the Internet to the popularity of video games and DVDs—many in the industry see the last seven years as a series of botched opportunities. And among the biggest, they say, was the labels' failure to address online piracy at the beginning by making peace with the first file-sharing service, Napster. "They left billions and billions of dollars on the table by suing Napster—that was the moment that the labels killed themselves," says Jeff Kwatinetz, CEO of management company the Firm. "The record business had an unbelievable opportunity there. They were all using the same service. It was as if everybody was listening to the same radio station. Then Napster shut down, and all those 30 or 40 million people went to other [file-sharing services]."

It all could have been different: Seven years ago, the music industry's top executives gathered for secret talks with Napster CEO Hank Barry. At a July 15th, 2000 meeting, the execs—including the CEO of Universal's parent company, Edgar Bronfman Jr.; Sony Corporation head Nobuyuki Idei; and Bertelsmann chief Thomas Middelhof—sat in a hotel in Sun Valley, Idaho with Barry and told him that they wanted to strike licensing deals with Napster. "Mr. Idei started the meeting," recalls Barry, now a director in the law firm Howard Rice. "He was talking about how Napster was something the customers wanted." The idea was to let Napster's 38 million users keep downloading for a monthly subscription fee—roughly $10—with revenues split between the service and the labels. But ultimately, despite a public offer of $1 billion from Napster, the companies never reached a settlement. "The record companies needed to jump off a cliff, and they couldn't bring themselves to jump," says Hilary Rosen, who was then CEO of the Recording Industry Association of America. "A lot of people say, 'The labels were dinosaurs and idiots, and what was the matter with them?' But they had retailers telling them, 'You better not sell anything online cheaper than in a store,' and they had artists saying, 'Don't screw up my WalMart sales.'" Adds Jim Guerinot, who manages Nine Inch Nails and Gwen Stefani, "Innovation meant cannibalizing their core business."

Even worse, the record companies waited almost two years after Napster's July 2nd, 2001 shutdown before licensing a user-friendly legal alternative to unauthorized file-sharing services: Apple's iTunes Music Store, which launched in the spring of 2003. Before that, labels started their own subscription services: PressPlay, which initially offered only Sony, Universal, and EMI music; and MusicNet, which had only EMI, Warner, and BMG music. The services failed. They were expensive, allowed little or no CD burning, and didn't work with many MP3 players then on the market.

Rosen and others see that 2001-03 period as disastrous for the business. "That's when we lost the users," Rosen says. "Peer-to-peer took hold. That's when we went from music having real value in people's minds to music having no economic value, just emotional value."

In the fall of 2003, the RIAA filed its first copyright-infringement lawsuits against file sharers. They've since sued more than 20,000 music fans. The RIAA maintains that the lawsuits are meant to spread the word that unauthorized downloading can have consequences. "It isn't being done on a punitive basis," says RIAA CEO Mitch Bainwol. But file-sharing isn't going away—there was a 4.4% increase in the number of peer-to-peer users in 2006, with about a billion tracks downloaded illegally per month, according to research group BigChampagne.

Despite the industry's woes, people are listening to at least as much music as ever. Consumers have bought more than 100 million iPods since their November 2001 introduction, and the touring business is thriving, earning a record $437 million last year. And according to research organization NPD Group, listenership to recorded music—whether from CDs, downloads, video games, satellite radio, terrestrial radio, online streams, or other sources—has increased since 2002. The problem the business faces is how to turn that interest into money. "How is it that the people that make the product of music are going bankrupt, while the use of the product is skyrocketing?" asks the Firm's Kwatinetz. "The model is wrong."

Kwatinetz sees other, leaner kinds of companies—from management firms like his own, which now doubles as a record label, to outsiders such as Starbucks—stepping in. Paul McCartney recently abandoned his longtime relationship with EMI Records to sign with Starbucks' fledgling Hear Music. Video-game giant Electronic Arts also started a label, exploiting the promotional value of its games, and the newly revived CBS Records will sell music featured in CBS TV shows.

Licensing music to video games, movies, TV shows, and online subscription services is becoming an increasing source of revenue. "We expect to be a brand licensing organization," says Cohen of Warner, which in May started a new division, Den of Thieves, devoted to producing TV shows and other video content from its music properties. And the record companies are looking to increase their takes in the booming music publishing business, which collects songwriting royalties from radio play and other sources. The performance-rights organization ASCAP reported a record $785 million in revenue in 2006, a 5% increase from 2005. Revenues are up "across the board," according to Martin Bandier, CEO of Sony/ATV Music Publishing, which controls the Beatles' publishing. "Music publishing will become a more important part of the business," he says. "If I worked for a record company, I'd be pulling my hair out. The recorded-music business is in total confusion, looking for a way out."

Nearly every corner of the record industry is feeling the pain. "A great American sector has been damaged enormously," says the RIAA's Bainwol, who blames piracy, "from songwriters to backup musicians to people who work at labels. The number of bands signed to labels has been compromised in a pretty severe fashion, roughly a third." Times are hard for record-company employees. "People feel threatened," says Rosen. "Their friends are getting laid off left and right." Adam Shore, general manager of the then-Atlantic Records-affiliated Vice Records, told *Rolling Stone* in January that his colleagues are having an "existential crisis." "We have great records, but we're less sure than ever that people are going to buy them" he says. "There's a sense around here of losing faith."

Follow-Up Activity

Questions for Discussion

1. Sales of recordings are down, but people are listening to more music. What accounts for these two seemingly contradictory facts, according to Hiatt and Serpick? How would Diamond account for the contradiction?

2. Discuss the way one or more of the factors that Diamond argues are responsible for the acceptance/rejection of innovation explains the decline of the record industry.

3. Explain why some people argue that music has no economic value to the artists, backup musicians, and record company employees who have lost their source of income because of file sharing. Why do you feel that this activity should or should not be illegal?

Assignment 5

In this unit you will be writing a paper in response to the writing topic for Clyde Kluckhohn's "Mirror for Man." This unit also asks you to read and discuss two related essays, "Body Rituals of the Nacirema" and "DNA as Destiny," and to think about how they connect to the topic of "Mirror for Man" and its thesis statement.

Mirror for Man

Essay

CLYDE KLUCKHOHN

Clyde Kluckhohn was a Rhodes Scholar from 1928–1930 and earned his Ph.D. from Harvard University, where he remained as a professor of social anthropology for the rest of his life. He was both an anthropologist and social theorist and is best known for his long-term study of the Navajo in the American Southwest.

One of the interesting things about human beings is that they try to understand themselves and their own behavior. While this has been particularly true of Europeans in recent times, there is no group which has not developed a scheme or schemes to explain human actions. To the insistent human query "why?" the most exciting illumination anthropology has to offer is that of the concept of culture. Its explanatory importance is comparable to categories such as evolution in biology, gravity in physics, disease in medicine.

Why do so many Chinese dislike milk and milk products? Why during World War II did Japanese soldiers die willingly in a Banzai charge that seemed senseless to Americans? Why do some nations trace descent through the father, others through the mother, still others through both parents? Not because different peoples have different instincts, not because they were destined by God or Fate to different habits, not because the weather is different in China and Japan and the United States. Sometimes shrewd common sense has an answer that is close to that of the anthropologist: "because they were brought up that way." By "culture" anthropology means the total life way of a people, the social legacy individuals acquire from their group. Or culture can be regarded as that part of the environment that is the creation of human beings.

This technical term has a wider meaning than the "culture" of history and literature. A humble cooking pot is as much a cultural product as is a Beethoven sonata. In ordinary speech "people of culture" are those who can speak languages other than their own, who are familiar with history, literature, philosophy, or the fine arts. To the anthropologist, however, to be human is to be cultured. There is culture in general, and then there are the specific cultures such as Russian, American, British, Hottentot, Inca. The general abstract notion serves to remind us that we cannot explain acts solely in terms of the biological properties of the people concerned, their individual past experience, and the immediate situation. The past experience of other people in the form of culture enters into almost every event. Each specific culture constitutes a kind of blueprint of all of life's activities.

A good deal of human behavior can be understood, and indeed predicted, if we know a people's design for living. Many acts are neither accidental nor due to personal peculiarities nor caused by supernatural forces nor simply mysterious. Even we Americans

(Continued)

who pride ourselves on our individualism follow most of the time a pattern not of our own making. We brush our teeth on arising. We put on pants—not a loincloth or a grass skirt. We eat three meals a day—not four or five or two. We sleep in a bed—not in a hammock or on a sheep pelt. I do not have to know individuals and their life histories to be able to predict these and countless other regularities, including many in the thinking process of all Americans who are not incarcerated in jails or hospitals for the insane.

To the American woman a system of plural wives seems "instinctively" abhorrent. She cannot understand how any woman can fail to be jealous and uncomfortable if she must share her husband with other women. She feels it "unnatural" to accept such a situation. On the other hand, a Koryak woman of Siberia, for example, would find it hard to understand how a woman could be so selfish and so undesirous of feminine companionship in the home as to wish to restrict her husband to one mate.

Some years ago I met in New York City a young man who did not speak a word of English and was obviously bewildered by American ways. By "blood" he was American, for his parents had gone from Indiana to China as missionaries. Orphaned in infancy, he was reared by a Chinese family in a remote village. All who met him found him more Chinese than American. The facts of his blue eyes and light hair were less impressive than a Chinese style of gait, Chinese arm and hand movements, Chinese facial expression, and Chinese modes of thought. The biological heritage was American, but the cultural training had been Chinese. He returned to China.

Another example of another kind: I once knew a trader's wife in Arizona who took a somewhat devilish interest in producing a cultural reaction. Guests who came her way were often served delicious sandwiches filled with a meat that seemed to be neither chicken nor tuna fish yet was reminiscent of both. To queries she gave no reply until each had eaten his or her fill. She then explained that what they had eaten was not chicken, not tuna fish, but the rich, white flesh of freshly killed rattlesnakes. The response was instantaneous, often violent vomiting. A biological process is caught in a cultural web.

All this does not mean that there is no such thing as raw human nature. The members of all human groups have about the same biological equipment. All people undergo the same poignant life experiences, such as birth, helplessness, illness, old age, and death. The biological potentialities of the species are the blocks with which cultures are built. Some patterns of every culture crystallize around focuses provided by biology: the difference between the sexes, the presence of persons of different ages, the varying physical strength and skill of individuals. The facts of nature also limit culture forms. No culture provides patterns for jumping over trees or for eating iron ore. There is thus no "either-or" between nature and that special form of nurture called culture. The two factors are interdependent. Culture arises out of human nature, and its forms are restricted both by human biology and by natural laws.

Adapted from *Mirror for Man* by Clyde Kluckhohn. Copyright © by Bruce Kluckhohn. Reprinted by permission.

Writing Topic
According to Kluckhohn, what accounts for the differences in peoples throughout the world? Do you accept his explanation? To develop your essay, be sure to support your position by using examples from your own experiences, your observations of others, and your readings.

Vocabulary and Dictionary Practice

Part I.

Look up the following words used in "Mirror for Man." For each, write the two most common definitions on the lines provided and include what part of speech each definition is (noun, verb, adjective, etc.). Then, under each of the two definitions, write a sentence that uses the word in a way that reflects that particular definition and part of speech.

1. query
2. comparable
3. descent
4. abstract
5. regularities
6. incarcerated
7. abhorrent
8. poignant
9. potentialities
10. interdependent

1. **query**

first definition: _____

_____

part of speech: _____

sentence: _____

_____

second definition: _____

_____

part of speech: _____

sentence: _____

_____

2. **comparable**

first definition: _____

_____

part of speech: _____

sentence: _____

_____

second definition: _____

_____

part of speech: _____

sentence: _____

_____

3. **descent**

first definition: _____

_____

part of speech: _____

sentence: _____

_____

second definition: _____

_____

part of speech: _____

sentence: _____

_____

4. **abstract**

first definition: _____

_____

part of speech: _____

sentence: _____

_____

second definition: _____

_____

part of speech: _____

sentence: _____

_____

5. **regularities**

first definition: _____

_____

part of speech: _____

sentence: _____

_____

second definition: _____

_____

part of speech: _____

sentence: _____

_____

6. **incarcerated**

first definition: _____

_____

part of speech: _____

sentence: _____

_____

second definition: _____

_____

part of speech: _____

sentence: _____

_____

7. **abhorrent**

first definition: _____

_____

part of speech: _____

sentence: _____

_____

second definition: _____

_____

part of speech: _____

sentence: _____

_____

8. **poignant**

first definition: _____

_____

part of speech: _____

sentence: _____

_____

second definition: _____

_____

part of speech: _____

sentence: _____

_____

9. **potentialities**

first definition: _____

_____

part of speech: _____

sentence: _____

_____

second definition: _____

_____

part of speech: _____

sentence: _____

_____

10. **interdependent**

first definition: _____

_____

part of speech: _____

sentence: _____

_____

second definition: _____

_____

part of speech: _____

sentence: _____

_____

Part II.

A. Write down each sentence from Kluckhohn's essay that contains the following words.

B. Tell which of the word's various definitions best fits the sentence.

C. Paraphrase the sentence without using the vocabulary word; in other words, write the sentence using your own words.

1. **query**

   A. _____

   _____

   B. _____

   _____

   C. _____

   _____

2. **comparable**

   A. _____

   _____

   B. _____

   _____

   C. _____

   _____

3. **descent**

   A. _____

   _____

   B. _____

   _____

   C. _____

   _____

4. **abstract**

   A. _____

   _____

   B. _____

   _____

   C. _____

   _____

5. **regularities**

   A. _____
   _____
   B. _____
   _____
   C. _____
   _____

6. **incarcerated**

   A. _____
   _____
   B. _____
   _____
   C. _____
   _____

7. **abhorrent**

   A. _____
   _____
   B. _____
   _____
   C. _____
   _____

8. **poignant**

   A. _____
   _____
   B. _____
   _____
   C. _____
   _____

9. **potentialities**

   A. _____
   _____

B. _____

_____

C. _____

_____

10. **interdependent**

A. _____

_____

B. _____

_____

C. _____

_____

Part III.

For each of these words from the essay, tell something new and interesting you learned about the word from the dictionary. For example, you might have found the correct way to pronounce a word you were already familiar with from reading but not from speaking, or you might have learned that a word you thought of as entirely English came from a foreign language.

1. **query**

_____

_____

2. **comparable**

_____

_____

3. **descent**

_____

_____

4. **abstract**

_____

_____

5. **regularities**

_____

_____

6. **incarcerated**

_____

_____

7. **abhorrent**

_____

_____

8. **poignant**

_____

_____

9. **potentialities**

_____

_____

10. **interdependent**

_____

_____

Follow-Up Activity

Write three sentences about your favorite pastime, making sure to include at least one of the vocabulary words in each sentence. Exchange papers with a partner. Look over each other's sentences and see if you can improve them. When everyone is finished, share one another's sentences by reading them aloud to the class.

Doing a Careful Reading of "Mirror for Man"

First, if time permits, begin by reading "Mirror for Man" aloud with the class. Take turns reading paragraphs. This exercise will allow you to listen to the essay as someone else speaks it, giving you a unique experience in absorbing the essay's ideas.

By now you should be aware of the importance of working systematically with a reading selection to make sure that you understand its purpose and ideas. In Assignments #1 and #2, you practiced some helpful techniques for a thoughtful reading of an essay; use them again now to better understand "Mirror for Man."

The steps are reproduced here, but your goal should be to memorize them so that they become a normal part of the writing process for you.

1. **Read the title again.**
   - The title will tell you something about the reading's main topic.
   - It may also tell you something about Kluckhohn's opinion on the topic.
   - Think about what you already know about the topic and what else you want to know.

2. **Learn about the author.**
   - Read the biographical information about Kluckhohn at the top of the selection.
   - As you go through the remaining steps below, take note of how Kluckhohn's life or work might connect with his topic.

3. **Read through the selection once quickly.**
   - Read quickly through the reading again so that you get a general fresh impression of what it is about and what Kluckhohn's attitude is toward the topic.
   - Notice the things—people, places, experiences, concepts, for example—he brings up to develop and support his opinion about the topic.

4. **Read again to identify the thesis.**
   - Now read the selection a second time, but more slowly and carefully, and *with a pen or highlighter in your hand.*
   - Find the thesis and underline it or write it in the margin. Remember, the thesis states Kluckhohn's overall opinion on the topic of the reading. Often the thesis is contained in a single sentence, but, in some cases, it takes several sentences to make the main argument of the reading selection clear. There are times, too, when the author does not state his or her thesis explicitly, but, if you read the selection carefully, you should be able to state it and then write it in the margin.
   - To help, ask yourself, "What does Kluckhohn seem to want readers to think about his topic?"

5. **Read slowly and methodically through the rest of the reading.**
   - Examine each body paragraph one at a time, and list or underline the kinds of evidence that Kluckhohn uses to support his thesis.
   - Look in each body paragraph for a *topic sentence*—a sentence that both presents an idea and tells how it gives support to the reading's overall opinion.

- As you read and study the selection, *be sure to write down any thoughts you have* about Kluckhohn's opinion and supporting evidence.
- It is your job to evaluate this evidence for its logic and validity, so be sure to *make notes in the margins* as you read.
- *Mark the points* that you found interesting or convincing and write a few words explaining your thoughts.
- Note, too, any weaknesses you find.
- When you look back at the notes you made in the margins, you should have a general idea of how convincing you found "Mirror for Man" and what you found to be its strengths and weaknesses.

6. **Read again for review.**

- Once you have thought through the reading selection, read it once more, looking for places where you don't quite understand what is being said.
- Underline any terms that you aren't familiar with, and look them up in a dictionary.
- Mark any places in the reading that don't fit with your understanding of the reading as a whole. Decide whether this is something that Kluckhohn should have revised, or whether it is something that you need to read again because you don't understand it. You may find that you need to go back to Step 4 and begin working through the reading again.
- Once you are certain that you understand the entire reading, you are prepared to discuss, summarize, and/or respond to the reading with your own essay.

Questions to Review Your Understanding of "Mirror for Man"

Answer the following questions to check your complete understanding of Kluckhohn's argument as a whole.

Paragraph 1

Explain the way Kluckhohn uses other disciplines to show the importance of the concept of culture to anthropology.

Paragraph 2

How does Kluckhohn define culture? How does culture explain the examples, such as that of the Banzai soldiers, which he cites?

Paragraph 3

Kluckhohn contrasts the anthropologist's definition of culture with the wider, more general way the word is used. Explain the difference. Give an example to illustrate each definition.

Paragraph 4

By knowing the culture, what things can Kluckhohn predict about an American male? Is he accurate? If so, in what way is his definition of culture responsible for his accuracy? If not, locate his error. Does the error point to a problem in his definition of culture?

Paragraph 5

How does culture explain Kluckhohn's example of attitudes toward plural wives?

Paragraphs 6-7

Summarize the two examples Kluckhohn gives in these paragraphs. What does each say about the relationship between culture and biology?

Paragraph 8

What similarities does Kluckhohn find in all human groups? How does nature restrict culture?

Responding to the Writing Topic

You have spent time with "Mirror for Man" and should now have a good understanding of its ideas and overall message. It is important now to look at the writing topic at the bottom of the selection because the essay you write must answer directly the questions in the writing topic. Here it is again, but this time formatted so that each part is on its own line:

Writing Topic

According to Kluckhohn, what accounts for the differences in peoples throughout the world?

Do you accept his explanation?

To develop your essay, be sure to support your position by using examples from your own experiences, your observations of others, and your readings.

Pay careful attention to all parts of the writing topic.

- You are first asked a question about a specific aspect of "Mirror for Man," a question that asks you to consider the ways that people are different in different parts of the world. When examining a writing topic, always underline the question words (who, what, why, how, when, where). In this writing topic, the first question asks *what:* what accounts for the differences in peoples? In other words, how does Kluckhohn *explain why* people of different races or from different cultures are so markedly different from one another? Note that he isn't talking about why you like Coke and your friend likes
Dr. Pepper. Kluckhohn is interested in differences of a greater significance.
- The second question in the writing topic asks you to state whether you think Kluckhohn's explanation seems valid to you. Does his point of view on difference seem to explain difference reasonably well, in your opinion? What do *you* think accounts for the differences in peoples throughout the world? Your answer to this question will become the thesis of your essay because it will state your overarching view on the topic.
- The third part of the writing topic tells you to support your opinion—your thesis—with clear examples taken from your own experiences. The following activity will help you begin to find some of those examples. Be sure to keep notes on your ideas so that you can turn back to them later.

Follow-Up Activity

1. Tell the class how your family celebrates a major holiday. Include all significant details such as special foods that are prepared or special clothing that is worn. Explain to the class why your family celebrates this holiday in the way that they do.
2. Look around the classroom and notice the clothing people are wearing. Have a discussion of why people choose the clothes they wear. What determines their choices?

Strategies to Help You Analyze a Reading Selection and Develop Your Ideas for Writing a Response

Students often say that they don't know what to write *about*—that is, they think they have no ideas to put into the essay. In fact, students have many thoughtful ideas; they just need a few techniques for accessing and clarifying their ideas. Try the ones below to analyze and think about "Mirror for Man."

Questioning

You will have already taken the first step toward writing your essay when you did a careful reading of "Mirror for Man" and the writing topic that follows it. Looking back at your annotations is a good way to remind yourself about things in the essay you thought were important. Now you need to enter the *question phase* of your prewriting. At this point, you can ask yourself several kinds of questions:

- questions focused on your annotations, such as:
  Why did I highlight/underline this part of the essay?

  How is this information important to the author's point?

  What is the relationship between this information and the question I am being asked to write about?

- questions about your comprehension of the reading, such as:
  What things in this essay do not make sense to me?

  Where do I think the author needed to explain further?

  How do the examples in the essay relate to the author's point?

- questions about the author's ideas, such as:
  What idea in this essay is completely new to me?

  What are some of the things that the author says that I am happy to hear someone say?

  What things that the author says seem true to me?

  What things that the author says seem wrong to me?

  What thing that the author says is most important to me?

What idea in this essay is completely new to me?

The answers to these questions will help you understand your own thoughts about the topic of the reading and help you see how you want to respond to the writing topic.

Freewriting

A further step in the prewriting process that you may want to take is *freewriting*. After having answered for yourself a number of the questions about the reading and topic, you still may be having trouble expanding on your initial reaction to the author's position on the topic. Pick one or more of your answers to the questions you have already answered, and just begin to write about it. While you are doing this writing, do not stop or censor yourself; just let the words come. Do this for about five or ten minutes without thinking about spelling, grammar, word choice, or even the sense of what you are saying. When you have completed this activity, you will want to take a break.

After your brief break, come back and read what you have written. Most of what you now have down on paper will not end up in your essay, but, as you read through your freewriting, you will find one or more sentences or ideas that seem interesting, important, or even compelling to you. Highlight these points and ideas.

Listing

Next, you may decide to make a list of your highlightings from all your freewritings. *Listing* is another technique for finding the ideas you want to write about. Be sure to list all the items from your freewriting that you thought were interesting. As you make this list, other ideas may come into your head. Put them on your list as well.

Study your list. Connect with some kind of mark all the ideas that seem related to each other. When you are done, one related group of ideas will probably be longer than the others. This group should provide insight into a topic for your paper.

Shaping Your Ideas into a Rough Draft

At this stage of the writing process, you are ready to begin planning your essay draft. It is important to understand the conventional structure of an academic essay because it will guide you when you are ready to put your ideas in writing. Go back to the writing topic for this assignment and reread it. Notice that it asks you to do three things:

1. **Summarize a topic** idea that Kluckhohn develops in his essay.

2. **Present your position** on this topic idea.

3. **Support and develop your position** using specific evidence taken from your own experiences and readings.

The first part of the writing topic for "Mirror for Man" asks:

"According to Kluckhohn, ***what accounts for*** the differences in peoples throughout the world?"

We have bolded the important action words to help you focus your response correctly. You should not summarize Kluckhohn's entire essay, only one particular aspect of it. This question is asking you to explain "what accounts for the differences in peoples." In other words, how does Kluckhohn reason out, reconcile, or think through an explanation for the differences among large groups of people in the world? Obviously, the idea of *differences* here means something other than, for example, one person can sing while another one cannot. What kinds of differences do you think Kluckhohn is interested in exploring?

Here are some questions that will help you answer the first part of the writing topic. Answer each one as thoroughly and carefully as you can; then, use your answers to draft an introductory paragraph that answers the first question.

1. Explain the difference Kluckhohn establishes between "culture in general" and "specific cultures." Is a "humble cooking pot" an artifact of culture in general or of a specific culture?

2. List all of the differences that Kluckhohn refers to in his essay. For each one, tell whether it is an example of "culture in general" or "specific culture."

3. What does Kluckhohn mean by "the social legacy individuals acquire from their group"? What are some of the things people do as a result of their "social legacy"?

4. Can biological processes be influenced by culture? To what extent?

5. Explain the distinction Kluckhohn makes between nature and culture.

Follow-Up Activity

Working with a partner or a small group, take turns reading your answers to the above questions and getting feedback from your partner or group members. For each answer, ask your partner or group:

1. How clearly written was my answer?
2. Did it thoroughly answer the question, or could more have been added to make it clear?
3. What suggestions can you make to help me improve my work?
4. Give everyone a chance to give and to receive feedback.

Drafting Your Directed Summary

- Begin drafting the directed summary by reviewing the writing topic for "Mirror for Man," paying particular attention to the first question asked. The answer you give to this question is called a *directed summary* because it summarizes only the parts of Kluckhohn's essay that answer this first question.
- As you learned in Part II, the question that calls for a directed summary often opens with a question word such as *what, how,* or *why.* In Kluckhohn's essay, the first question asks "***what accounts for*** the differences in peoples throughout the world?" You will have to go back to his essay to find his explanation. It will not be enough simply to tell what these differences are; you will also have to summarize *how* Kluckhohn accounts for them.
- You might find it helpful to turn back to "Mirror for Man" and mark the sentences that respond directly to the directed summary question. When writing your directed summary, be very careful to use your own words to *paraphrase* his ideas, as you learned to do in Part II.
- You should avoid including any of the following in a *directed summary*:
  1. a summary of the entire essay rather than a summary that pays attention only to what is asked for in the first question of the writing topic
  2. minor details or points that are irrelevant to the question
  3. your own opinion or ideas
  4. examples of your own, and, unless particularly helpful, those of the author

Once you have written a directed summary, you will be ready to draft your essay's introductory paragraph. These steps will help guide you:

- Introduce Kluckhohn's essay by giving its title and the full name of its author.
- Follow these opening sentences with the directed summary.
- Last, present your thesis statement, or the answer to the second question in the writing topic. To develop your thesis statement, use the guides in the following section.

Follow-Up Activity

1. After the class as a whole has discussed the important points from "Mirror for Man" that need to be included in the directed summary, form small groups. Have each member of the group read his or her summary aloud. Then, discuss the correctness and completeness of each summary.
2. Discuss with the class the differences among these terms:
   people
   peoples
   people's

Developing Your Thesis Statement

As you know by now, your answer to the second question will be the *thesis* of your essay. The rest of your essay will be built around your answer to the second question in the writing topic, "Do you accept his explanation?" because this question is directing you to explain your own understanding of why there are differences among peoples of the world. Do you think the differences in the customs and behaviors of people are a result of their different cultures, as Kluckhohn does? However you decide to respond, you will have to state your position clearly and support it with explanation and evidence. Begin by taking special notice of the important words.

Do you **accept** his **explanation**?

As you consider your response, go back through "Mirror for Man" and look at Kluckhohn's evidence ("We put on pants—not a loincloth or a grass skirt") and go back over his attempt to account for these differences. Does his reasoning seem sound to you? Or do you have a different viewpoint that accounts for differences among peoples? Look through the activities and exercises you've done in this unit; they will help you to develop your thoughts and insights.

To help focus your thoughts, ask yourself the following questions;
- What is the subject of Kluckhohn's argument?

Notice that, although we can say that "differences among peoples" is the topic idea of Kluckhohn's essay, in fact it is the impact of culture on human behavior that is the actual subject of his argument.
- Based on his own experiences, what is his opinion about the subject?

Kluckhohn, an expert in anthropology, argues that differing cultural practices account for the differences among peoples in the world. Notice that he lived and studied more than fifty years ago. Is there a more modern understanding of difference, or do Kluckhohn's ideas still hold true? What explanation do you have for the differences among peoples of the world?

- Do I think that his understanding of the way societies' cultures account for human differences makes sense?

What alternative explanations might there be to account for differences among peoples in the world? Perhaps family traditions? Could it be gene pools? Could difference be the result of random developments that are unexplainable? Is human nature universal, or do some people's basic nature differ from other people's? You will have to think carefully and sort through your own experiences and knowledge to determine the position you want to take.

Now, use these answers to help write your own thesis. Your thesis will need to include:
- the subject being considered
- the author's opinion about the subject
- your opinion about the subject

Fill in your answers on the line below to form your thesis statement.

subject/author's idea about the subject   your opinion about the subject

_____

_____

_____

_____

_____

After you have finished writing your sentence, review your statement to see that it contains the following elements:

- Kluckhohn's point of view on the subject
- your point of view on the subject

If either of these elements is missing, rewrite your thesis statement so that both are included.

Developing Body Paragraphs for an Essay That Presents a Thesis

Body paragraphs make up the largest part of an essay.

- The job of each body paragraph is to develop one point that supports the thesis statement.
- These points taken together build the argument of the essay.
- Writing an effective body paragraph can be easy once you understand the criteria that the body paragraph must fulfill.

Here are the three most important criteria for paragraphs in an argumentative essay:

Body Paragraphs Need:

1. an appropriate or suitable topic
2. evidence (fact, example, and/or idea)
3. a link to the thesis

An appropriate or suitable topic

First, write a topic sentence that states the point you wish to make in this paragraph. The point must be on topic; that is, it must state an idea that is relevant to the claim you make in your thesis.

Evidence

The major part of the paragraph will be devoted to evidence. In your essays, that evidence will most often be an example, but specific facts, quotations, and ideas can also help support the topic sentence of your paragraph. You must be careful to choose a clear example, one that clearly demonstrates the point of the paragraph. Then you must explain the example with details.

A link to the thesis

After you have given all the evidence and supplied all the details that support the topic sentence of the paragraph, you must show the way this evidence links back to the thesis of your essay. It is not enough to just provide an example. You have to tell the reader the reason this particular example connects to the main argument of your essay.

A Basic Outline Form for an Essay That Presents a Thesis

All of the work you have done so far—reading and carefully annotating "Mirror for Man," analyzing its ideas, writing a directed summary in response to the first question in the writing topic, thinking about your own experiences and deciding on your thesis statement, and drafting your essay's introduction—should be gathered together now into a shape that will become your essay, your response to the writing topic at the bottom of "Mirror for Man."

- Remember that you should follow the basic structure of an academic essay.
- To refresh your memory, turn back to Part II and review the diagram of the academic essay format.
- As you begin filling in this diagram form, you should be able to turn back to material you have already drafted as you worked through the exercises in this unit.
- Fill in the diagram form as fully as you can. A good plan will help you draft an essay that is clear and coherent.

I. **Introductory Paragraph:**

   A. one or two opening sentences that give the reading selection's title, author, and main topic:

   _____

   _____

   _____

   B. the main points that will be included in the directed summary:

   1.

   2.

   3.

   4.

   C. your thesis statement: Be sure that it presents a clear position in response to the writing topic. State your thesis in your own words.

   _____

   _____

   _____

II. Body Paragraphs: For each body paragraph you will include in your essay, plan the following parts:

Write down the topic idea for the paragraph.

_____

_____

_____

List the evidence you will use to support your topic idea (fact, example, etc.).

_____

_____

_____

_____

_____

Tell how the evidence and your ideas link to the thesis statement.

_____

_____

_____

_____

_____

(Repeat this part of the outline as often as necessary to plan all of your body paragraphs.)

III. Conclusion: What are some general remarks you can make to close your essay? Perhaps you will remind your readers of the main argument of your paper, for example.

_____

_____

_____

Drafting Your Essay

Now that you have a basic plan for the structure of your essay and a map of its various parts, you are ready to begin drafting.

- Turn back to the helpful guidelines in Part II before you begin. These guidelines will help you to evaluate the parts of your draft and your essay as a whole.

- If your thinking changes as you draft, return to your outline and make necessary adjustments. Every time you decide to revise your outline and essay, remember that this is a good sign, a sign that your thinking is developing and becoming more thoughtful and convincing.

- Keep turning back to all of the activities in this unit as you draft your essay. Try to recall some of your reactions, thoughts, and ideas as you worked on these activities. This may help you to strengthen, expand on, or more fully develop your essay's argument.

Follow-Up Activity

Your draft will always benefit from careful rereadings. Even better is to let others hear or read your draft and give you their feedback. Sometimes, a classmate or family member can spot places in your draft where you aren't clear, or where you have neglected to fix a grammar error.

1. Read a classmate's rough draft. Then choose the paragraph or group of sentences that, in your opinion, are the strongest part of the essay. Read the sentences out loud to the writer of the draft and explain why you chose them.

2. Using three different colors of ink or pencil, exchange drafts with a classmate, read the draft, and then do the following:

   Put a bracket in the margin around the directed summary.

   Underline the thesis statement.

   In each body paragraph, and using three different colors, underline the three elements required: the appropriate topic, the evidence, and the link to the thesis.

   Return the draft to its writer and discuss your markings. Be sure to mention any questions, concerns, or suggestions you have for improving the draft.

Supplemental Reading

Read the following essays and practice the strategies of annotating, questioning, listing, and freewriting so that you comprehend the arguments and explanations of each. Then consider them in terms of Kluckhohn's ideas. This activity will help you to work through your own ideas and write a thesis statement that you can support with compelling explanations and evidence. Some of that evidence may come from the essays here.

Body Ritual Among the Nacirema

Essay

HORACE MINER

> *Horace Miner was an anthropologist, and this essay originally appeared in the journal* American Anthropologist *in June 1956.*

The anthropologist has become so familiar with the diversity of ways in which different peoples behave in similar situations that he is not apt to be surprised by even the most exotic customs. In fact, if all of the logically possible combinations of behavior have not been found somewhere in the world, he is apt to suspect that they must be present in some yet undescribed tribe. In this light, the magical beliefs and practices of the Nacirema present such unusual aspects that it seems desirable to describe them as an example of the extremes to which human behavior can go.

Professor Linton first brought the ritual of the Nacirema to the attention of anthropologists twenty years ago, but the culture of this people is still very poorly understood. They are a North American group living in the territory between the Canadian Cree, the Yaqui and Tarahumare of Mexico, and the Carib and Arawak of the Antilles. Little is known of their origin, although tradition states that they came from the east. According to Nacirema mythology, their nation was originated by a culture hero, Notgnishaw, who is otherwise known for two great feats of strength—the throwing of a piece of wampum across the river Pa-To-Mac and the chopping down of a cherry tree in which the Spirit of Truth resided.

Nacirema culture is characterized by a highly developed market economy which has evolved in a rich natural habitat. While much of the people's time is devoted to economic pursuits, a large part of the fruits of these labors and a considerable portion of the day are spent in ritual activity. The focus of this activity is the human body, the appearance and health of which loom as a dominant concern in the ethos of the people. While such a concern is certainly not unusual, its ceremonial aspects and associated philosophy are unique.

The fundamental belief underlying the whole system appears to be that the human body is ugly and that its natural tendency is to debility and disease. Incarcerated in such a body, man's only hope is to avert these characteristics through the use of the powerful influences of ritual and ceremony. Every household has one or more shrines devoted to this purpose. The more powerful individuals in the society have several shrines in their houses and, in fact, the opulence of a house is often referred to in terms of the number of such ritual centers it possesses. Most houses are of wattle and daub construction, but the shrine rooms of the more wealthy are walled with stone. Poorer families imitate the rich by applying pottery plaques to their shrine walls.

While each family has at least one such shrine, the rituals associated with it are not family ceremonies but are private and secret. The rites are normally only discussed with children, and then only during the period when they are being initiated into these mysteries. I was able, however, to establish sufficient rapport with the natives to examine these shrines and to have the rituals described to me.

The focal point of the shrine is a box or chest which is built into the wall. In this chest are kept the many charms and magical potions without which no native believes he could live. These preparations are secured from a variety of specialized practitioners. The most powerful of these are the medicine men, whose assistance must be rewarded with substantial gifts. However, the medicine men do not provide the curative potions for their clients, but decide what the ingredients should be and then write them down in an ancient and secret language. This writing is understood only by the medicine men and by the herbalists who, for another gift, provide the required charm.

The charm is not disposed of after it has served its purpose, but is placed in the charm-box of the household shrine. As these magical materials are specific for certain ills, and the real or imagined maladies of the people are many, the charm-box is usually full to overflowing. The magical packets are so numerous that people forget what their purposes were and fear to use them again. While the natives are very vague on this point, we can only assume that the idea in retaining all the old magical materials is that their presence in the charm-box, before which the body rituals are conducted, will in some way protect the worshipper.

Beneath the charm-box is a small font. Each day every member of the family, in succession, enters the shrine room, bows his head before the charm-box, mingles different sorts of holy water in the font, and proceeds with a brief rite of ablution. The holy waters are secured from the Water Temple of the community, where the priests conduct elaborate ceremonies to make the liquid ritually pure.

In the hierarchy of magical practitioners, and below the medicine men in prestige, are specialists whose designation is best translated "holy-mouth-men." The Nacirema have an almost pathological horror and fascination with the mouth, the condition of which is believed to have a supernatural influence on all social relationships. Were it not for the rituals of the mouth, they believe that their teeth would fall out, their gums bleed, their jaws shrink, their friends desert them, and their lovers reject them. (They also believe that a strong relationship exists between oral and moral characteristics. For example, there is a ritual ablution of the mouth for children which is supposed to improve their moral fiber.)

The daily body ritual performed by everyone includes a mouth-rite. Despite the fact that these people are so punctilious about care of the mouth, this rite involves a practice which strikes the uninitiated stranger as revolting. It was reported to me that the ritual consists of inserting a small bundle of hog hairs into the mouth, along with certain magical powders, and then moving the bundle in a highly formalized series of gestures.

In addition to the private mouth-rite, the people seek out a holy-mouth-man once or twice a year. These practitioners have an impressive set of paraphernalia, consisting of a variety of augers, awls, probes, and prods. The use of these objects in the exorcism of the evils of the mouth involves almost unbelievable ritual torture of the client. The holy-mouth-man opens the client's mouth and, using the above-mentioned tools, enlarges any holes which decay may have created in the teeth. Magical materials are put into these holes. If there are no naturally occurring holes in the teeth, large sections of one or more teeth are gouged out so that the supernatural substance can be applied. In the client's view, the purpose of these ministrations is to arrest decay and to draw friends. The extremely sacred and traditional character of the rite is evident in the fact that the natives return to the holy-mouth-men year after year, despite the fact that their teeth continue to decay.

It is to be hoped that, when a thorough study of the Nacirema is made, there will be a careful inquiry into the personality structure of these people. One has but to watch the gleam in the eye of a holy-mouth-man, as he jabs an awl into an exposed nerve, to suspect that a certain amount of sadism is involved. If this can be established, a very interesting pattern emerges, for most of the population shows definite masochistic tendencies. It was to these that Professor Linton referred in discussing a distinctive part of the daily body ritual which is performed only by men. This part of the rite involves scraping and lacerating the surface of the face with a sharp instrument. Special women's

(Continued)

rites are performed only four times during each lunar month, but what they lack in frequency is made up in barbarity. As part of this ceremony, women bake their heads in small ovens for about an hour. The theoretically interesting point is that what seems to be a preponderantly masochistic people have developed sadistic specialists.

The medicine men have an imposing temple, or *latipso*, in every community of any size. The more elaborate ceremonies required to treat very sick patients can only be performed at this temple. These ceremonies involve not only the thaumaturge but a permanent group of vestal maidens who move sedately about the temple chambers in distinctive costume and headdress. The *latipso* ceremonies are so harsh that it is phenomenal that a fair proportion of the really sick natives who enter the temple ever recover. Small children whose indoctrination is still incomplete have been known to resist attempts to take them to the temple because "that is where you go to die." Despite this fact, sick adults are not only willing but eager to undergo the protracted ritual purification, if they can afford to do so. No matter how ill the supplicant or how grave the emergency, the guardians of many temples will not admit a client if he cannot give a rich gift to the custodian. Even after one has gained admission and survived the ceremonies, the guardians will not permit the neophyte to leave until he makes still another gift.

The supplicant entering the temple is first stripped of all his or her clothes. In everyday life the Nacirema avoids exposure of his body and its natural functions. Bathing and excretory acts are performed only in the secrecy of the household shrine, where they are ritualized as part of the body-rites. Psychological shock results from the fact that body secrecy is suddenly lost upon entry into the *latipso*. A man, whose own wife has never seen him in an excretory act, suddenly finds himself naked and assisted by a vestal maiden while he performs his natural functions into a sacred vessel. This sort of ceremonial treatment is necessitated by the fact that the excreta are used by a diviner to ascertain the course and nature of the client's sickness. Female clients, on the other hand, find their naked bodies are subjected to the scrutiny, manipulation, and prodding of the medicine men.

Few supplicants in the temple are well enough to do anything but lie on their hard beds. The daily ceremonies, like the rites of the holy-mouth-men, involve discomfort and torture. With ritual precision, the vestals awaken their miserable charges each dawn and roll them about on their beds of pain while performing ablutions, in the formal movements of which the maidens are highly trained. At other times they insert magic wands in the supplicant's mouth or force him to eat substances which are supposed to be healing. From time to time the medicine men come to their clients and jab magically treated needles into their flesh. The fact that these temple ceremonies may not cure, and may even kill the neophyte, in no way decreases the people's faith in the medicine men.

There remains one other kind of practitioner, known as a "listener." This witch-doctor has the power to exorcise the devils that lodge in the heads of people who have been bewitched. The Nacirema believe that parents bewitch their own children. Mothers are particularly suspected of putting a curse on children while teaching them the secret body rituals. The counter-magic of the witch-doctor is unusual in its lack of ritual. The patient simply tells the "listener" all his troubles and fears, beginning with the earliest difficulties he can remember. The memory displayed by the Nacirema in these exorcism sessions is truly remarkable. It is not uncommon for the patient to bemoan the rejection he felt upon being weaned as a babe, and a few individuals even see their troubles going back to the traumatic effects of their own birth.

In conclusion, mention must be made of certain practices which have their base in native esthetics but which depend upon the pervasive aversion to the natural body and its functions. There are ritual fasts to make fat people thin and ceremonial feasts to make thin people fat. Still other rites are used to make women's breasts large if they are small, and smaller if they are large. General dissatisfaction with breast shape is symbolized in the fact that the ideal form is virtually outside the range of human variation. A few women afflicted with almost inhuman hyper-mammary development are so idolized that they make a handsome living by simply going from village to village and permitting the natives to stare at them for a fee.

Reference has already been made to the fact that excretory functions are ritualized, routinized, and relegated to secrecy. Natural reproductive functions are similarly distorted. Intercourse is taboo as a topic and scheduled as an act. Efforts are made to avoid pregnancy by the use of magical materials or by limiting intercourse to certain phases of the moon. Conception is actually very infrequent. When pregnant, women dress so as to hide their condition. Parturition takes place in secret, without friends or relatives to assist, and the majority of women do not nurse their infants.

Our review of the ritual life of the Nacirema has certainly shown them to be a magic-ridden people. It is hard to understand how they have managed to exist so long under the burdens which they have imposed upon themselves. But even such exotic customs as these take on real meaning when they are viewed with the insight provided by Malinowski when he wrote:

"Looking from far and above, from our high places of safety in the developed civilization, it is easy to see all the crudity and irrelevance of magic. But without its power and guidance early man could not have mastered his practical difficulties as he has done, nor could man have advanced to the higher stages of civilization."

Follow-Up Activity

Questions for Discussion

1. This essay is a piece of social satire that is meant to amuse readers (note the backward spelling of "Nacirema," for example), but do you think the writer has a serious purpose that is served by the satire? How does satire help him accomplish this purpose?

2. What is the essay's point of view, i.e., whose perspective does it present? Explain.

3. What are the "shrines" that are used to help the Nacirema avert their "natural tendency . . . to debility and disease" described in paragraph 4? What is the focal point of the shrine described in paragraph 6?

4. What is another name for the "holy-mouth-men" mentioned in paragraph 9?

5. Torture, exorcism, and magic are terms used to describe the ritual practices of the Nacirema. What kinds of cultures are usually associated with these practices? Why does Miner use these terms here?

6. What is our common term for the temple, or "latipso," described in paragraphs 13-15? Identify some of the unexpected terms he uses to describe this "temple" and explore their effect on the reader.

7. What is the tone of the essay, and what effect does the tone have on its readers? Do you think you respond differently to the essay than an anthropologist would? Explain.

8. How does Miner's choice of subject—our concerns with appearance and health—and the social customs we use to address those concerns connect with Kluckhohn's idea that "biological process[es] . . . [are always] caught in a cultural web"?

DNA as Destiny

DAVID EWING DUNCAN

David Ewing Duncan is the Founding Director of the Center of Life Science Policy at University of California, Berkeley. He is an author, journalist, and film producer, and a writer for the New York Times, Fortune, Wired, and National Geographic. His most recent book is titled When I'm 164: The New Science of Radical Life Extension, and What Happens If It Succeeds *(2012).*

I feel naked. Exposed. As if my skin, bone, muscle tissue, cells, have all been peeled back, down to a tidy swirl of DNA. It's the basic stuff of life, the billions of nucleotides that keep me breathing, walking, craving, and just being. Eight hours ago, I gave a few cells, swabbed from inside my cheek, to a team of geneticists. They've spent the day extracting DNA and checking it for dozens of hidden diseases. Eventually, I will be tested for hundreds more. They include, as I will discover, a nucleic time bomb ticking inside my chromosomes that might one day kill me.

For now I remain blissfully ignorant, awaiting the results in an office at Sequenom, one of scores of biotech startups incubating in the canyons north of San Diego. I'm waiting to find out if I have a genetic proclivity for cancer, cardiac disease, deafness, Alzheimer's, or schizophrenia.

This, I'm told, is the first time a healthy human has ever been screened for the full gamut of genetic disease markers. Everyone has errors in his or her DNA, glitches that may trigger a heart spasm or cause a brain tumor. I'm here to learn mine.

Waiting, I wonder if I carry some sort of Pandora gene, a hereditary predisposition to peek into places I shouldn't. Morbid curiosity is an occupational hazard for a writer, I suppose, but I've never been bothered by it before. Yet now I find myself growing nervous and slightly flushed. I can feel my pulse rising, a cardiovascular response that I will soon discover has, for me, dire implications.

In the coming days, I'll seek a second opinion, of sorts. Curious about where my genes come from, I'll travel to Oxford and visit an "ancestral geneticist" who has agreed to examine my DNA for links back to progenitors whose mutations have been passed on to me. He will reveal the seeds of my individuality and the roots of the diseases that may kill me—and my children.

For now, I wait in an office at Sequenom, a sneak preview of a trip to the DNA doctor, circa 2008. The personalized medicine being pioneered here and elsewhere prefigures a day when everyone's genome will be deposited on a chip or stored on a gene card tucked into a wallet. Physicians will forecast illnesses and prescribe preventive drugs custom-fitted to a patient's DNA, rather than the one-size-fits-all pharmaceuticals that people take today. Gene cards might also be used to find that best-suited career, or a DNA-compatible mate, or, more darkly, to deny someone jobs, dates, and meds because their nucleotides don't measure up. It's a scenario Andrew Niccol imagined in his 1997 film, *Gattaca*, where embryos in a not-too-distant future are bio-engineered for perfection and where genism—discrimination based on one's DNA—condemns the lesser-gened to scrubbing toilets.

The *Gattaca*-like engineering of defect-free embryos is at least twenty or thirty years away, but Sequenom and others plan to take DNA testing to the masses in just a year or two. The prize: a projected $5 billion market for personalized medicine by 2006 and billions, possibly hundreds of billions, more for those companies that can translate the errors in my genome and yours into custom pharmaceuticals.

(Continued)

Sitting across from me is the man responsible for my gene scan: Andi Braun, chief medical officer at Sequenom. Tall and sinewy, with a long neck, glasses, and short gray hair, Braun, forty-six, is both jovial and German. Genetic tests are already publicly available for Huntington's disease and cystic fibrosis, but Braun points out that these illnesses are relatively rare. "We are targeting diseases that impact millions," he says in a deep Bavarian accent, envisioning a day when genetic kits that can assay the whole range of human misery will be available at Wal-Mart, as easy to use as a home pregnancy test.

But a kit won't tell me if I'll definitely get a disease, just if I have a bum gene. What Sequenom and others are working toward is pinning down the probability that, for example, a colon cancer gene will actually trigger a tumor. To know this, Braun must analyze the DNA of thousands of people and tally how many have the colon cancer gene, how many actually get the disease, and how many don't. Once these data are gathered and crunched, Braun will be able to tell you, for instance, that if you have the defective DNA, you have a 40 percent chance, or maybe a 75 percent chance, of getting the disease by age fifty, or ninety. Environmental factors such as eating right—or wrong—and smoking also weigh in. "It's a little like predicting the weather," says Charles Cantor, the company's cofounder and chief scientific officer.

The sun sets outside Braun's office as my results arrive, splayed across his computer screen like tarot cards. I'm trying to maintain a steely, reportorial façade, but my heart continues to race.

Names of SNPs [pronounced "snips," the tiny genetic variations that account for nearly all differences in humans] pop up on the screen: connexin 26, implicated in hearing loss; factor V leiden, which causes blood clots; and alpha-1 antitrypsin deficiency, linked to lung and liver disease. Beside each SNP are codes that mean nothing to me: 13q11-q12, 1q23, 14q32.1. Braun explains that these are addresses on the human genome, the P.O. box numbers of life. For instance, 1q23 is the address for a mutant gene that causes vessels to shrink and impede the flow of blood—it's on chromosome 1. Thankfully, my result is negative. "So, David, you will not get the varicose veins. That's good, ja?" says Braun. One gene down, dozens to go.

Next up is the hemochromatosis gene. This causes one's blood to retain too much iron, which can damage the liver. As Braun explains it, somewhere in the past, an isolated human community lived in an area where the food was poor in iron. Those who developed a mutation that stores high levels of iron survived, and those who didn't became anemic and died, failing to reproduce. However, in these iron-rich times, hemochromatosis is a liability. Today's treatment? Regular bleeding. "You tested negative for this mutation," says Braun. "You do not have to be bled." I'm also clean for cystic fibrosis and for a SNP connected to lung cancer.

Then comes the bad news. A line of results on Braun's monitor shows up red and is marked "MT," for mutant type. My body's programming code is faulty. There's a glitch in my system. Named ACE (for angiotensin-I converting enzyme), this SNP means my body makes an enzyme that keeps my blood pressure spiked. In plain English, I'm a heart attack risk.

By the time I get home, I realize that all I've really learned is, I might get heart disease, and I could get diabetes. And I should avoid smoking and unsafe sex—as if I didn't already know this. Obviously, I'll now watch my blood pressure, exercise more, and lay off the Cap'n Crunch. But beyond this, I have no idea what to make of the message Andi Braun has divined from a trace of my spit.

After probing my genetic future, I jet to England to investigate my DNA past. Who are these people who have bequeathed me this tainted bloodline? From my grandfather Duncan, an avid genealogist, I already know that my paternal ancestors came from Perth, in south-central Scotland. We can trace the name back to an Anglican priest murdered in

Glasgow in 1680 by a mob of Puritans. His six sons escaped and settled in Shippensburg, Pennsylvania, where their descendants lived until my great-great-grandfather moved west to Kansas City in the 1860s.

In an Oxford restaurant, over a lean steak and a heart-healthy merlot, I talk with geneticist Bryan Sykes, a linebacker-sized fifty-five-year-old with a baby face and an impish smile. He's a molecular biologist at the university's Institute of Molecular Medicine and the author of the bestselling *Seven Daughters of Eve*. Sykes first made headlines in 1994 when he used DNA to directly link a 5,000-year-old body discovered frozen and intact in an Austrian glacier to a twentieth-century Dorset woman named Marie Mosley. This stunning genetic connection between housewife and hunter-gatherer launched Sykes's career as a globe-trotting genetic gumshoe. In 1995, he confirmed that bones dug up near Ekaterinburg, Russia, were the remains of Czar Nicholas II and his family by comparing the body's DNA with that of the czar's living relatives, including Britain's Prince Philip. Sykes debunked explorer Thor Heyerdahl's *Kon-Tiki* theory by tracing Polynesian genes to Asia, not the Americas, and similarly put the lie to the *Clan of the Cave Bear* hypothesis, which held that the Neanderthal interbred with our ancestors, the Cro-Magnon, when the two subspecies coexisted in Europe 15,000 years ago.

Sykes explains to me that a bit of DNA called mtDNA is key to his investigations. A circular band of genes residing separately from the twenty-three chromosomes of the double helix, mtDNA is passed down solely through the maternal line. Sykes used mtDNA to discover something astounding: Nearly every European can be traced back to just seven women living 10,000 to 45,000 years ago. In his book, Sykes gives these seven ancestors hokey names and tells us where they most likely lived: Ursula, in Greece (circa 43,000 B.C.) and Velda, in northern Spain (circa 15,000 B.C.), to name two of the "seven daughters of Eve." (Eve was the ur-mother who lived 150,000 years ago in Africa.).

Sykes has taken swab samples from the cheeks of more than 10,000 people, charging $220 to individually determine a person's mtDNA type. "It's not serious genetics," Sykes admits, "but people like to know their roots. It makes genetics less scary and shows us that, through our genes, we are all very closely related." He recently expanded his tests to include non-Europeans. The Asian daughters of Eve are named Emiko, Nene, and Yumio, and their African sisters are Lamia, Latifa, and Ulla, among others.

Before heading to England, I had mailed Sykes a swab of my cheek cells. Over our desserts in Oxford he finally offers up the results. "You are descended from Helena," he pronounces. "She's the most common daughter of Eve, accounting for some 40 percent of Europeans." He hands me a colorful certificate, signed by him, that heralds my many-times-great-grandma and tells me that she lived 20,000 years ago in Dordogne Valley of France. More interesting is the string of genetic letters from my mtDNA readout that indicate I'm mostly Celtic, which makes sense. But other bits of code reveal traces of Southeast Asian DNA, and even a smidgen of Native American and African.

This doesn't quite have the impact of discovering that I'm likely to die of a heart attack. Nor am I surprised about the African and Indian DNA, since my mother's family has lived in the American South since the seventeenth century. But Southeast Asian? Sykes laughs. "We are all mutts," he says. "There is no ethnic purity. Somewhere over the years, one of the thousands of ancestors who contributed to your DNA had a child with someone from Southeast Asia." He tells me a story about a blond, blue-eyed surfer from Southern California who went to Hawaii to apply for monies awarded only to those who could prove native Hawaiian descent. The grant-givers laughed—until his DNA turned up traces of Hawaiian.

Follow-Up Activity

Questions for Discussion

1. What are SNPs?

2. Explain how our genes make each of us a unique individual and connect us to those who come before and after us.

3. In your own words, what does an "ancestral geneticist" do?

4. Explain Bryan Sykes's discovery of the "seven daughters of Eve." Do you think this discovery is important? Explain.

5. Why does Sykes say that, "through our genes, we are all very closely related"? Do you agree? Why or why not?

6. Does Sykes's theory about human individuality and human connectedness have anything in common with Kluckhohn's idea of "culture in general" and "specific culture"?

A Glossary of Key Terms

annotation
a comment, underline, or other marking that a reader makes on a reading or in its margins to understand and critically evaluate the text

argument
in a paragraph's topic sentence or an essay's thesis statement, a declaration of the point of view that the author wants to persuade readers is true or valid; also, the act of trying to persuade others of a particular opinion

argument essay
a type of writing that tries to persuade readers that a certain opinion is valid or correct

body
the main section of an essay, often consisting of several paragraphs, that develops and supports the author's thesis and that appears between the introduction and conclusion

conclusion
the closing section of an essay that may restate the thesis and its supporting points, offer the reader an emotional appeal, or relate an interesting anecdote that gracefully signals the end of an essay

copyright
the legal ownership of published material

directed summary
a type of focused writing that summarizes a particular aspect of a reading selection in response to an essay topic

drafting
a stage of the writing process where a writer develops and organizes the ideas in a paper in an effort to present the essay's points with clarity and effectiveness

editing
the stage in the writing process where work is checked for grammatical and mechanical errors

evidence
specific details that support an argument and that usually appear in the form of anecdotes (personal stories), examples, statistics, facts, or authorities (quoted experts)

freewriting
a prewriting activity in which the writer quickly puts down on paper random thoughts and ideas on a topic as a method of discovery

handbook
a text that guides the writer through the various stages of writing and provides complete information on the grammar, mechanics, and conventions of written English

homophones
two words that sound the same and may be spelled the same but that have different meanings

idiom
a phrase or expression whose meaning differs from the obvious, literal meaning and whose significance is expected to be automatically understood when used by people from a particular district, community, class, city, region, or nation

index
an alphabetical list of all subjects mentioned in the text, followed by the page numbers on which those subjects appear

introduction
the opening paragraph or paragraphs of an essay that provide a context for the material that follows

listing
a prewriting activity in which a writer lists his or her ideas about a topic as a way of generating useful material for an essay

literacy
a well-developed ability to read and write

outline
a brief list of an essay's thesis statement, main points, main supporting ideas, and specific details

paragraph
related sentences grouped around a central idea or thought

paraphrase
a restatement of an author's piece of writing, expressed with different wording and sentence structure but conveying the same meaning in about the same number of words

part of speech
the idea and function a word has in a sentence

plagiarism
the act of using another author's ideas or words as one's own without crediting the source

post-grade evaluation
a process in which a writer, after receiving instructor feedback on a paper, determines patterns of weakness and strength in his or her writing and formulates a plan for improvement

prewriting
invention techniques or strategies—such as clustering, questioning, freewriting, or listing—for exploring ideas about a topic

questioning
a prewriting activity in which the writer asks and answers questions about the topic as a way to generate useful material for an essay

quotation
a restatement of an author's *exact* words, enclosed in quotation marks

revising
the process of rethinking and rewriting the initial draft

scoring rubric
a guide for evaluating the strengths and weaknesses of an essay

summary
a short presentation in the writer's own words of the argument and main point of a reading

syllable
the smallest unit of pronunciation in a word

syllabus
a plan or summary outline of a course of study

table of contents
a topical list at the beginning of a text that shows at a glance the text's chapters and subjects and the pages on which they are located

theme
a topic or issue of focus and concern

thesis statement
a sentence or sentences found in an essay's introduction that give the essay's central argument, the perspective or idea that locks the other components of the essay together

timed essay
usually a response to a question or topic written in a supervised setting in a designated amount of time

topic
the subject of a piece of writing or speech

topic sentence
the sentence in a paragraph that states the paragraph's main point

transition
a word, phrase, or device used to provide a connection between sentences or paragraphs

vocabulary
a collection or stock of words used in a language to express thoughts and ideas

writing process
the stages of writing that include prewriting, drafting, revising, and editing

Index

Carpentry
Workbook

Third Edition

Timothy Lockley
Floyd Vogt

Africa • Australia • Canada • Denmark • Japan • Mexico • New Zealand • Philippines
Puerto Rico • Singapore • Spain • United Kingdom • United States

NOTICE TO THE READER

Publisher and author do not warrant or guarantee any of the products described herein. Publisher and author do not perform any independent analysis in connection with any of the product information contained herein. Publisher and author do not assume, and expressly disclaim, any obligation to obtain and include information other than that provided to it by the manufacturer.

The reader is expressly warned to consider and adopt all safety precautions that might be indicated by the activities herein and to avoid all potential hazards. By following the instructions contained herein, the reader willingly assumes all risks in connection with such instructions.

The publisher and author make no representations or warranties of any kind, whether express or implied, including but not limited to, the warranties of fitness for particular purpose or merchantability, nor are any such representations implied with respect to the material set forth herein, its reliability, completeness, correctness, accuracy, legality, practicality or operativeness and the publisher and author do not take any responsibility with respect to such material. The publisher and author shall not be liable for any special, consequential, or exemplary damages resulting, in whole or in part, from the readers' use of, or reliance upon, this material. The material contained herein does not in any way constitute and is not intended to be legal advice, or any promise, guarantee or binding statement of the state of the law.

Delmar Staff
Business Unit Director: Alar Elken
Executive Editor: Sandy Clark
Aquisitions Editor: Mark Huth
Developmental Editor: Jeanne Mesick
Editorial Assistant: Dawn Daugherty
Executive Marketing Manager: Maura Theriault
Channel Manager: Mona Caron
Marketing Coordinator: Kasey Young
Executive Production Manager: Mary Ellen Black
Project Editor: Barbara L. Diaz
Art Director: Rachael Baker

Printed in the United States of America
 2 3 4 5 6 7 8 9 10 XXX 06 05 04 03 02 01

For more information, contact: Delmar, 3 Columbia Circle, PO Box 15015, Albany, NY 12212-5015;
or find us on the World Wide Web at http://www.delmar.com

Library of Congress Catalog Card Number: 99-057913
ISBN: 0-7668-1082-8

Contents

Preface

In order to meet the needs of students with various learning styles and abilities, a well-rounded educational program needs to include a variety of resource material. The use of this workbook will help address this need. It is designed to be used with *Carpentry* by Gaspar Lewis and Floyd Vogt. Each chapter in *Carpentry* has a corresponding chapter of exercises in the workbook. The objective of these exercises is to provide the student with learning reinforcement of the material in the main text.

After reading each chapter in *Carpentry*, the student should also read the related chapter in the workbook. If need be, it is acceptable for the student to refer back to the textbook for the correct answers. The exercises are comprised of multiple choice, completion, matching, identification, and discussion. Several of the discussion questions are open-ended without exact correct or incorrect answers. These questions are intended to stimulate thought and discussion between the students and instructor.

CHAPTER 1   WOOD

Multiple Choice

Write the letter for the correct answer on the line next to the number of the sentence.

_____ 1. The carpenter must understand the nature and characteristics of wood to _____ .
- A. protect it from decay
- B. select it for the appropriate use
- C. work it with the proper tools
- D. A , B, and C

_____ 2. The insulating value of 1″ of wood is the equivalent of _____ of brick.
- A. 6″
- B. 10″
- C. 14″
- D. 18″

_____ 3. _____ is a wood that is known for its elasticity.
- A. Oak
- B. Maple
- C. Pine
- D. Hickory

_____ 4. The natural substance that holds wood's many hollow cells together is called _____ .
- A. pith
- B. cambium layer
- C. lignin
- D. sapwood

_____ 5. Tree growth takes place in the _____ .
- A. heartwood
- B. medullary rays
- C. pith
- D. cambium layer

_____ 6. The central part of the tree that is usually darker in color is called the _____ .
- A. sapwood
- B. heartwood
- C. springwood
- D. medullary rays

_____ 7. Wood growth that is rapid and takes place in the _____ is usually light in color and rather porous.
- A. spring
- B. summer
- C. fall
- D. winter

_____ 8. Periods of fast or slow growth can be determined by _____ of the tree.
    A. counting the annual rings
    B. measuring the height
    C. studying the width of the annual rings
    D. measuring the circumference

_____ 9. _____ is an example of a hardwood that is softer than some softwoods.
    A. Basswood
    B. Oak
    C. Redwood
    D. Cherry

_____ 10. All softwoods are _____ .
    A. close-grained
    B. cone-bearing
    C. open-grained
    D. A and B

Completion

Complete each sentence by inserting the correct answer on the line near the number.

_____ 1. _____ trees lose their leaves once a year.

_____ 2. Softwoods come from _____ trees, commonly known as evergreens.

_____ 3. Water passes upward through the tree in the _____ .

_____ 4. Wood that comes from deciduous trees is classified as _____ .

_____ 5. Fir comes from the _____ classification of wood.

_____ 6. Oak is an example of _____ -grained wood.

_____ 7. The _____ of cedar, cypress, and redwood are extremely resistant to decay.

_____ 8. Open-grained lumber has large _____ that show tiny openings or pores in the surface.

_____ 9. Cedar can always be identified by its characteristic _____ .

_____ 10. The best way to learn the different types of wood is by _____ with them.

Identification: Cross-section of Wood

Identify each term, and write the letter of the correct answer on the line next to each number.

_____ 1. pith

_____ 2. sapwood

_____ 3. cambium layer

_____ 4. medullary rays

_____ 5. heartwood

_____ 6. annual rings

_____ 7. bark

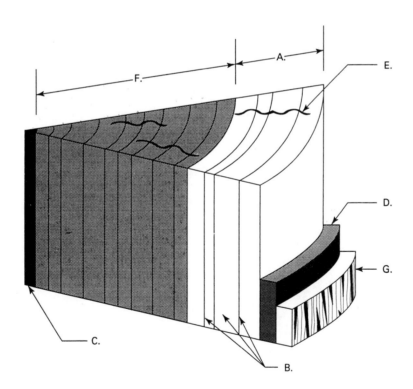

CHAPTER 2   LUMBER

Multiple Choice

Write the letter for the correct answer on the line next to the number of the sentence.

_____ 1. The process of restacking lumber in a way that allows air to circulate between the
            pieces is known as _____.
            A. blocking
            B. spacing
            C. sticking
            D. airing

_____ 2. The best appearing side of a piece of lumber is its _____ side.
            A. face
            B. visage
            C. veneer
            D. select

_____ 3. Most logs are sawed using the _____ method.
            A. plain-sawed
            B. quarter-sawed
            C. edge-grained
            D. a combination of the plain and quarter-sawed

_____ 4. Cracked ceilings, sticking doors, squeaking floors, and many other problems can
            occur from using _____ lumber.
            A. recycled
            B. green
            C. seasoned
            D. quarter-sawed

_____ 5. The moisture content of lumber is expressed as a percentage _____ .
            A. of its total weight
            B. of its total volume
            C. of the weight of its free water
            D. of weight to volume

_____ 6. Wood has reached its _____ when all of the free water is gone.
            A. equilibrium moisture content
            B. stabilization point
            C. fiber-saturation point
            D. dehydration point

_____ 7. Lumber that is under 2″ thick has the classification of _____ .
            A. timbers
            B. boards
            C. dimensional
            D. joists

_____ 8. Dimensional lumber is in the following category: _____
   A. under 2″ thick
   B. 2″–4″ thick
   C. 5″ and thicker
   D. open-grained only

_____ 9. The best grade of hardwood as established by the National Hardwood Association
   is _____ .
   A. select
   B. first and seconds
   C. No. 1 commons
   D. choice

_____ 10. Parallel cracks between the annual rings in wood that are sometimes caused by
   storm damage are known as _____ .
   A. shakes
   B. crooks
   C. checks
   D. cups

Completion

Complete each sentence by inserting the correct answer on the line near the number.

_____ 1. _____ -sawed lumber is the least expensive method of sawing.

_____ 2. _____ -sawed lumber is less likely to warp or shrink.

_____ 3. The _____ uses a great amount of skill in determining the most
   efficient and conservative way to cut a log.

_____ 4. When lumber is first cut from the log it is called _____ lumber.

_____ 5. The heavy weight of green lumber is due to its high _____ content.

_____ 6. The low form of plant life that causes wood to decay is known as
   _____ .

_____ 7. Wood with a moisture content of below _____ percent will not decay.

_____ 8. Lumber used for framing should not have a moisture content over
   _____ percent.

_____ 9. Lumber used for interior finish should not have a moisture content
   over _____ percent.

_____ 10. _____ moisture content occurs when the moisture content of
   the lumber is the same as the surrounding air.

_____ 11. S4S means the lumber was surfaced on _____ sides.

_____ 12. Crooks, bows, twists, and cups are classified as _____ .

_____ 13. Four boards 1″ × 6″ × 12′ contain _____ board feet.

_____ 14. Twenty-four boards 2″ × 4″ × 16′ contain _____ board feet.

Identification: Cut Lumber

Identify each term, and write the letter of the correct answer on the line next to each number.

_____ 1. crook

_____ 2. quarter-sawed

_____ 3. twist

_____ 4. cup

_____ 5. check

_____ 6. bow

_____ 7. plain-sawed

A.

B.

C.

D.

E.

F.

G.

Discussion

Write your answer(s) on the lines below.

1. Describe the difference between air dried and kiln dried lumber.

_____

_____

_____

2. Describe the difference between nominal and actual dimensions.

_____

_____

_____

3. Describe some of the factors one must keep in mind when properly storing lumber on the job site.

_____

_____

_____

_____

CHAPTER 3   RATED PLYWOOD AND PANELS

Multiple Choice

Write the letter for the correct answer on the line next to the number of the sentence.

_____ 1. A/an _____ is a very thin layer of wood.
- A. underlayment
- B. com-ply
- C. span
- D. veneer

_____ 2. With the use of engineered panels _____ .
- A. construction progresses faster
- B. more surface protection is provided than with solid lumber
- C. lumber resources are more efficiently used
- D. A, B, and C

_____ 3. Cross-graining in the manufacture of plywood refers to _____ .
- A. touch sanding the grain
- B. the use of open-grained hardwoods
- C. the grain of each succesive layer is at a right angle to the next one
- D. the placement of the peeler log on the lath

_____ 4. The American Plywood Association is concerned with quality supervision and testing of _____ .
- A. waferboards
- B. composites
- C. oriented strand board
- D. A, B, and C

_____ 5. The letters A, B, C, and D indicate _____ .
- A. span rating
- B. exposure durability classification
- C. the quality of the panel veneers
- D. strength grades

_____ 6. Douglas fir and southern pine are classified in the _____ strength grade.
- A. plugged C
- B. group 1
- C. 303
- D. 32/16

_____ 7. A performance rated panel meets the requirements of the _____ .
- A. panel's end use
- B. sawyer
- C. EPA
- D. United States Forest Service

_____ 8. The left-hand number in a span rating denotes the maximum recommended suport spacing when the panel is used for _____.
   A. roof sheathing
   B. subflooring
   C. siding
   D. underlayment

Completion

Complete each sentence by inserting the correct answer on the line near the number.

_____ 1. The _____ is the largest trade association that tests the quality of plywood and other engineered panels.

_____ 2. The sheets of veneer that are bonded together to form plywood are also known as _____ .

_____ 3. Plywood usually contains a/an _____ number of layers.

_____ 4. Specially selected logs mounted on a huge lath are known as _____ logs.

_____ 5. The highest appearance quality of a panel veneer is designated by the letter _____.

_____ 6. Panels with a _____ grade or better are always sanded smooth.

_____ 7. V-groove, channel groove, striated, brushed, and rough-sawed, are all special surfaces used in the manufacture of _____ .

_____ 8. Most panels manufactured with oriented strands or wafers are known as _____.

_____ 9. Composite panels rated by the American Plywood Association are known as _____ .

_____ 10. Exposure durability of a panel is located on the _____ .

Matching

Write the letter for the correct answer on the line near the number to which it corresponds.

_____ 1. composite panels

_____ 2. span rating

_____ 3. exposure 1

_____ 4. exposure 2

_____ 5. exterior

_____ 6. plywood

_____ 7. aspenite

_____ 8. grade stamp

A. may be exposed to weather during moderate delays

B. is a specific brand of oriented strand board

C. cross-laminated, layered plies glued and bonded under pressure

D. may be exposed to weather during long delays

E. wood veneer bonded to both sides of reconstituted wood panels

F. appears as two numbers separated by a /

G. may be permanently exposed to weather or moisture

H. assures the product has met quality and performance requirements

Identification: Label Information

Identify each term, and write the letter of the correct answer on the line next to each number.

_____ 1. thickness

_____ 2. mill number

_____ 3. panel grade

_____ 4. national research board report number

_____ 5. exposure durability classification

_____ 6. span rating

APA
A. ➞ RATED SHEATHING
B. ➞ 32/16 1/2 INCH ⟵ D.
SIZED FOR SPACING
C. ➞ EXPOSURE 2
000 ⟵ E.
NRB-108 ⟵ F.

CHAPTER 4   NON-STRUCTURAL PANELS

Multiple Choice

Write the letter for the correct answer on the line next to the number of the sentence.

_____ 1. Non-structural particleboard is used in the construction industry for _____ .
    A. cabinet construction
    B. kitchen countertops
    C. the core of veneer doors
    D. A, B, and C

_____ 2. The highest quality particleboard _____ .
    A. contains the same size particles throughout
    B. is 100% sawdust
    C. has large wood flakes in the center with the particle size decreasing the closer to the surface
    D. usually has a rough surface texture

_____ 3. High density fiberboards are called _____ .
    A. particleboard
    B. softboard
    C. oriented strand board
    D. hardboard

_____ 4. *Masonite* is a brand name for _____ .
    A. softboard
    B. duraflake
    C. hardboard
    D. particleboard

_____ 5. Hardboard is widely used for _____ .
    A. sound control purposes
    B. exterior siding and interior wall paneling
    C. roof sheathing
    D. insulation

_____ 6. _____ is a brand name for softboard.
    A. *Celotex*
    B. *Fibrepine*
    C. *Masonite*
    D. A, B, and C

_____ 7. To protect exterior softboard wall sheathing from moisture during construction it is impregnated with _____ .
    A. lignin
    B. asphalt
    C. oil
    D. ceresote

_____ 8. _____ is a well-known reference on products used in the construction industries.
   A. The Dodge Report
   B. Dunn and Bradstreet
   C. Sweets Architectural File
   D. Thompson's Products

Completion

Complete each sentence by inserting the correct answer on the line near the number.

_____ 1. _____ plywood is frequently used on the interior of buildings for wall paneling and cabinets.

_____ 2. The quality of _____ is indicated by its density per cubic foot.

_____ 3. _____ are manufactured as high density, medium density, and low density boards.

_____ 4. Lignin is utilized in the manufacturing process of _____ .

_____ 5. Tempered hardboard panels are coated with _____ and baked.

_____ 6. Most hardboard producers belong to the _____ .

_____ 7. *Medite*, *Baraboard*, and *Fibrepine* are brand names for _____ .

_____ 8. Decorative ceiling panels for suspended ceilings are often made from _____ .

Math

Add the following numbers.

1)	2)	3)	4)	5)	6)	7)
23	54	89	91	11	74	22
55	77	31	82	14	42	61
9	45	81	8	46	98	51
27	65	58	94	32	21	53

8)	9)	10)	11)	12)	13)	14)
74	81	93	32	37	80	22
26	47	92	18	21	27	32
56	55	11	19	67	29	56
81	97	45	33	72	85	11

CHAPTER 5   LAMINATED VENEER LUMBER

Multiple Choice

Write the letter for the correct answer on the line next to the number of the sentence.

_____ 1. During the manufacture of laminated veneer lumber, the grain in each layer of veneer is placed _____ to the previous one.
   A. parallel
   B. at right angles
   C. diagonally
   D. at 22.5°

_____ 2. Laminated veneer lumber was first used to make _____ .
   A. automobile frames
   B. airplane propellers
   C. underlayment
   D. canoes

_____ 3. The first commercially produced laminated veneer lumber for building construction was patented as _____ .
   A. *Micro-Lam*
   B. *Gang-Lam*
   C. *Struclam*
   D. *Versa-Lam*

_____ 4. Laminated veneer lumber uses _____ in its construction.
   A. basswood
   B. poplar and aspen
   C. Douglas fir or southern pine
   D. mostly hardwoods

_____ 5. Laminated veneer lumber is widely used in _____ .
   A. wood frame construction
   B. subflooring
   C. exterior siding
   D. interior paneling

_____ 6. A typical 1¾ inch beam of laminated veneer lumber contains _____ layers of veneer.
   A. 3–5
   B. 5–8
   C. 10–15
   D. 15–20

_____ 7. The thickness of LVL veneers ranges from _____ of an inch.
   A. $\frac{1}{32}$–$\frac{1}{8}$
   B. $\frac{1}{10}$–$\frac{3}{16}$
   C. ¼–$\frac{3}{8}$
   D. $\frac{5}{16}$–$\frac{7}{16}$

_____ 8. Laminated veneer lumber is suited for _____ .
   A. load-carrying beams over window and door openings
   B. scaffold planks
   C. concrete forming
   D. A, B, and C

_____ 9. During its manufacture, LVL veneers are _____ .
   A. expanded
   B. densified
   C. coated with oil
   D. bonded with an interior adhesive

_____10. The usual thickness of LVL is _____ .
   A. ¾"
   B. 1"
   C. 2" and 4"
   D. 1½" and 1¾"

Math

Add the following numbers.

1)	2)	3)	4)	5)	6)	7)
22	63	82	84	31	66	11
74	49	95	32	39	21	8
48	50	37	71	19	46	23
41	92	28	62	92	65	16
7	44	3	51	73	38	31

8)	9)	10)	11)	12)	13)	14)
67	52	29	90	31	73	71
4	64	32	17	73	51	52
83	31	78	92	11	13	84
45	5	12	94	78	42	31
89	91	39	73	25	28	52
73	24	31	52	37	25	82

CHAPTER 6 PARALLEL STRAND AND LAMINATED STRAND LUMBER

Multiple Choice

Write the letter for the correct answer on the line next to the number of the sentence.

_____ 1. Parallel strand lumber provides the building industry with _____ .
   A. sheet materials
   B. small dimension lumber
   C. large dimension lumber
   D. A, B, and C

_____ 2. Parallel strand lumber meets an environmental concern by using _____ .
   A. strands not made of wood
   B. small diameter second growth trees
   C. only old-growth trees
   D. mostly hardwoods

_____ 3. Parallel strand lumber is manufactured _____ .
   A. using a process that is identical to plywood
   B. much the same as particleboard
   C. using a microwave pressing process
   D. using ultrasound to bond the strands

_____ 4. Parallel strand lumber is a material _____ .
   A. that is available in 4′ × 8′ sheets
   B. that sometimes contains defects like knots and shakes
   C. that can be used wherever there is a need for a large beam or post
   D. whose demand will decrease in the future

_____ 5. In comparison to solid lumber, parallel strand lumber _____ .
   A. is consistent in strength throughout its length
   B. has few differences
   C. lengths are not as long
   D. may contain checks

_____ 6. The registered brand name for laminated strand lumber is _____ .
   A. *Lam-stran*
   B. *Parallam*
   C. *TimberStrand*
   D. *Struclam*

_____ 7. Laminated strand lumber presently is made from _____ .
   A. Douglas fir only
   B. longer strands than those used in parallel strand lumber
   C. surplus over-mature aspen trees
   D. southern pine

_____ 8. Laminated strand lumber _____ .
   A. is made of wood strands under 12" long
   B. is not designed to carry heavy loads
   C. can be made from very small logs
   D. A, B, and C

Math

Subtract the following numbers.

1) 542
   −289

2) 752
   −697

3) 812
   − 34

4) 720
   −436

5) 835
   −749

6) 639
   −621

7) 982
   −326

8) 822
   −599

9) 278
   − 89

10) 298
    −129

11) 8229
    −6545

12) 426
    −239

13) 619
    −250

14) 812
    −301

15) 121
    − 72

16) 921
    − 39

17) 273
    −194

18) 721
    −653

19) 103
    − 59

20) 611
    −282

CHAPTER **7**   WOOD I-BEAMS

Completion

Complete each sentence by inserting the correct answer on the line near the number.

_____ 1. The "I" shape utilized in a wood I-beam increases its _____ .

_____ 2. The _____ of a wood I-beam may be made from laminated veneer lumber or specially selected finger-jointed solid wood lumber.

_____ 3. Plywood, laminated veneer lumber, or oriented strand board may be used in the _____ of the beam.

_____ 4. The manufacturing process of wood I-beams consists of _____ top and bottom flanges to a web.

_____ 5. Wood I-beams are produced to approximate _____ moisture content.

_____ 6. Wood I-beams are available in depths from _____ to _____ inches.

_____ 7. Beams with larger webs and flanges are designed to carry _____ loads.

_____ 8. Wood I-beams are available in lengths of up to _____ feet long.

Math

Multiply the following numbers.

1) 529 × 29   2) 738 × 77   3) 627 × 52   4) 982 × 72   5) 901 × 68

6) 833 × 72   7) 436 × 639   8) 889 × 29   9) 256 × 34   10) 449 × 22

11) 739 × 592   12) 812 × 323   13) 822 × 859   14) 162 × 451   15) 449 × 724

16) 374   17) 176   18) 525   19) 866   20) 929
    ×771   ×725   ×828   ×377   ×499

21) 303   22) 574   23) 829   24) 293   25) 117
    × 45   × 91   ×782   ×236   × 33

CHAPTER 8 GLUED LAMINATED BEAMS

Completion

Complete each sentence by inserting the correct answer on the line near the number.

_____ 1. Glued laminated lumber is commonly called _____ .

_____ 2. Glued laminated beams and joists are _____ than natural wood of the same size.

_____ 3. Aside from structural strength, glued laminated beams are _____ as well.

_____ 4. The individual pieces of stock in glued laminated lumber are known as _____ .

_____ 5. When a load is imposed on a glulam beam that is supported on both ends, the topmost lams are said to be in _____ .

_____ 6. _____ is a force applied to a member that tends to increase its length.

_____ 7. The lower stressed sections of glued laminated lumber are located in the beam's _____ .

_____ 8. The sequence of lam grades from the bottom to top of glued laminated lumber is referred to as _____ .

_____ 9. Glued laminated beams come with one edge stamped _____ .

_____ 10. Glued laminated lumber is manufactured in three different grades for _____ .

_____ _____ 11. Glued laminated beams are usually available in lengths from _____ to _____ feet in 2 foot increments.

_____ _____ 12. The widths of glued laminated beams range from _____ to _____ inches.

Discussion

Write your answer(s) on the lines below.

1. What are some of the reasons use of engineered lumber products will surpass solid lumber products in the future?

_____

_____

_____

2. Over time, will the engineered lumber products industry help or harm the lumber industry?

_____

_____

_____

Math

Divide the following numbers and round off each answer.

1) $452 \div 7$ _____

2) $763 \div 52$ _____

3) $525 \div 9$ _____

4) $1,868 \div 11$ _____

5) $778 \div 11$ _____

6) $663 \div 5$ _____

7) $1,586 \div 80$ _____

8) $80,549 \div 333$ _____

9) $12,732 \div 1.65$ _____

10) $978.9 \div 4.3$ _____

CHAPTER 9 NAILS, SCREWS, AND BOLTS

Completion

Complete each sentence by inserting the correct answer on the line near the number.

_____ 1. Steel nails that are uncoated are called _____ nails.

_____ 2. Steel nails that are coated with zinc to prevent rusting are called _____ .

_____ 3. _____ galvanized nails have a heavier coating than electroplated galvanized.

_____ 4. Moisture reacting with two different types of metal causes _____ , which, in time, results in disintegration of one of the metals.

_____ 5. The diameter or thickness of a nail is referred to as its _____ .

_____ 6. Wedge-shaped nails that are stamped from thin sheets of metal are known as _____ nails.

_____ 7. The preferred nail for fastening exterior finish is the _____ nail.

_____ 8. Small finishing nails sized according to gauge and length in inches are known as _____ .

_____ 9. To prevent them from bending, masonry nails are made from _____ steel.

_____ 10. The pointed end of the screw is called the _____ point.

_____ 11. Steel screws that have no coating are known as _____ screws.

_____ 12. _____ screws are larger than wood screws and are turned with a wrench instead of a screwdriver.

_____ 13. The square section under the oval head of a carriage bolt prevents the bolt from _____ as the nut is being turned.

_____ 14. The proper tool used to turn a stove bolt is a _____ .

Identification: Nails, Screws, and Bolts

Identify each term, and write the letter of the correct answer on the line next to each number.

_____ 1. duplex nail

_____ 2. finish nail

_____ 3. casing nail

_____ 4. roofing nail

_____ 5. common nail

_____ 6. gimlet point

_____ 7. threads

_____ 8. shank

_____ 9. lag screw

_____ 10. carriage bolt

_____ 11. machine bolt

_____ 12. stove bolt

_____ 13. staple

CHAPTER 10 ANCHORS AND ADHESIVES

Multiple Choice

Write the letter for the correct answer on the line next to the number of the sentence.

_____ 1. A _____ is a heavy duty anchor.
   A. wedge anchor
   B. coil anchor
   C. nylon nail anchor
   D. concrete screw

_____ 2. Holes may be drilled directly in the masonry through the mounting holes of the fixture being installed if the _____ is used.
   A. toggle bolt
   B. drop-in anchor
   C. stud anchor
   D. conical screw

_____ 3. The concrete screw is a _____ type of anchor.
   A. heavy duty
   B. medium duty
   C. light duty
   D. A, B, and C

_____ 4. Lead and plastic anchors are also called _____ .
   A. split-fast anchors
   B. lag shields
   C. hollow wall fasteners
   D. inserts

_____ 5. When using chemical anchoring systems, it is important to _____ .
   A. thoroughly clear the hole of all dust
   B. properly torque the bolt into the system
   C. immediately stress test the bond
   D. A, B, and C

_____ 6. A disadvantage of using toggle bolts is that _____ .
   A. their use is limited to solid walls
   B. if removed the toggle falls off inside the wall
   C. the diameter of the hole has to be the same as the bolt
   D. hole depth is critical

_____ 7. A common name for a hollow wall expansion anchor is _____ .
   A. universal plug
   B. conical screw
   C. self-drilling anchor
   D. molly screw

_____ 8. Conical screws are used on _____ .
   A. gypsum board
   B. cement block
   C. strand board
   D. A and C

_____ 9. Joist hangers are a form of _____ .
   A. universal anchor
   B. wood to wood connector
   C. hollow wall connector
   D. wood to concrete connector

_____ 10. Polyvinyl acetate is a _____ glue.
   A. yellow
   B. mastic
   C. contact
   D. white

_____ 11. Contact cement is widely used for _____ .
   A. applying plastic laminates on countertops
   B. interior trim
   C. exterior finish
   D. framing

_____ 12. _____ is a moisture-resistant glue.
   A. Yellow
   B. White
   C. Plastic resin
   D. Aliphatic resin

_____ 13. _____ is a type of mastic that may be used in cold weather, even on wet or frozen wood.
   A. Urea resin
   B. Resorcinol resin
   C. Contact cement
   D. Construction adhesive

_____ 14. When applying troweled mastics it is important to _____ .
   A. apply heavily
   B. be sure the depth and spacing of trowel's notches are correct
   C. thoroughly brush as well as trowel the mastic
   D. mix the proper ratio of hardener to the mastic

Identification: Anchors, Bolt, and Screw

Identify each term, and write the letter of the correct answer on the line next to each number.

_____ 1. self-drilling anchor

_____ 2. stud anchor

_____ 3. sleeve anchor

_____ 4. drop-in anchor

_____ 5. coil anchor

_____ 6. nylon nail anchor

_____ 7. toggle bolt

_____ 8. expansion anchor

_____ 9. conical screw

A.

B.

C.

D.

E.

F.

G.

H.

I.

CHAPTER 11   LAYOUT TOOLS

Multiple Choice

Write the letter for the correct answer on the line next to the number of the sentence.

_____   1. Early in carpenter training it is important that _____ is mastered.
      A. the essex board foot table
      B. quick and accurate measuring
      C. finger gauging
      D. the octagon scale

_____   2. Most of the rules and tapes used by the carpenter have clearly marked increments of _____ .
      A. yards
      B. 32nds of an inch
      C. 16 inches
      D. metric conversions

_____   3. Pocket tapes are available in _____ lengths.
      A. 50 and 100 foot
      B. 35 and 50 foot
      C. 6 to 35 foot
      D. A, B, and C

_____   4. A helpful and accurate device for laying out stock that has to be fitted between two surfaces is a _____ .
      A. slipstick
      B. framing square
      C. speed square
      D. sliding T-bevel

_____   5. The combination square functions as _____ .
      A. a depth gauge
      B. a layout or test device for 90° and 45° angles
      C. a marking gauge
      D. A, B, and C

_____   6. The rafter layout tool that can double as a guide for a portable power saw is the _____ .
      A. speed square
      B. combination square
      C. trammel point
      D. framing square

_____   7. The side of the framing square known as the face is the one that has the _____ on it.
      A. essex board foot table
      B. brace table
      C. hundredths scale
      D. manufacturer's name stamped

_____ 8. The most used table on the framing square is the _____ .
   A. rafter table
   B. brace table
   C. essex board foot table
   D. hundredths scale

_____ 9. The _____ is used to lay out or test angles other than those laid out with squares.
   A. trammel point
   B. butt gauge
   C. slipstick
   D. sliding T-bevel

_____ 10. In the absence of trammel points, the same type of layout can be made with _____ .
   A. a plumb bob
   B. a thin strip of wood with a brad through it for a center point
   C. butt markers
   D. a line level

Completion

Complete each sentence by inserting the correct answer on the line near the number.

_____ 1. The longer of the two legs of a framing square is known as the _____ .

_____ 2. In construction the term level is used to indicate that which is _____ .

_____ 3. The term _____ is used to mean the same as vertical.

_____ 4. The _____ is used to test both level and plumb surfaces.

_____ 5. The pair of tubes located in the center of the level is used to determine _____ .

_____ 6. When using the line level, it is important that the level is placed as close to the _____ of the line as possible.

_____ 7. Although very accurate indoors, the _____ can be difficult to use outside when the wind is blowing.

_____ 8. _____ is the technique of laying out stock to fit against an irregular surface.

Matching

Write the letter for the correct answer on the line near the number to which it corresponds.

_____ 1. folding rule

_____ 2. pocket tape

_____ 3. framing square

_____ 4. plumb bob

_____ 5. chalk line

_____ 6. butt marker

_____ 7. line level

_____ 8. wing dividers

A. gives only an approximate levelness; is not accurate

B. practically useless when wet

C. joints must be oiled occasionally

D. used to mark hinge gains

E. is often called a scriber

F. hook slides back and forth slightly

G. is suspended from a line

H. outside corner is called the heel

Measuring

Refer to Figure 11.1 (on page 32) to complete the following sentences. Write your answer on the line near the number.

_____ 1. The length of line A is _____ inches.

_____ 2. The length of line B is _____ inches.

_____ 3. The length of line C is _____ inches.

_____ 4. The length of line D is _____ inches.

_____ 5. The length of line E is _____ inches.

_____ 6. The length of line F is _____ inches.

_____ 7. The length of line G is _____ inches.

_____ 8. The length of line H is _____ inches.

_____ 9. The length of line I is _____ inches.

_____ 10. The length of line J is _____ inches.

_____ 11. The length of line K is _____ inches.

_____ 12. The length of line L is _____ inches.

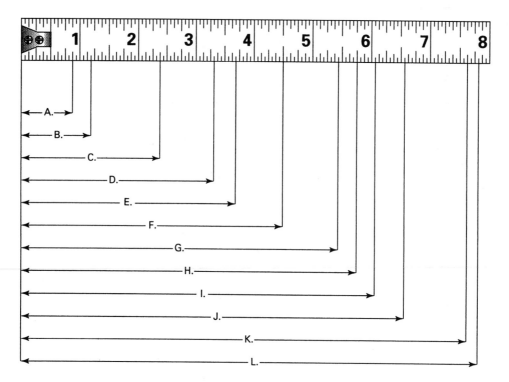

Figure 11.1

CHAPTER 12   BORING AND CUTTING TOOLS

Multiple Choice

Write the letter for the correct answer on the line next to the number of the sentence.

_____ 1. Firmer chisels are used mostly on _____ .
   A. finish work
   B. millwork
   C. heavy framing
   D. locksets

_____ 2. The longest bench plane is a _____ plane.
   A. jointer
   B. jack
   C. smooth
   D. block

_____ 3. A bevel that is referred to as hollow ground is one with a surface that is _____ .
   A. convex
   B. concave
   C. flat
   D. raised

_____ 4. When reshaping the bevel on a wood chisel by grinding, it is important to _____ .
   A. use safety goggles
   B. cool the blade by dipping it in water frequently
   C. maintain a width to the bevel that is approximately twice the thickness of the blade
   D. A, B, and C

_____ 5. Chisels and plane irons need to be ground _____ .
   A. every time they become dull
   B. before each time they are used
   C. when the bevel has lost its hollow ground shape
   D. to reestablish a new wire-edge on the tool's back

_____ 6. The handsaw that is designed to cut with the grain is the _____ .
   A. crosscut saw
   B. compass saw
   C. hacksaw
   D. ripsaw

_____ 7. When using the crosscut saw, the saw should be held at _____ .
   A. about 60° to the stock
   B. about 30° to the stock
   C. about 45° to the stock
   D. the same angle to the stock as the ripsaw

_____ 8. Stock is handsawn with the face side up because _____ .
     A. the action of the saw will splinter the bottom side
     B. it prevents the saw from jumping at the start of the cut
     C. it keeps the saw from binding in the cut
     D. the motion of the saw is built up before it hits the bottom of the board

_____ 9. The _____ is used to make circular cuts in wood.
     A. ripsaw
     B. hacksaw
     C. compass saw
     D. miterbox

_____ 10. The _____ crosscut saw is used to cut across the grain of trim and finished boards.
     A. 11- or 12-point
     B. 5½-point
     C. 7- or 8-point
     D. 4½-point

Completion

Complete each sentence by inserting the correct answer on the line near the number.

_____ 1. The term _____ is often used to denote cutting larger holes in wood.

_____ 2. The diameter of the circle made by the handle of a bit brace is known as its _____ .

_____ 3. As an auger bit is turned, the _____ score the circle in advance of the cutting lips.

_____ 4. The number of sixteenths of an inch in the diameter of an auger bit designates its _____ .

_____ 5. The _____ is usually used to bore holes over 1″ in diameter.

_____ 6. The _____ forms a recess for a flat head screw to set flush with the surface of the material in which it is driven.

_____ 7. The _____ is used to cut recesses in wood for such things as door hinges and locksets.

_____ 8. _____ come in several sizes and are used for smoothing rough surfaces and to bring work down to size.

_____ 9. The _____ is a small plane designed to be held in one hand.

_____ 10. A/An _____ is used to shape the bevel on a wood chisel or plane iron.

_____ 11. To produce a keen edge on a chisel it must be whetted using a/an _____ .

_____ 12. When whetting the flat side of a chisel or plane iron, always hold the tool _____ on the stone.

_____ 13. _____ are generally used to cut straight lines on thin metal.

_____ 14. Handsaws used to cut across the grain of lumber are called _____ saws.

_____ 15. The _____ saw is used to make circular cuts in wood.

_____ 16. Coping and hacksaw blades are usually installed with the teeth pointing _____ from the blade.

_____ 17. The proper hacksaw blade for fast cutting in thick metal is the _____ -toothed blade.

_____ 18. A saw similar to the compass saw, but designed especially for gypsum board, is the _____ saw.

_____ 19. The _____ is used to cut angles of various degrees in finish lumber.

_____ 20. Ripsaws have teeth shaped like rows of tiny _____ .

Discussion

Write your answer(s) on the lines below.

1. Why, in a time when power tools are available, is it essential that carpenters know how to choose and skillfully use hand tools?

_____

_____

_____

2. Why is it important for the carpenter to purchase good quality tools?

_____

_____

_____

CHAPTER 13 FASTENING AND DISMANTLING TOOLS

Multiple Choice

Write the letter for the correct answer on the line next to the number of the sentence.

_____ 1. The 22-ounce hammer is most popularly used on _____ .
- A. finish work
- B. rough work
- C. general work
- D. A, B, and C

_____ 2. The tip of a nail set is _____ to prevent it from slipping off the nail head.
- A. flattened
- B. convexed
- C. concave
- D. pointed

_____ 3. A hammer should be held _____ .
- A. firmly and close to the end of the handle
- B. firmly and in the middle of the handle
- C. in different places on the handle depending on the nails you are using
- D. loosely and in the middle

_____ 4. Toenailing is a technique of driving nails _____ .
- A. at an angle to fasten the end of one piece to another
- B. overhead in hard-to-reach places
- C. straight in to hardwood
- D. sideways in to end grain

_____ 5. To prevent wood from splitting or the nail from bending in hardwood, _____ .
- A. presoak the wood
- B. angle the nail
- C. use hardened nails
- D. drill a hole slightly smaller than the nail shank

_____ 6. The higher the number of the point size of a Phillips screwdriver, the _____ .
- A. higher the quality of the steel
- B. deeper the depth of the cross shaped tip
- C. larger the diameter of the point
- D. lower the steel's quality

_____ 7. If a screw has a flat head _____ .
- A. the shank hole must be countersunk
- B. a bit brace must be used to drive the screw
- C. a spiral screwdriver must be used
- D. a washer must be used under the head

_____ 8. The _____ is a dismantling tool available in lengths from 12"–36" that is used to withdraw spikes and for prying purposes.
A. nail claw
B. pry bar
C. wrecking bar
D. cats paw

_____ 9. C-clamp sizes are designated by _____ .
A. their overall length
B. the sweep of their handle
C. their throat opening
D. the outside length of the C

_____ 10. The proper smoothing tool to use when a considerable amount of stock is to be removed is the _____ .
A. flat file
B. half-round file
C. triangular file
D. rasp

Completion

Complete each sentence by inserting the correct answer on the line near the number.

_____ 1. The most popular hammer for general use is the _____ .

_____ 2. As a general rule, use nails that are _____ longer than the thickness of the material being fastened.

_____ 3. To prevent the filler from falling out, it is important that finish nails are set at least _____ deep.

_____ 4. Blunting or cutting off the point of a nail helps to prevent _____ the wood.

_____ 5. In preparation for driving a screw, a shank hole and a _____ hole must be drilled.

_____ 6. When drilling the shank hole, use a _____ to prevent drilling too deep.

_____ 7. If the material to be fastened is thick, the screw may be set below the surface by _____ to gain additional penetration without resorting to a longer screw.

_____ 8. The nail claw is commonly called a _____ .

_____ 9. To turn nuts, lag screws, bolts, and other objects, a/an _____ is often used.

Math

Add the following fractions.

1) $\frac{7}{8} + 4\frac{3}{4}$ = _____

2) $\frac{3}{8} + \frac{5}{16}$ = _____

3) $\frac{11}{16} + 9\frac{1}{2}$ = _____

4) $\frac{1}{8} + \frac{5}{8}$ = _____

5) $\frac{3}{4} + 5\frac{1}{16}$ = _____

6) $4\frac{1}{2} + \frac{9}{16}$ = _____

7) $\frac{1}{4} + \frac{1}{2}$ = _____

8) $7\frac{5}{8} + 3\frac{1}{16}$ = _____

9) $\frac{3}{4} + \frac{1}{2}$ = _____

10) $2\frac{1}{2} + 10\frac{3}{8}$ = _____

11) $\frac{7}{8} + \frac{1}{4}$ = _____

12) $\frac{3}{4} + 1\frac{3}{4}$ = _____

CHAPTER **14** SAWS, DRILLS, AND DRIVERS

Multiple Choice

Write the letter for the correct answer on the line next to the number of the sentence.

_____ 1. The _____ is the most used portable power tool the carpenter uses.
- A. saber saw
- B. electric circular saw
- C. heavy-duty drill
- D. reciprocating saw

_____ 2. The size of a portable circular saw is determined by _____ .
- A. its horsepower rating
- B. the length of the saw's base
- C. the saw's amperage
- D. the blade diameter

_____ 3. When operating the portable circular saw, _____ .
- A. keep the saw clear of the body until the blade has completely stopped
- B. follow the layout line closely
- C. be sure the stock's waste is over the end of the supports, not between them
- D. A, B, and C

_____ 4. Splintering occurs along the _____ with the portable circular saw.
- A. layout line of the stock
- B. opposite side of the stock from the saw
- C. beginning of the cut
- D. bottom of the kerf

_____ 5. When using the portable circular saw, the best way to prevent splintering is to _____ .
- A. lay out and cut on the finish side of the stock
- B. score the layout line with a sharp knife before cutting
- C. lay out and cut on the side opposite the finish side
- D. B and C

_____ 6. The more teeth per inch a saber saw blade has determines _____ .
- A. the faster, but rougher it cuts
- B. the slower, but smoother it cuts
- C. the stroke range of saw
- D. if plunge cuts are posssible

_____ 7. The reciprocating saw is primarily used for _____ .
- A. cutting straight lines
- B. finish cuts
- C. bevel and miter cuts
- D. roughing-in

_____ 8. The _____ saw would be the carpenters' most likely choice for cutting roof sheathing.
   A. circular
   B. saber
   C. reciprocating
   D. bayonet

_____ 9. _____ are more efficent when used in a hammer drill.
   A. Spade bits
   B. Hole saws
   C. Twist drills
   D. Masonry bits

_____ 10. The size of a portable power drill is determined by the _____ .
   A. maximum opening of its chuck
   B. maximum revolutions per minute it can achieve
   C. horsepower of its motor
   D. maximum torque rating it has received

Completion

Complete each sentence by inserting the correct answer on the line near the number.

_____ 1. To prevent fatal accidents from shock, make sure the tool is properly _____ and a GFCI is in the circuit being used.

_____ 2. It is important to use the proper size _____ to prevent excessive voltage drop.

_____ 3. _____ circular saw blades stay sharper longer than high speed steel blades.

_____ 4. When following a layout line with a circular saw, any deviation from the line can cause the saw to bind and possibly _____ .

_____ 5. To cut out the hole for a sink in a countertop, it is necessary to make a _____ cut.

_____ 6. Saber saws cut on the _____ .

_____ 7. For fast cutting in wood, the reciprocating saw should be set in the _____ mode.

_____ 8. Drills that have a D-shaped handle generally are classified as _____ duty.

_____ 9. A disadvantage of a _____ is that a hole cannot be made partially through the stock.

_____ 10. Holes in metal must always be _____ to prevent the drill from wandering off center.

Matching

Write the letter for the correct answer on the line near the number to which it corresponds.

_____ 1. GFCI

_____ 2. electric circular saw

_____ 3. saber saw

_____ 4. reciprocating saw

_____ 5. light-duty drills

_____ 6. heavy-duty drills

_____ 7. twist drills

_____ 8. spade bit

A. sometimes called a jigsaw

B. ¼″ or ⅜″ chuck capacity

C. used for boring holes in rough work

D. makes small holes in wood or metal

E. ½″ chuck capacity

F. will trip at 5 milliamperes

G. sometimes called a sawzall

H. commonly called the skilsaw

Discussion

Write your answer(s) on the lines below.

1. Discuss the role that attitude plays in portable power tool safety.

_____

_____

_____

2. List some general safety rules that apply to all portable power tools.

_____

_____

_____

CHAPTER 15 PLANES, ROUTERS, AND SANDERS

Multiple Choice

Write the letter for the correct answer on the line next to the number of the sentence.

_____ 1. _____ can be used to sand masonry or metal.
    A. The power jointer plane
    B. The power bench plane
    C. The abrasive plane
    D. The belt sander

_____ 2. The power jointer plane can take up to _____ off the stock with one pass.
    A. $\frac{1}{8}''$
    B. $\frac{1}{4}''$
    C. $\frac{1}{16}''$
    D. $\frac{5}{16}''$

_____ 3. A major advantage of the abrasive plane is that _____ .
    A. its depth of cut is deeper than other power planes
    B. the surface is left sanded and ready for finishing
    C. it can use the same belts as the belt sander
    D. A, B, and C

_____ 4. The part of the router that holds the bit is known as the _____ .
    A. cutter head
    B. template
    C. pilot guide
    D. chuck

_____ 5. Always advance the router into the stock in a direction that is _____ .
    A. clockwise on outside edges and ends
    B. counterclockwise when making internal cuts
    C. against the rotation of the bit
    D. with the rotation of the bit

_____ 6. Extreme care must be taken while sanding when a _____ is applied.
    A. painted coating
    B. transparent coating
    C. penetrating stain
    D. A, B, and C

_____ 7. The adjusting screw on the front of a belt sander is used to _____ .
    A. retract the front roller when changing belts
    B. track the belt and center it on the roller
    C. control the belt's speed
    D. retract the belt's guard

_____ 8. When operating the belt sander, it is important to always _____ .
    A. exert downward pressure on the sander
    B. sand against the grain
    C. tilt the sander in several different directions
    D. keep the electrical cord clear of the tool

_____ 9. A major disadvantage of operating the finish sander in the orbital mode is that
    _____ .
    A. it is slower than the oscillating mode
    B. it leaves scratches across the grain
    C. it is more likely to overheat the sander
    D. the belt needs to be tracked frequently

_____ 10. Commonly used grits for finish sanding are _____ .
    A. 100 or 120
    B. 60 or 80
    C. 30 or 36
    D. 12 or 16

Completion

Complete each sentence by inserting the correct answer on the line near the number.

_____ 1. The power _____ is used to smoothe and straighten long
    edges, such as when fitting doors to openings.

_____ 2. The motor on a power plane turns a _____ .

_____ 3. The power _____ plane is ordinarily operated with one hand.

_____ 4. The _____ plane is similar to a power block plane but has a
    heavy-duty sleeve instead of a cutter head.

_____ 5. The _____ is used to make many different cuts such as
    grooves, dadoes, rabbets, and dovetails.

_____ 6. At least ½" of the router bit must be inserted into the router's
    _____ .

_____ 7. Caution must always be exercised when operating the router, because
    the _____ is unguarded.

_____ 8. Improper use of the _____ has probably ruined more work
    than any other tool.

_____ 9. The most widely used sandpaper on wood is coated with
    _____ .

_____ 10. Sandpaper _____ refers to the size of the abrasive particles.

Math

Subtract the following fractions.

1) $\frac{7}{8} - \frac{3}{8}$ = _____

2) $6\frac{1}{2} - 3\frac{1}{4}$ = _____

3) $\frac{13}{16} - \frac{1}{4}$ = _____

4) $5\frac{1}{8} - \frac{3}{4}$ = _____

5) $\frac{1}{2} - \frac{7}{16}$ = _____

6) $\frac{3}{4} - \frac{3}{8}$ = _____

7) $8\frac{3}{8} - 2\frac{7}{8}$ = _____

8) $\frac{3}{4} - \frac{1}{2}$ = _____

9) $10\frac{1}{2} - 7\frac{3}{4}$ = _____

10) $\frac{7}{8} - \frac{3}{8}$ = _____

11) $6\frac{5}{8} - \frac{3}{4}$ = _____

12) $\frac{1}{2} - \frac{3}{16}$ = _____

CHAPTER 16 FASTENING TOOLS

Multiple Choice

Write the letter for the correct answer on the line next to the number of the sentence.

_____ 1. Pneumatic fastening tools are powered by _____ .
   A. explosive powder cartridges
   B. mechanical leverage
   C. compressed air
   D. disposable fuel cells

_____ 2. A _____ would be used to fasten subfloor.
   A. finish nailer
   B. brad nailer
   C. roofing stapler
   D. light duty framing gun

_____ 3. Nails come _____ for easy insertion into the framing gun's magazine.
   A. glued in strips
   B. attached end to end
   C. in preloaded plastic cassettes
   D. individually packed

_____ 4. Cordless nailing guns eliminate the need for _____ .
   A. air compressors
   B. long lengths of air hoses
   C. extra set-up time
   D. A, B, and C

_____ 5. A battery and spark plug is found in _____ nailing guns.
   A. pneumatic
   B. cordless
   C. powder-actuated
   D. mechanical leverage

_____ 6. The fuel cell in a cordless framing nailer can deliver enough energy to drive about _____ nails.
   A. 1,200
   B. 2,500
   C. 3,200
   D. 4,000

_____ 7. When the nailing gun's trigger is depressed, a fastener is _____ .
   A. immediately driven
   B. driven when the gun's nose touches the work
   C. repeatedly ejected from the gun
   D. automatically actuated

_____ 8. Many states require certification to operate _____ .
   A. pneumatic nailers
   B. cordless nailers
   C. powder-actuated drivers
   D. mechanical staplers

_____ 9. The strength of a powder charge can be determined by its _____ .
   A. color code
   B. diameter
   C. number
   D. length

_____ 10. In selecting a powder charge, always use _____ .
   A. a charge that has more than enough power
   B. the weakest charge that will do the job
   C. a charge that will penetrate the drive pin below the surface
   D. A and C

Completion

Complete each sentence by inserting the correct answer on the line near the number.

_____ 1. A nail set is not required and the possibility of marring the wood is avoided when using the _____ nailer.

_____ 2. Nails for roof nailers come in _____ of 120, which are easily loaded in a nail canister.

_____ 3. Air compressors are needed to operate _____ nailers.

_____ 4. The _____ nailer is used to fasten small moldings and trim.

_____ 5. Within the cordless nailer is a/an _____ engine that forces a piston down to drive the fastener.

_____ 6. A cordless finish nailer will drive about _____ nails before the battery needs to be charged.

_____ 7. A nailing gun can operate only when the work contact element is firmly _____ against the work and the trigger pulled.

_____ 8. Never leave an unattended gun with the _____ attached.

_____ 9. Specially designed pins are driven into masonry and steel by _____ drivers.

_____ 10. Never pry a powder charge out with a screwdriver or knife, as this could result in an _____ .

CHAPTER **17**   CIRCULAR SAW BLADES

Multiple Choice

Write the letter for the correct answer on the line next to the number of the sentence.

_____   1. The more teeth on a circular saw blade, the _____ cut.
      A. faster it can
      B. rougher the surface of the
      C. smoother the surface of the
      D. longer between sharpening it can

_____   2. If a blade is allowed to overheat, it is likely to _____ .
      A. loose its shape and wobble at high speed
      B. bind in the cut
      C. possibly cause a kickback
      D. A, B, and C

_____   3. Coarse-tooth blades are suited for cutting _____ .
      A. thin, dry material
      B. heavy, rough lumber
      C. plastic laminated material
      D. where the quality of the cut surface is important

_____   4. A _____ blade stays sharper longer when cutting materials that contain adhesives.
      A. carbide-tipped
      B. taper-ground
      C. planner
      D. high-speed steel

_____   5. Every tooth on the _____ blade is filed or ground at right angles to the face of the blade.
      A. crosscut saw
      B. ripsaw
      C. combination
      D. A and C

_____   6. The sides of all the teeth on a _____ blade are alternately filed or ground on a bevel.
      A. crosscut saw
      B. ripsaw
      C. combination
      D. B and C

_____   7. Taper-ground blades are _____ .
      A. thinner at the tips and wider toward the center
      B. wider at the tips and thinner toward the center
      C. set to ensure the necessary clearance
      D. an excellent choice for rough, wet, heavy lumber

_____ 8. The ideal carbide-tipped blade for cutting plastic laminated material is the
_____ .
   A. triple chip grind
   B. alternative top bevel
   C. square grind
   D. combination

_____ 9. The arbor nut is always loosened by turning it in the _____ .
   A. opposite direction the blade rotates
   B. same direction the blade rotates
   C. direction of a right-handed thread
   D. direction of a left-handed thread

Completion

Complete each sentence by inserting the correct answer on the line near the number.

_____ 1. Carbide-tipped blades are so hard that they must be sharpened by
_____ -impregnated grinding wheels.

_____ 2. Most of the saw blades being used at present are _____ .

_____ 3. The _____ saw blade is suited for when a variety of crosscutting and ripping is to be done, and it eliminates the need for
changing blades.

_____ 4. A circular saw blade may overheat if the rate of feed is too _____ .

_____ 5. The teeth on a _____ saw blade act like a series of small chisels.

_____ 6. To keep from binding, all saw blades must have some provision for
_____ in the saw cut.

_____ 7. The teeth on a _____ carbide-tipped blade are similar
to the rip teeth on a high speed steel blade.

_____ 8. The versatile carbide-tipped _____ blade is probably the most
widely used by carpenters.

_____ 9. The valleys between the teeth on a saw blade are known as
_____ .

_____ 10. Arbors are always threaded in a direction that will prevent the nut
from becoming _____ during operation.

Identification: Blades

Identify each term, and write the letter of the correct answer on the line next to each number.

_____ 1. crosscut blade

_____ 2. ripsaw blade

_____ 3. combination blade

_____ 4. chisel-point

_____ 5. square grind

_____ 6. alternate bevel

_____ 7. triple chip

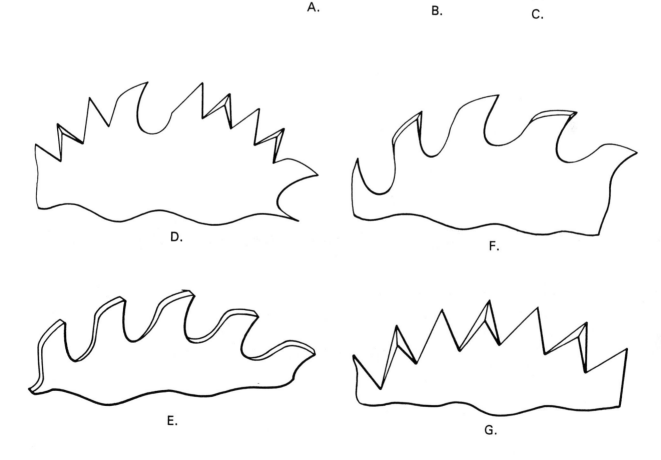

A.

B.

C.

D.

F.

E.

G.

CHAPTER 18 RADIAL ARM AND MITER SAW

Multiple Choice

Write the letter for the correct answer on the line next to the number of the sentence.

_____ 1. The size of the radial arm saw is determined by the _____ .
   A. the width of the board it can rip
   B. the length of the table
   C. the diameter of the largest blade it can use
   D. the horsepower of the motor

_____ 2. The depth of cut is controlled by _____ .
   A. raising or lowering the table
   B. horizontally swinging the arm
   C. tilting the motor unit
   D. raising or lowering the arm

_____ 3. Adjust the depth of cut on the radial arm saw so that the saw blade is about _____ below the surface of the table.
   A. ½″
   B. ⅜″
   C. ¾″
   D. 1/16″

_____ 4. When cutting thick material on the radial arm saw, _____ .
   A. pull the saw through the stock rapidly
   B. pull the saw slowly or hold it back (hesitate) somewhat
   C. never use a stop block
   D. remove the saw's guard

_____ 5. Flat miters are cut on the radial arm saw by _____ .
   A. tilting the saw blade
   B. swinging the arm and simultaneously tilting the motor
   C. positioning the motor parallel to the fence
   D. rotating the arm to the desired angle

_____ 6. Compound miter cuts are frequently used on some types of _____ .
   A. headers
   B. floor joists
   C. roof rafters
   D. collar ties

_____ 7. A stop block is fastened to the table of the radial arm saw when _____ .
   A. ripping stock
   B. cutting many pieces the same length
   C. cutting various sized pieces
   D. the saw is in the out-rip position

_____ 8. Upon completing a cut on the radial arm saw, always _____ .
    A. raise the blade up out of the table
    B. return the saw to the starting point behind the fence
    C. place the saw directly in front of the fence
    D. lower the blade to where it contacts the table

_____ 9. The power miter saw is also called the _____ .
    A. power miter box
    B. radial arm saw
    C. hew saw
    D. A and B

_____ 10. The most common sizes of power miter saws are _____ .
    A. 7½″ and 8½″
    B. 6″ and 8″
    C. 10″ and 12″
    D. 5″ and 7″

Completion

Complete each sentence by inserting the correct answer on the line near the number.

_____ 1. The _____ saw is used primarily for crosscutting framing members.

_____ 2. The _____ saw is specifically designed to crosscut interior and exterior trim.

_____ 3. The arm of a radial arm saw moves horizontally in a complete _____ .

_____ 4. The least obscured view when cutting miters on a radial arm saw occurs when the arm is swung to the _____ .

_____ 5. The _____ locks the arm of a radial arm saw into position.

_____ 6. A/an _____ miter is cut in the same manner as a crosscut except that the radial arm saw's blade is tilted to the desired angle.

_____ 7. When ripping wide material, the motor unit is locked in the _____ position.

_____ 8. When ripping thin stock, always use a _____ to guide the stock between the blade and the fence.

_____ 9. The adjustable dado head is commonly called a/an _____ .

_____ 10. The _____ is widely used to cut and fit molding.

CHAPTER 19 TABLE SAWS

Multiple Choice

Write the letter for the correct answer on the line next to the number of the sentence.

_____ 1. _____ when operating the table saw.
   A. Never cut freehand
   B. Always use the rip fence for ripping
   C. Never reach over a running blade
   D. A, B, and C

_____ 2. A _____ can be cut by making multiple passes across a table saw.
   A. dado
   B. rabbet
   C. V-groove
   D. A, B, and C

_____ 3. When the miter gauge is turned and the blade is tilted, the resulting cut is a
   _____ .
   A. flat miter
   B. compound miter
   C. end miter
   D. bevel

_____ 4. _____ are useful aids to hold work against the fence and down on the
   table surface during ripping operations.
   A. Stop blocks
   B. Feather boards
   C. Taper-ripping jigs
   D. Miter jigs

_____ 5. The most common size table saw used on construction sites is the _____
   model.
   A. 6″
   B. 8″
   C. 10″
   D. 12″

_____ 6. The table saw is favored over the radial arm saw for _____ .
   A. ripping
   B. crosscutting
   C. miter cuts on long stock
   D. dado cuts

_____ 7. When ripping on the table saw, always use a push stick if the stock is under
   _____ .
   A. 2″
   B. 3″
   C. 4″
   D. 5″

_____ 8. An auxiliary tabletop can _____ .
    A. prevent thin stock from slipping under the fence
    B. prevent narrow rippings from slipping between the saw blade and the table insert
    C. help prevent accidents
    D. A, B, and C

Completion

Complete each sentence by inserting the correct answer on the line near the number.

_____ 1. The size of the table saw is determined by the diameter of the _____ .

_____ 2. The table saw's blade can be tilted up to a _____ -degree angle.

_____ 3. Handwheels on a table saw are used to adjust the _____ .

_____ 4. During the ripping operation, the stock is guided by the _____ .

_____ 5. The _____ slides in grooves on the table saw's surface.

_____ 6. Blade height is to be adjusted to about _____ above the stock.

_____ 7. A table saw operator should never stand directly in back of the _____ .

_____ 8. Cut stock that is left between a running blade and the fence may result in possible _____ that could injure those in its path.

_____ 9. Ripping on a _____ is done the same as straight ripping, except the blade is tilted.

_____ 10. When crosscutting stock, the _____ is used to guide the stock past the blade.

Discussion

Write your answer(s) on the lines below.

1. Make a list of general safety rules for the table saw.

_____

_____

_____

2. What advantages does the radial arm saw have over the table saw?

_____

_____

_____

3. What advantages does the table saw have over the radial arm saw?

_____

_____

_____

CHAPTER 20   UNDERSTANDING DRAWINGS

Completion

Complete each sentence by inserting the correct answer on the line near the number.

_____   1. Multi-view drawings, also called _____ drawings, convey most of the information needed for construction.

_____   2. The lines in a/an _____ drawing diminish in size as they approach a vanishing point.

_____   3. Presentation drawings are usually the _____ type.

_____   4. The _____ plan simulates a view looking down from a considerable height.

_____   5. The direction and spacing of floor and roof framing is shown on the _____ plan.

_____   6. The drawings that show the shape and finishes of all sides of the exterior of a building are called _____ .

_____   7. Window _____ give information about the location, size, and type of windows to be installed in a building.

_____   8. For complex commercial projects, a _____ guide has been developed by the Construction Specifications Institute.

_____   9. The triangular_____ scale is used to scale lines when making drawings.

_____   10. The most commonly used scale on blueprints is _____ inch(es) equals one foot.

Matching

Write the letter for the correct answer on the line near the number to which it corresponds.

_____ 1. pictorial drawings

_____ 2. multi-view

_____ 3. isometric drawing

_____ 4. presentation drawing

_____ 5. plot plan

_____ 6. interior elevations

_____ 7. modular measure

_____ 8. section

_____ 9. specifications

_____ 10. dimensions

A. take precedence over the drawing if a conflict arises

B. used to show the appearance of the completed building

C. a dash is always placed between the foot and the inch

D. most common ones show the kitchen and bath cabinets

E. the horizontal lines are drawn at 30° angles

F. two-dimensional drawings that convey the most information

G. shows information about the lot

H. three-dimensional isometric or perspective drawing

I. buildings designed using a grid with a unit of 4"

J. shows a vertical cut through all or part of a construction

Identification: Lines

Identify each term, and write the letter of the correct answer on the line next to each number.

_____ 1. object line

_____ 2. hidden line

_____ 3. centerline

_____ 4. section reference

_____ 5. break line

_____ 6. dimension line

_____ 7. extension line

_____ 8. leader line

H. ————————————

G. ⟵————————————⟶

F. ————————————

E. ------------------------------

D. —·—·—·—·—·—·—·—·—

C. ⟵———— ·· —— ·· ————⟶

B. ⟍/⟍/⟍/⟍

A. ⟋————————

CHAPTER 21 FLOOR PLANS

Completion

Refer to Figure 21.1 to complete the following sentences.

_____ 1. The overall length of the building is _____ .

_____ _____ 2. The dimensions of the utility room are _____ by _____ .

_____ 3. The fireplace is located in the _____ room.

_____ 4. The exterior door symbol in the dining room is that of a _____ .

_____ 5. The size of the floor joists in the living room and the kitchen is _____ .

_____ 6. In heated areas, all exterior studs are to be _____ placed 16″ on center.

_____ _____ 7. The dimensions of the garage are _____ by _____ .

_____ 8. Not counting the garage door, there are _____ entrance doors into the garage.

_____ 9. The _____ can be entered only through the garage.

_____ 10. The plan is drawn to a scale of _____ = 1′-0″.

_____ 11. A _____ door is on the pantry.

_____ _____ 12. The dimensions of the living room are _____ by _____ .

_____ 13. In the living room, the number of electrical outlets that can be controlled by switches is _____ .

_____ 14. Attic access is located in the _____ .

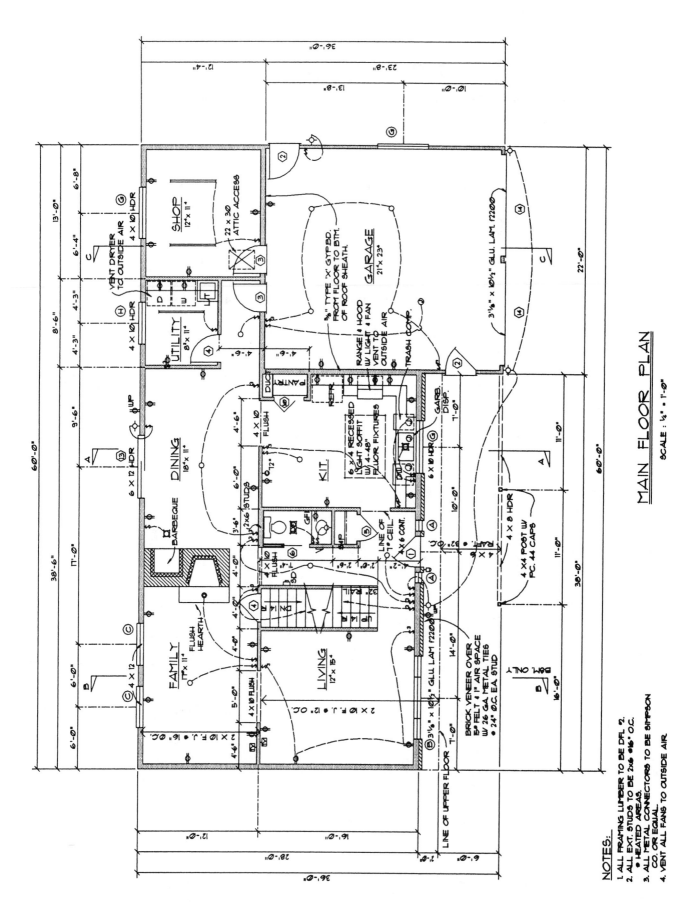

Figure 21.1

Sketch: Floor Plan Symbols

Please sketch each described item in the space provided.

1. exterior sliding door

2. pocket door

3. bifold door

4. double-hung window

5. casement window

6. awning window

7. sliding window

8. water closet

9. standard tub

10. standard shower

Discussion

Write your answer(s) on the lines below.

1. Refer to Figure 21.1 again. If you were building the home on the floor plan for yourself to live in, what changes might you make to improve the design of the home?

_____

_____

_____

CHAPTER 22 SECTIONS AND ELEVATIONS

Completion

Base your answers to questions 1–10 on Figure 22.1.

_____ 1. While floor plans are views of a horizontal cut, sections show _____ cuts.

_____ 2. Sections are usually drawn at a scale of _____ = 1'-0".

_____ 3. _____ are cut across the width or through the length of the entire building.

_____ 4. Enlargements of part of a section, which are done to convey additional needed information, are called _____ .

_____ 5. According to section A-A, the bottom of the footer must be located _____ inches below grade.

_____ 6. The insulation between the crawl space and the subfloor has an R value of _____ in section A-A.

_____ 7. In section A-A, a minimum distance of _____ inches must be maintained between the .006 black vapor barrier and the bottom of the floor joists.

_____ 8. The insulation in the attic has a thickness of _____ inches in section A-A.

_____ 9. The roof has a _____-12 slope in section A-A.

_____ 10. The plywood sheathing on the roof calls for a thickness of _____ in section A-A.

Base your answers to questions 11–17 on Figure 22.2.

_____ 11. The rafters are framed with _____ by _____ stock in section A-8.

_____ 12. The thickness of the basement floor is _____ in section A-8.

_____ 13. In section A-8, the basement wall is _____ inches thick.

_____ 14. Section A-8 is drawn to a scale of _____ " equal 1'-0".

_____ 15. The insulation on the outside of the basement wall is _____ inches thick in section A-8.

_____ _____ 16. In section A-8, the floor joists are framed with _____ by _____ stock.

_____ 17. The footer in section A-8 is _____ inch(es) thick.

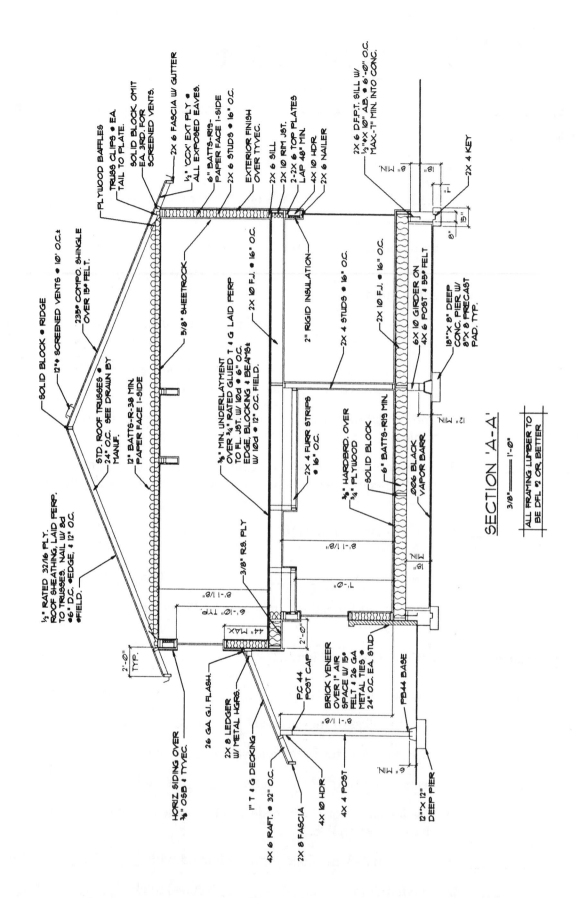

Figure 22.1

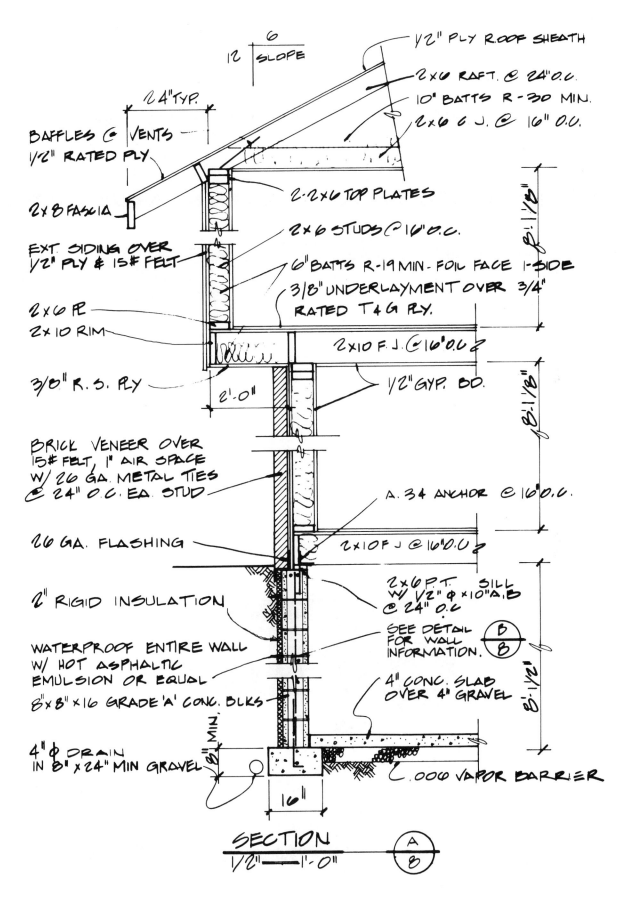

12 | 6 SLOPE

24" TYP.

BAFFLES @ VENTS
1/2" RATED PLY

2×8 FASCIA

EXT. SIDING OVER
1/2" PLY & 15# FELT

2×6 PL
2×10 RIM

3/8" R.S. PLY

BRICK VENEER OVER
15# FELT, 1" AIR SPACE
W/ 26 GA. METAL TIES
@ 24" O.C. EA. STUD

26 GA. FLASHING

2" RIGID INSULATION

WATERPROOF ENTIRE WALL
W/ HOT ASPHALTIC
EMULSION OR EQUAL

8"×8"×16 GRADE 'A' CONC. BLKS.

4" ⌀ DRAIN
IN 8"×24" MIN GRAVEL

1/2" PLY ROOF SHEATH

2×6 RAFT. @ 24" O.C.
10" BATTS R-30 MIN.
2×6 C.J. @ 16" O.C.

2·2×6 TOP PLATES

2×6 STUDS @ 16" O.C.

6" BATTS R-19 MIN. FOIL FACE 1-SIDE
3/8" UNDERLAYMENT OVER 3/4"
RATED T&G PLY.

2×10 F.J. @ 16" O.C.

1/2" GYP. BD.

2'-0"

A.34 ANCHOR @ 16" O.C.

2×10 F.J. @ 16" O.C.

2×6 P.T. SILL
W/ 1/2" ⌀ ×10" A.B.
@ 24" O.C.

SEE DETAIL
FOR WALL
INFORMATION. B/B

4" CONC. SLAB
OVER 4" GRAVEL

3" MIN.

.0006 VAPOR BARRIER

16"

8'-1 1/2"

8'-1 1/2"

8'-1 1/2"

SECTION
1/2" —— 1'-0"   A/B

Figure 22.2

Refer to Figures 22.1–22.3 to complete the following sentences.

_____ 18. According to the accompanying detail, there are _____ inches of gravel under the concrete floor.

_____ 19. The gypsum wallboard on the detail drawing has a thickness of _____ inch(es).

_____ 20. The thickness of the insulation of the exterior wall in Figure 22.3 is _____ inch(es).

_____ 21. Elevations are usually drawn at the same scale as the _____ .

_____ 22. There are usually _____ elevations in each set of drawings.

_____ 23. In relation to other drawings, elevations have few _____ .

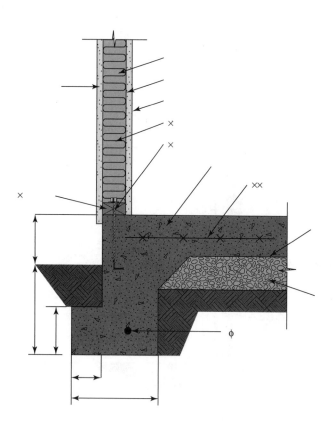

Figure 22.3

CHAPTER 23 PLOT AND FOUNDATION PLANS

Multiple Choice

Write the letter for the correct answer on the line next to the number of the sentence.

_____ 1. The plot plan must show _____ .
   A. a frontal view of the completed structure
   B. the direction and spacing of the framing members
   C. compliance with zoning and health regulations
   D. A, B, and C

_____ 2. Metes and bounds on a plot plan refer to _____ .
   A. elevation
   B. boundary lines
   C. utility easements
   D. the slope of the finish grade

_____ 3. When contour lines are spaced close together, _____ .
   A. a new grade is being indicated
   B. a gradual slope is indicated
   C. they are closer to sea level
   D. a steep slope is indicated

_____ 4. Instead of contour lines, the slope of the finish grade can be indicated by
   _____ .
   A. an arrow
   B. metes and bounds
   C. easements
   D. the measurement of rods

_____ 5. The distance from the property line to the building is known as _____ .
   A. the point of beginning
   B. setbacks
   C. variances
   D. bearings

_____ 6. The location of the footer on a foundation plan is indicated by _____ .
   A. solid lines
   B. solid lines with a dash in the center
   C. dashed lines
   D. object lines

_____ 7. A recess in a foundation wall to support a girder is called a _____ .
   A. benchmark
   B. pocket
   C. casement
   D. seat

_____ 8. On foundation plans, the walls are dimensioned from the _____ .
   A. centerlines of opposing walls
   B. inside of one wall to the inside of the next
   C. outside area of the footer
   D. face of one wall to the face of the next

Completion

Refer to Figure 23.1 to complete the following sentences.

_____ 1. The elevation of the finished floor on the accompanying plot plan is
                       _____ .

_____ 2. The setback distance of the home from the front boundary line is
                       _____ on the plot plan.

_____ 3. The plot plan is drawn on a scale of 1" equals _____ feet.

_____ _____ 4. The dimensions of the home on the plot plan are _____ by _____ .

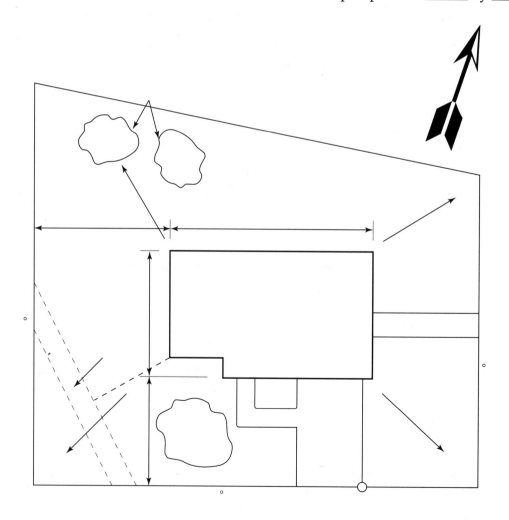

Figure 23.1

_____ 5. The longest property boundary on the plot plan is _____ feet.

_____ 6. The driveway connects to _____ Road.

_____ 7. The driveway is _____ feet long.

_____ 8. The foundation drain connects to the _____ .

_____ 9. The side of the home the water and sewer lines are connected to faces the street named _____ .

_____ 10. The front property boundary is _____ feet long.

Math

The following elevations contain decimals of a foot. Convert the decimals of a foot to inches and sixteenths of an inch, as found on a rule.

1) 96.75' _____

2) 99.10' _____

3) 97.40' _____

4) 99.85' _____

5) 104.35' _____

6) 93.60' _____

7) 90.25' _____

8) 93.10' _____

Discussion

Write your answer(s) on the lines below.

1. What are some of the reasons municipal planning officials insist on a plot plan prior to issuance of a building permit?

_____

_____

_____

CHAPTER 24 BUILDING CODES AND REGULATIONS

Multiple Choice

Write the letter for the correct answer on the line next to the number of the sentence.

_____ 1. Similar size and purpose buildings are limited to various areas of cities and towns by _____ .
A. building codes
B. construction techniques
C. zoning regulations
D. labor unions

_____ 2. Green space refers to the _____ .
A. minimum lot width
B. amount of landscaped area
C. structure's maximum ground coverage
D. off-street parking required

_____ 3. Structures built prior to zoning regulations that do not exist within their proper zone are called _____ .
A. unreformed
B. nonsanctioned
C. nonconfirming
D. preapproved

_____ 4. Hardships imposed by zoning regulations may be relieved by a _____ granted by the zoning board.
A. dissention
B. objection
C. variance
D. reassessment

_____ 5. Minimum standards of safety concerning the design and construction of buildings are regulated by _____ .
A. zoning laws
B. an appeals committee
C. construction costs
D. building codes

_____ 6. The building code primarily used in the Northeast and Midwest is the _____ .
A. Basic National Building Code
B. Uniform Building Code
C. Standard Building Code
D. Primary Building Code

_____ 7. An area of importance in residential building codes is _____ .
    A. exit facilities
    B. room dimensions
    C. requirements for bath, kitchens, and hot and cold water
    D. A, B, and C

_____ 8. The building permit fee is usually based on the _____ .
    A. square footage of the building
    B. estimated cost of construction
    C. occupant load
    D. location of the building

_____ 9. Foundation inspections occur prior to the _____ .
    A. placement of concrete
    B. erection of forms
    C. placement of reinforcement rod
    D. removal of the forms

_____ 10. It is the responsibility of the _____ to notify the Building Official when it is time for a scheduled inspection.
    A. loan officer
    B. zoning officer
    C. contractor
    D. business agent

Discussion

Write your answer(s) on the lines below.

1. Although zoning is intended to protect the rights of the property owners, how might it at the same time infringe on these very rights?

_____

_____

_____

2. Select a recent current event covered by the media where the existence of building codes has played a positive factor. Describe it below and then discuss it with your class.

_____

_____

_____

3. For the most part, a good rapport exists between inspectors and builders. Why is it important for those entering the trade to be aware of this and strive to continue it?

_____

_____

_____

CHAPTER 25 LEVELING AND LAYOUT INSTRUMENTS

Completion

Complete each sentence by inserting the correct answer on the line near the number.

_____ 1. If no other tools are available, a long straightedge and a _____ may be used to level across the building area.

_____ 2. An accurate tool dating back centuries and used for leveling from one point to another is the _____ level.

_____ 3. The _____ level consists of a telescope mounted in a fixed horizontal position with a spirit level attached.

_____ 4. Automatic levels have an internal compensator that uses _____ to maintain a true level line of sight.

_____ 5. Before a level can be used, it must be placed on a _____ or some other means of support.

_____ 6. When adjusting any level, never apply excessive pressure to the _____ .

_____ 7. The folding rule is a favored target over the tape measure because of the _____ of the tape.

_____ 8. The _____ is the ideal target for longer sightings because of its clearer graduations.

_____ 9. A starting point of known elevations used to determine other elevations is known as a _____ .

_____ 10. When the base of the rod is at the desired elevation, the reading on the rod is known as _____ rod.

_____ 11. The height of an instrument is determined by placing the rod on the _____ and adding that reading to the elevation of the bench-mark.

_____ 12. When recording readings of elevation differences, all _____ sights are known as plus sights.

_____ 13. When the level must be set up directly over a particular point, a _____ is attached to a hook centered below the instrument.

_____ 14. A horizontal circle scale on the instrument is divided into quadrants of _____ degrees each.

_____ 15. The horizontal vernier is used to read _____ of a degree.

_____ 16. When laying out a horizontal angle, the instrument must be centered and leveled over the _____ of the angle.

_____ 17. By rotating a full _____ degrees, the laser level creates a level plane of light.

_____ 18. A battery-powered electronic sensor is attached to the leveling rod to detect _____ .

_____ 19. Laser level safety requires that whenever possible the laser be set up so that it is above or below _____ level.

_____ 20. All _____ instruments are required to have warning labels attached to them.

Matching

Write the letter for the correct answer on the line near the number to which it corresponds.

_____ 1. water level

_____ 2. builder's level

_____ 3. transit level

_____ 4. horizontal crosshairs

_____ 5. vertical crosshairs

_____ 6. foresights

_____ 7. horizontal circle scale

_____ 8. vertex

_____ 9. laser level

_____ 10. suspended ceiling grids

A. minus sights

B. the point of an angle

C. magnetic or clip on targets are attached to

D. may rotate up to 40 RPS

E. outside ring

F. has a horizontally fixed telescope

G. crosshairs used when laying out angles

H. limited by the length of the plastic tube

I. telescope can be moved up and down

J. crosshairs used for reading elevations

CHAPTER 26 LAYING OUT FOUNDATION LINES

Multiple Choice

Write the letter for the correct answer on the line next to the number of the sentence.

_____ 1. It is usually the responsibility of the _____ to lay out building lines.
   A. mason
   B. architect
   C. carpenter
   D. foundation inspector

_____ 2. Before any layout can be made, it is important to determine _____ .
   A. the dimensions of the building and its location on the site from the plot plan
   B. a starting corner by the 6-8-10 method
   C. a level plane to measure from
   D. a proper benchmark

_____ 3. Measure in on each side from the front property line the specified setback to establish the _____ .
   A. approximate boundaries of the property
   B. benchmark
   C. the front line of the building
   D. different elevation points

_____ 4. In the absence of a transit or builder's level, a right triangle may be laid out using the _____.
   A. speed square
   B. water level
   C. plot plan
   D. Pythagorean Theorem

_____ 5. The diagonal of a rectangular building that measures 34'-6" × 46'-0" is _____ .
   A. 57'-5"
   B. 57'-6"
   C. 57'-6¾"
   D. 80'-6"

_____ 6. If the lengths of opposite sides of a rectangular layout are equal and the diagonal measurements are also equal, then the corners are _____ .
   A. parallel
   B. square
   C. divergent
   D. obtuse or acute angles

_____ 7. All corner stakes are located by measuring from _____ .
   A. diagonal points
   B. a benchmark
   C. a point of beginning
   D. the established front and side building lines

_____ 8. _____ are wood frames to which building lines are secured.
   A. Grade rods
   B. Batter boards
   C. Line anchors
   D. Transome boards

_____ 9. Ledgers are usually _____ .
   A. vertical 2" × 4" stakes
   B. horizontal 1" × 6" boards
   C. precast concrete
   D. fastened below the top of the footer

_____ 10. Batter boards must be erected in such a manner that they _____ .
   A. will last for years
   B. will withstand sideways force when the footer is poured
   C. will not be disturbed during excavation
   D. can support large amounts of downward pressure

Measuring

Refer to Figure 26.1 to complete the following sentences.

_____ 1. The length of line A is _____ inches.

_____ 2. The length of line B is _____ inches.

_____ 3. The length of line C is _____ inches.

_____ 4. The length of line D is _____ inches.

_____ 5. The length of line E is _____ inches.

_____ 6. The length of line F is _____ inches.

_____ 7. The length of line G is _____ inches.

_____ 8. The length of line H is _____ inches

_____ 9. The length of line I is _____ inches.

_____ 10. The length of line J is _____ inches.

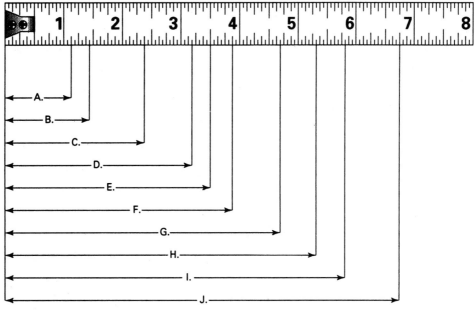

Figure 26.1

Discussion

Write your answer(s) on the lines below.

1. List and discuss some of the serious problems that could happen if a mistake were to occur during foundation layout.

   _____

   _____

   _____

2. How important is the knowledge of layout instruments and an understanding of plans to the foundation layout?

   _____

   _____

   _____

CHAPTER **27** CHARACTERISTICS OF CONCRETE

Multiple Choice

Write the letter for the correct answer on the line next to the number of the sentence.

_____ 1. Concrete form construction is usually the responsibility of the _____ .
   A. laborers
   B. masons
   C. carpenters
   D. ready-mix plant

_____ 2. A chemical reaction called _____ causes cement to harden.
   A. aggregation
   B. aeration
   C. adhesion
   D. hydration

_____ 3. Hardening of concrete can continue for _____ .
   A. days
   B. weeks
   C. months
   D. years

_____ 4. A bag of portland cement contains one cubic foot and weighs _____ pounds.
   A. 70
   B. 82
   C. 94
   D. 100

_____ 5. Type IA is an air-entraining cement used to _____ .
   A. improve resistance to freezing and thawing
   B. withstand great compression
   C. seal oil wells
   D. withstand high temperatures

_____ 6. The quality of concrete is greatly affected by _____ .
   A. the water-cement ratios
   B. rapid evaporation of the water
   C. freezing of the water
   D. A, B, and C

_____ 7. Aggregates serve as a _____ in concrete.
   A. bonding agent
   B. stabilizer
   C. filler
   D. corrosion inhibitor

_____ 8. A cubic yard contains _____ cubic feet.
   A. 27
   B. 81
   C. 36
   D. 18

_____ 9. Concrete must be delivered within _____ after water has been added to the mix.
   A. 30 minutes
   B. 3½ hours
   C. 15 minutes
   D. 1½ hours

_____ 10. Steel bars are added to concrete to increase its _____ .
   A. compressive strength
   B. tensile strength
   C. resistance to freezing
   D. curing time

Completion

Complete each sentence by inserting the correct answer on the line near the number.

_____ 1. A #6 rebar has a diameter of _____ inch(es).

_____ 2. Welded wire mesh is identified by the gauge and spacing of the _____ .

_____ 3. To ease their removal, the inside surfaces of forms are brushed with _____ .

_____ 4. Concrete without admixtures having a slump of greater than _____ inches should not be used.

_____ 5. Vibrating or hand-spading is done to eliminate voids or _____ in the concrete.

_____ 6. Excessive vibration causes concrete to become more liquid, causing more _____ on forms.

_____ 7. Flooding or constant sprinkling of the surface with water after the concrete has set is the most effective method of _____ concrete.

_____ 8. Permanent damage is almost certain if the concrete becomes _____ within the first 24 hours of being placed.

_____ 9. In cold weather, _____ are sometimes added to the concrete to shorten the setting time.

_____ 10. Concrete should be protected from freezing for at least _____ days.

Discussion

Write your answer(s) on the lines below.

1. Why is it so important for the carpenter to have a knowledge of concrete?

_____

_____

_____

CHAPTER 28 FORMS FOR SLABS, WALKS, AND DRIVEWAYS

Multiple Choice

Write the letter for the correct answer on the line next to the number of the sentence.

_____ 1. Slab-on-grade construction permits the structure to have _____ .
   A. lower construction costs
   B. a basement
   C. a crawl space
   D. a higher profile

_____ 2. For good drainage with slab-on-grade construction, the top of the slab should be

_____ .
   A. not more than 4″ below grade
   B. level with the grade
   C. not more than 4″ above grade
   D. not less than 8″ above grade

_____ 3. The soil under a slab is sometimes treated with chemicals to _____ .
   A. reduce settling
   B. prevent frost from lifting the slab
   C. control termites
   D. improve drainage

_____ 4. Prior to pouring the slab for a slab-on-grade structure, _____ .
   A. a vapor barrier should be installed
   B. all water and sewer lines must be installed
   C. top soil must be removed
   D. A, B, and C

_____ 5. With a monolithic slab, _____ .
   A. no footer is necessary
   B. the slab and footer are one piece
   C. a basement is included
   D. no reinforcement is needed in the slab

_____ 6. In an area where the ground freezes to an appreciable depth, the type of slab-on-grade construction that must be used is known as _____ .
   A. a monolithic slab
   B. an independent slab
   C. a detached slab
   D. a thickened edge slab

_____ 7. To reduce heat loss, rigid insulation is placed _____ .
   A. on top of the slab
   B. under the footing
   C. under the perimeter of the slab
   D. A, B, and C

_____ 8. Forms for walks and driveways should be built so that _____ .
   A. water will drain from their surfaces
   B. they may be left in place to save on labor cost
   C. the concrete will rest on sod when possible
   D. A, B, and C

_____ 9. When building forms for curved walks or driveways, it is helpful to _____ .
   A. use hardwood
   B. install the grain horizontally if using plywood
   C. wet the stock before bending
   D. prestress the form for several days prior to the pour

_____ 10. When bending curves with a long radius, _____ may be used for forms.
   A. 2″ × 4″s
   B. ridged insulation
   C. 1″ × 4″s
   D. A and B

Completion

Complete each sentence by inserting the correct answer on the line near the number.

_____ 1. The _____ for a foundation provides a base to spread the load of the structure over a wide area of the earth.

_____ 2. To provide support for posts and columns, a _____ footing is used.

_____ 3. In residential construction, the width of the footing is usually _____ the thickness of the wall.

_____ 4. Reinforcement rods of specified size and spacing are placed in footings of larger buildings to increase their _____ strength.

_____ 5. The depth of footings must be below the _____ line.

_____ 6. If the soil is stable, form work is not necessary and the concrete can be carefully placed in a _____ of proper width and depth.

_____ 7. When constructing forms, the use of _____ nails ensures easy removal.

_____ 8. _____ are nailed to the top edges of the form to tie them together and keep them from expanding.

_____ 9. A _____ is formed in a footing by pressing 2″ × 4″ lumber into freshly poured concrete.

_____ 10. Sometimes it is necessary to _____ the footing if it is built on sloped land.

_____ 11. Another name for a thickened edge slab is a _____ slab.

_____ 12. Forms for walks and driveways should be built so that water will _____ from the concrete's surface.

_____ 13. When forming curves with ¼″ plywood, install it with the grain _____ for easier bending.

_____ 14. _____ the stock also sometimes helps the bending process when forming curves.

Discussion

Write your answer(s) on the lines below.

1. There is an old saying among builders, "If you don't have a good foundation, you don't have anything." Explain the reasoning behind this statement.

   _____

   _____

   _____

2. Why is it so important to place a footer below the frost level?

   _____

   _____

   _____

CHAPTER 29 WALL AND COLUMN FORMS

Multiple Choice

Write the letter for the correct answer on the line next to the number of the sentence.

_____ 1. To increase the efficiency of forming foundation walls, _____ .
- A. the forms are custom-built in place
- B. panels and panel systems are used
- C. snap ties are eliminated
- D. ⅝″ plywood is used to construct the walers

_____ 2. A typical _____ size is 2′ wide by 8′ high.
- A. waler
- B. strongback
- C. girder pocket
- D. panel

_____ 3. Snap ties are used to _____ .
- A. hold the wall forms together at the desired distance
- B. support the wall forms against the lateral pressure of the concrete
- C. reduce the need for external bracing
- D. A, B, and C

_____ 4. The projecting ends of snap ties are snapped off _____ .
- A. prior to placing the concrete
- B. inside the concrete after the removal of the forms
- C. slightly protruding from the concrete after it is placed
- D. when erecting the panels

_____ 5. Walers are _____ .
- A. spaced at right angles to the panel frame members
- B. always run horizontally
- C. constructed of ⅝″ plywood
- D. A, B, and C

_____ 6. The higher a concrete wall, the _____ .
- A. more lateral pressure on the top of the form
- B. less lateral pressure at the bottom of the form
- C. fewer snap ties needed at the bottom of the form
- D. greater the lateral pressure on the bottom of the form

_____ 7. To provide a smooth face to the hardened concrete and for easy stripping of the forms, _____ .
- A. all panel faces should be oiled or treated with a chemical-releasing agent
- B. the panels should be placed horizontally
- C. the concrete must not be vibrated
- D. it is recommended that the panels not be placed on plates

_____ 8. When concrete walls are to be reinforced, the rebars are _____ .
   A. installed after the walers are spaced
   B. added after the concrete is placed
   C. used instead of snap ties
   D. tied in place before the inside panels are erected

_____ 9. A _____ is a thickened portion of the wall added for strength or support for beams.
   A. strongback
   B. pilaster
   C. gusset
   D. parapet

_____ 10. Anchor bolts are set in the wall _____ .
   A. after the concrete has partially set
   B. at the same time as the rebar
   C. as soon as the wall is screeded
   D. when the concrete is placed

_____ 11. It is important that anchor bolts be _____ .
   A. staggered and placed at various heights
   B. attached to the rebar
   C. set at the correct height and at the specified locations
   D. A and B

_____ 12. A _____ is a form that provides an opening in a foundation wall for things such as ducts, pipes, doors, and windows.
   A. domeform
   B. sleeper
   C. keyway
   D. buck

Completion

Complete each sentence by inserting the correct answer on the line near the number.

_____ 1. A radius can be formed on the corners of a concrete column by fastening _____ molding to the panel edges.

_____ 2. Quarter-round molding can be attached to the panels to form a _____ shape.

_____ 3. By attaching triangular-shaped strips of wood to the edges of a panel, a _____ is formed on the column's corners.

_____ 4. A column may be decorated with flutes by attaching vertical strips of _____ molding spaced on the panel faces.

_____ 5. _____ are often used to provide the face of the column with various textures, such as wood, brick, and stone.

_____ 6. The number and spacing of yokes depends on the _____ of the column.

_____ 7. With column form construction, vertical _____ are installed between the overlapping ends of the yokes.

_____ 8. A concrete _____ consists of manufactured items for concrete form construction.

CHAPTER **30** STAIR FORMS

Completion

Complete each sentence by inserting the correct answer on the line near the number.

_____ 1. To conserve on concrete when forming stairs, it may be necessary to lay out the stairs before the _____ is placed.

_____ 2. When forming earth-supported stairs between two existing walls, the _____ and the _____ are laid out on the inside of the existing walls.

_____ 3. When forming stairs, planks are ripped to width to correspond to the height of each _____ .

_____ 4. When forming stairs, it is important to _____ the bottoms of the planks used to form the risers. This permits the mason to trowel the entire edge of the tread.

_____ 5. Riser planks are braced from top to bottom between their ends to keep them from _____ due to the concrete's pressure.

_____ 6. Suspended stairs must be designed and reinforced to support not only their own weight but also the weight of the _____ .

_____ 7. On suspended stairs with open ends, the layout is made on the _____ used for forming the stairs' ends.

_____ 8. Short lengths of narrow boards known as _____ are fastened across joints in forms to strengthen them.

_____ 9. A _____ is a thin piece of plywood that has the width of the tread and the height of the riser laid out on it. It is used to mark the tread and riser locations on the form.

_____ 10. Economical concrete construction depends a great deal on the _____ of form.

Measuring

Refer to Figure 30.1 to complete the following sentences.

_____ 1. The length of line A is _____ inches.

_____ 2. The length of line B is _____ inches.

_____ 3. The length of line C is _____ inches.

_____ 4. The length of line D is _____ inches.

_____ 5. The length of line E is _____ inches.

_____ 6. The length of line F is _____ inches.

_____ 7. The length of line G is _____ inches.

_____ 8. The length of line H is _____ inches

_____ 9. The length of line I is _____ inches.

_____ 10. The length of line J is _____ inches.

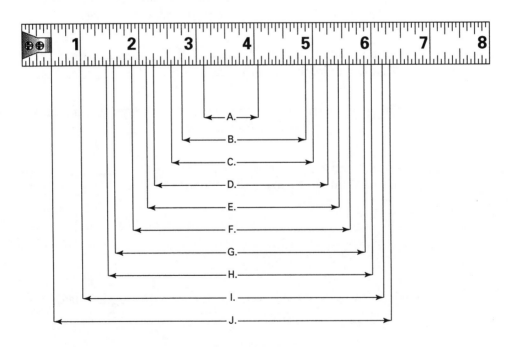

Figure 30.1

CHAPTER **31** TYPES OF FRAME CONSTRUCTION

Multiple Choice

Write the letter for the correct answer on the line next to the number of the sentence.

_____ 1. The most widely used framing method in residential construction is _____ .
   A. balloon frame construction
   B. platform frame construction
   C. post and beam frame construction
   D. the Arkansas system

_____ 2. A platform frame is easy to construct because _____ .
   A. the second floor joists rest on 1″ × 4″ ribbon
   B. at each level a flat surface is provided to work on
   C. the studs run uninterruptedly the entire height of the building
   D. it uses fewer but larger pieces

_____ 3. Lumber shrinks mostly _____ .
   A. across its width
   B. across its thickness
   C. from end to end
   D. A and B

_____ 4. A larger amount of settling occurs in _____ .
   A. platform frame construction
   B. balloon frame construction
   C. post and beam frame construction
   D. B and C

_____ 5. In balloon frame construction, it is important that _____ .
   A. firestops be installed in the walls at several locations
   B. the second floor platform is erected on top of the walls of the first floor
   C. brick or stucco not be used to finish the outside walls
   D. interior design be planned around the supporting roof beam posts

_____ 6. Wood frame construction is used for residential and light commercial construction because _____ .
   A. the cost is usually less than other types
   B. it provides for better insulation
   C. it is very durable and will last indefinitely if properly maintained
   D. A, B, and C

_____ 7. A post and beam roof is usually _____ .
   A. not insulated
   B. insulated on top of the deck
   C. insulated below the deck
   D. more labor- and material-consuming than conventional roof framing

_____ 8. House depths that are not evenly divided by four _____ .
   A. conserve material
   B. waste material
   C. save on labor costs
   D. A and C

_____ 9. Reducing the clear span of floor joists _____ .
   A. makes it necessary to use larger joists
   B. can be accomplished by using narrower sill plates
   C. can make it possible to use smaller-sized joists
   D. can always result in higher costs if wider sill plates must be used

_____ 10. An energy-saving construction system that uses 2″ × 6′ wall studs spaced 24″ on center is called _____ .
   A. the Arkansas system
   B. the 24″ Module Method
   C. the western frame
   D. post and beam construction

Discussion

Write your answer(s) on the lines below.

1. Explain in detail the reason it is important that building dimensions be divisible by four.

   _____

   _____

   _____

2. Given a choice between platform, balloon, or post and beam construction in a home you would be building for yourself, which would you choose and why?

   _____

   _____

   _____

Name_____   Date _____

CHAPTER **32** LAYOUT AND CONSTRUCTION OF THE FLOOR FRAME

Multiple Choice

Write the letter for the correct answer on the line next to the number of the sentence.

_____ 1. Heavy beams that support the inner ends of the floor joists are called _____ .
   A. sill plates
   B. girders
   C. subflooring
   D. bridging

_____ 2. If the blueprints do not specify the kind or size of structural component, _____ .
   A. the job foreman may have to estimate this data
   B. always oversize the material to be safe
   C. have the design checked by a professional engineer
   D. consult with an insurance expert

_____ 3. Pockets should be large enough to provide at least a _____ bearing for the girder.
   A. 12″
   B. 1½″
   C. 8″
   D. 4″

_____ 4. Anchor bolts are used to attach the _____ to the foundation.
   A. floor joists
   B. sill plate
   C. girder
   D. A, B, and C

_____ 5. When tightening the nuts on anchor bolts, be sure to _____ .
   A. replace the washers first
   B. not overtighten them
   C. tighten them as tight as possible
   D. A and B

_____ 6. In conventional framing, floor joists are usually placed _____ .
   A. 16″ on center
   B. prior to the girder
   C. 18″ on center
   D. below the sill plate

_____ 7. Notches in the bottom or top of sawn lumber floor joists should not _____ .
   A. exceed ⅜ the joist depth
   B. be in the middle third of the joist span
   C. be in the first third of the joist span
   D. exceed ½ the joist depth

99

_____ 8. When measuring for floor joist layout, it is best to _____ .
- A. mark the joist locations on top of the foundation
- B. measure and mark each joist individually
- C. have the ends of the plywood fall directly on the edge of the joists
- D. use a tape stretched along the length of the building

_____ 9. Joists are installed with the _____ .
- A. crown down
- B. lap-spiked together over the sill plate
- C. crown up
- D. A and B

_____ 10. When installing plywood subflooring _____ .
- A. leave a ¹⁄₁₆″ space at all panel end joints
- B. leave an ⅛″ between panel edges
- C. all end joints are made over joists
- D. A, B, and C

Completion

Complete each sentence by inserting the correct answer on the line near the number.

_____ 1. Sill plates lie directly on the foundation wall and provide bearing for the _____ .

_____ 2. If joists are lapped over the girder, the minimum amount of lap is _____ inches.

_____ 3. Holes bored in joists for piping or wiring should not be larger than _____ of the joist depth.

_____ 4. Shortened floor joists at the ends of floor openings are called _____ joists.

_____ 5. It is important that the floor joist layout permits the plywood sheets to fall directly on the _____ of the joists.

_____ 6. The area of a rectangular floor is determined by multiplying the length by its _____ .

_____ 7. To determine the number of rated panels of subflooring required, divide the floor area by _____ .

_____ 8. A one-story home with the dimensions of 28′ × 48′ would require _____ rated panels for the subfloor.

_____ 9. To determine the total linear feet of wood cross-bridging needed, multiply the length of the building by _____ for every row of bridging.

Identification: Floor Frame

Identify each term, and write the letter of the correct answer on the line next to each number.

_____ 1. girder

_____ 2. floor joist

_____ 3. rim joists

_____ 4. sill plate

_____ 5. foundation wall

_____ 6. column footing

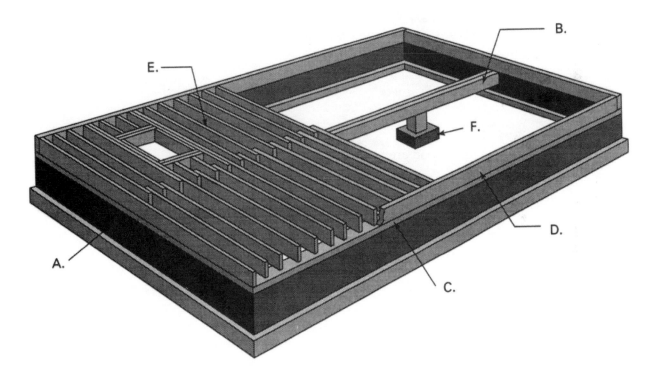

Figure 32.1

Math

The following questions concern estimating the necessary material to construct a floor frame on a foundation measuring 28′ × 40′.

1. Using 2″ × 6″s for the sill plate, how many board feet must be ordered?

2. If the floor joists are placed 16″ on center and none are to be doubled, how many are needed?

3. How many sheets of plywood are needed for the subfloor?

CHAPTER 33 CONSTRUCTION TO PREVENT TERMITES AND FUNGI

Multiple Choice

Write the letter for the correct answer on the line next to the number of the sentence.

_____ 1. For effective treatment against dry wood termites, it is usually necessary to
_____ .
    A. install earth-to-wood termite barriers, and chemically treat the foundation and
        soil
    B. tent-fumigate the whole home with a toxic gas
    C. eliminate any moisture that is reaching the wood and allow the wood to dry
        out
    D. spray the infested area with over-the-counter insecticides

_____ 2. The most destructive species of termite is the _____ .
    A. dry wood termite
    B. damp wood termite
    C. subterranean termite
    D. northern pine termite

_____ 3. Protection against subterranean termites should be considered _____ .
    A. at the first sign of an infestation
    B. when planning and during construction of a building
    C. prior to occupation of the building
    D. after the elimination of the queen

_____ 4. Prevention of termite attacks is based on _____ .
    A. keeping the wood dry
    B. making it as difficult as possible for termites to get to the wood
    C. chemical treatment of the soil
    D. A, B, and C

_____ 5. In crawl spaces, clearance between the ground and the bottom of the floor joists
should be at least _____ .
    A. 8″
    B. 12″
    C. 14″
    D. 18″

_____ 6. The _____ foundation provides the home with the best protection against
termites.
    A. slab-on grade
    B. monolithic slab
    C. two core concrete block
    D. independent slab

_____ 7. Wall siding should not extend more than _____ below the top of the foundation wall.
    A. 2"
    B. 4"
    C. 6"
    D. 8"

_____ 8. Research has shown that due to _____ termite shields have not been effective in preventing infestations.
    A. improper installation
    B. the failure to frequently inspect for signs of shelter tubes
    C. the shields' rapid deterioration
    D. A and B

_____ 9. To safely work with pressure treated lumber, it is important _____ .
    A. to wear eye protection and a dust mask when sawing or machining it
    B. upon completion of the work to wash your hands before eating and drinking
    C. not to burn the leftover scraps
    D. A, B, and C

_____ 10. Clothing that accumulates sawdust from pressure treated wood should be _____ .
    A. disposed of
    B. treated with a disinfectant
    C. laundered separately from other clothing and before reuse
    D. washed in boiling water, then dried outdoors

Completion

Complete each sentence by inserting the correct answer on the line near the number.

_____ 1. _____ termites tend to cause less damage to buildings than other types of termites.

_____ 2. Discovery of a leak sometimes reveals a _____ termite infestation.

_____ 3. All wood scraps should be _____ from the area before backfilling around the foundation.

_____ 4. A pit in the ground filled with stones used to absorb drainage water is called a _____ .

_____ 5. Cracks as little as _____ of an inch permit the passage of termites.

_____ 6. Wall siding should be at least _____ above the finish grade.

_____ 7. _____ grade pressure treated lumber is used for sill plates, joists, girders, and decks.

_____ 8. Termites will not usually eat treated wood; however, they will _____ over it to reach wood that is not treated.

CHAPTER 34 EXTERIOR WALL FRAME PARTS

Multiple Choice

Write the letter for the correct answer on the line next to the number of the sentence.

_____ 1. It is important for the carpentry student to be able to know the _____ of the different parts of the wall frame.
   A. names
   B. functions
   C. locations
   D. A, B, and C

_____ 2. Names given to different parts of a structure _____ .
   A. are the same nationwide
   B. may differ with the geographical area
   C. always include the size of the framing member
   D. change if engineered lumber is used

_____ 3. The bottom horizontal member of a wall frame is called the _____ .
   A. sole plate
   B. top plate
   C. double plate
   D. sill plate

_____ 4. Vertical members of the wall frame that run full length between the plates are known as _____ .
   A. ribbons
   B. trimmers
   C. braces
   D. studs

_____ 5. It is necessary that headers be _____ .
   A. installed wherever interior partitions meet exterior walls
   B. left in until the wall section is erected
   C. strong enough to support the load over the opening
   D. placed under the rough sill

_____ 6. When headers are built to fit a 4″ wall, they consist of _____ .
   A. two pieces of 2″ lumber
   B. three pieces of 2″ lumber
   C. two pieces of 2″ lumber with ½″ plywood or strand board sandwiched in between
   D. two pieces of 2″ lumber with ¾″ plywood or strand board sandwiched in between

_____ 7. Some carpenters prefer to double the rough sills to _____ .
   A. bear the weight over the window
   B. cut down on insulation
   C. provide more surface to nail window trim
   D. fasten the drywall to

_____ 8. Shortened studs that carry the weight of the header are called _____ .
   A. trimmers
   B. door jacks
   C. braces
   D. A and B

_____ 9. Ribbons are horizontal members that support the second floor _____ .
   A. partition intersections
   B. joists in balloon construction
   C. corner posts
   D. headers

_____ 10. Generally, corner bracing is not needed if _____ is used on the corners.
   A. softboard
   B. Celotex
   C. insulated board sheathing
   D. rated panel wall sheathing

Completion

Complete each sentence by inserting the correct answer on the line near the number.

_____ 1. Studs are usually _____ , unless 6″ insulation is desired in the exterior wall.

_____ 2. Studs are usually spaced _____ or 24″ on center.

_____ 3. The depth of the header depends on the _____ of the opening.

_____ 4. Headers in _____ walls may be made up of three pieces of 2″ lumber and two pieces of ½″ plywood or strand board.

_____ 5. The use of _____ lumber for headers permits the spanning of wide openings that otherwise might need additional support.

_____ 6. Rough sills are members used to form the bottom of a _____ opening.

_____ 7. Corner posts may be constructed of _____ 2″ × 4″s.

_____ 8. Ribbons are usually made of _____ stock.

_____ 9. When needed, corners are braced using 1″ × 4″s that are set into the face of the studs, top plate, and sole plate, and run _____ .

Identification: Exterior Wall Frame Parts

Identify each term, and write the letter of the correct answer on the line next to each number.

_____ 1. corner post

_____ 2. top plate

_____ 3. sole plate

_____ 4. stud

_____ 5. cripple stud

_____ 6. corner brace

_____ 7. partition intersection

_____ 8. trimmer

_____ 9. rough sill

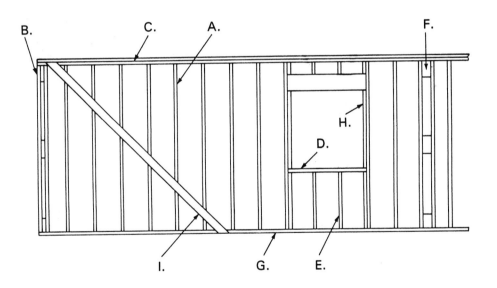

Figure 34.1

CHAPTER **35** FRAMING THE EXTERIOR WALL

Multiple Choice

Write the letter for the correct answer on the line next to the number of the sentence.

_____ 1. To determine stud length, the carpenter must know the _____ .
   A. thickness of the finished floor
   B. thickness of the ceiling below the ceiling joists
   C. height from the finished floor to the finished ceiling
   D. A, B, and C

_____ 2. The carpenter must determine _____ sizes from information contained in the door and window schedules.
   A. header
   B. corner post
   C. rough opening
   D. A and B

_____ 3. When laying out a rough opening, a clearance of _____ is usually maintained between the door frame and the rough opening.
   A. ¼"
   B. ½"
   C. ¾"
   D. 1"

_____ 4. The sides and tops of a door frame are called _____ .
   A. stops
   B. rabbets
   C. jambs
   D. door sets

_____ 5. Interior partitions on blueprints are usually _____ .
   A. dimensioned to their centerlines
   B. shown on the plot plan
   C. eliminated
   D. represented by dotted lines on the floor plan

_____ 6. When laying out studs, _____ .
   A. vary their spacing between 8" and 10"
   B. keep the studs directly in line with the joists below
   C. mark their location on the sill plate
   D. A, B, and C

_____ 7. Prior to bracing the end sections of a wall, an easy and effective way to check the wall section for square is to _____ .
   A. use a framing square
   B. measure the corner posts to see if they are the same
   C. measure the wall from corner to corner both ways to see if they are the same
   D. check the window openings with a combination square

_____ 8. For accurate plumbing of corner posts use _____ .
   A. a transit level
   B. a plumb bob
   C. a 6' level with accessory aluminum blocks attached to each end
   D. A, B, and C

_____ 9. A job-built combination wall aligner and brace is called a/an _____ .
   A. spring brace
   B. wall jack
   C. aligner strut
   D. partition brace

_____ 10. All softboard sheathing is fastened to the wall using _____ nails.
   A. 6d
   B. 12d
   C. duplex
   D. roofing

Completion

Complete each sentence by inserting the correct answer on the line near the number.

_____ 1. A _____ is an opening framed in the wall in which to install doors and windows.

_____ 2. The bottom member of a door frame is called a _____ .

_____ 3. Consulting the manufacturers' _____ is the best way to determine window rough openings.

_____ 4. The first step in laying out wall openings is to consult the blueprints to find the _____ dimension of all the openings.

_____ 5. To avoid problems when installing finish work, it is important that all edges of frame members be kept _____ wherever they join each other.

_____ 6. All studs in a wall should have their crowned edges facing in the _____ direction.

_____ 7. When applying temporary bracing to an erected wall, use _____ nails or drive the nails only partway into the lumber.

_____ 8. Partitions that carry a load are referred to as _____ partitions.

_____ 9. Wall _____ covers the exterior walls.

_____ 10. When estimating material for an exterior wall with a layout that is 16″ on center, figure _____ stud(s) for each linear foot.

Math

The following problems concern estimating the necessary material needed to frame the outside walls for a building that measures 24′ by 32′. The studs are placed 16″ on center and are 2″ × 4″s.

1. How many linear feet of 2″ × 4″s should be ordered for the plates?

2. How many studs should be ordered?

3. If the wall is 8′ high, how many sheets of fiber board sheathing will be needed to cover it?

CHAPTER 36 CEILING JOISTS AND PARTITIONS

Multiple Choice

Write the letter for the correct answer on the line next to the number of the sentence.

_____ 1. Because of the added weight on bearing walls, it is required that _____ .
   A. the top plate be doubled
   B. the sole plate be doubled
   C. they be erected after the roof is on
   D. they be erected in a manner different than exterior walls

_____ 2. Roof trusses eliminate the need for bearing partitions because _____ .
   A. they distribute all the weight on the interior walls
   B. the girder carries the weight
   C. they transmit the weight to the exterior walls
   D. they weigh less than conventional roof framing

_____ 3. Rough opening widths for interior doors are equal to the _____ .
   A. door width plus 1" and the thickness of the finish floor
   B. door width plus 1" and twice the thickness of the door stop
   C. door width plus 1" and twice the thickness of the door jamb
   D. width of the door plus 1¾"

_____ 4. At exterior walls, ceiling joists are placed so that _____ .
   A. the sole plate is attached to them
   B. the rafters can be attached to their sides
   C. they will support the roof trusses until they are set into place
   D. A and C

_____ 5. When ceiling joists are installed in line, _____ .
   A. their ends must butt together at the center line of the bearing partition
   B. a scab must be installed at the splice
   C. the exterior wall location for either side of the span is on the same side of the rafter
   D. A, B, and C

_____ 6. The ends of ceiling joists on the exterior wall must be cut _____ .
   A. if additional head room is needed
   B. slightly above the rafter at the same angle as the roof's slope
   C. flush or slightly below the top edge of the rafter
   D. only if the roof has a very steep pitch

_____ 7. When low-pitched hip roofs are used, _____ .
   A. roof trusses are a necessity
   B. ceiling joists must be doubled
   C. stub joists must be installed
   D. ceiling joists may be eliminated

_____ 8. Ceiling joists on each end of the building are placed so that _____ .
   A. the outside face is flush with the inside of the wall
   B. the outside face is flush with the outside of the wall
   C. there is a 1½" gap between the joists and outside wall
   D. there is access for the electrician to run wiring through them

_____ 9. The top plate of a bearing partition _____ .
   A. laps the plate of the exterior wall
   B. is a single member
   C. butts the top plate of the exterior wall
   D. is applied after the ceiling joists are installed

_____ 10. Most building codes state that the studs of nonbearing partitions may be spaced up to _____ on center.
   A. 16"
   B. 24"
   C. 28"
   D. 32"

Completion

Complete each sentence by inserting the correct answer on the line near the number.

_____ 1. Ceiling joists tie the exterior side walls together and provide a base for the ceiling _____ .

_____ 2. Size and spacing of ceiling joists are determined by the _____ or from local building codes.

_____ 3. _____ prevent the roof from exerting outward pressure on the wall, which would cause the walls to spread.

_____ 4. When joists are installed, be sure the crowned edges are pointed _____ .

_____ 5. When cutting the taper on the ends of ceiling joists, be sure the taper length does not exceed _____ times the depth of the member.

_____ 6. A _____ is a small opening in ceiling joists that allows access to the attic.

_____ 7. Joists are to be toenailed into the plates with at least two _____ penny nails.

_____ 8. Ceiling joists may be installed butting a girder with each joist supported by a _____ .

_____ 9. Because nonbearing partitions carry no load, headers are usually doubled _____ .

_____ 10. Bathroom and kitchen walls sometimes must be made thicker to accommodate _____ later installed in those walls.

_____ 11. A rough opening width of _____" is needed for a 32" interior door, if the jamb stock is ½" thick.

114

CHAPTER **37** BACKING, BLOCKING, AND BASES

Completion

Complete each sentence by inserting the correct answer on the line near the number.

_____ 1. A short block of lumber that is installed in floor, wall, and ceiling cavities to provide fastening for various fixtures and parts is known as _____ .

_____ 2. The placement of blocking and backing is not usually found in a set of _____ .

_____ 3. Wall blocking is needed at the _____ edges of wall sheathing panels permanently exposed to the weather.

_____ 4. Blocking is required between studs in walls over _____ high.

_____ 5. It is easier to install blocking in a _____ line than in a straight one.

_____ 6. The white mineral mined from the earth that plaster is made from is called _____ .

_____ 7. The thin wood strips that in the past were used for a plaster base are known as _____ .

_____ 8. _____ and metal lath are the plaster bases that are commonly used today.

_____ 9. Gypsum lath that is ⅜″ thick may be used if the framing is spaced _____″ on center.

_____ 10. The standard width of gypsum lath is 16″ and the standard length is _____″.

_____ 11. Metal lath is formed from sheet metal that has been slit and _____ to form numerous small openings to key the plaster.

_____ 12. Specialists called _____ install metal lath on large commercial jobs.

_____ 13. Gypsum lath requires _____ coats of plaster.

_____ 14. To prevent cracks, metal lath called _____ is installed at inside corners for reinforcement.

_____ 15. All exterior corners must have _____ of expanded metal installed on them.

_____ 16. Plasterers use _____ as guides to control the plaster's thickness.

Identification: Blocking and Backing

Identify each term, and write the letter of the correct answer on the line next to each number.

_____ 1. faucet backing

_____ 2. tub support blocking

_____ 3. showerhead backing

_____ 4. outlet backing

_____ 5. shower curtain rod backing

_____ 6. lavatory backing

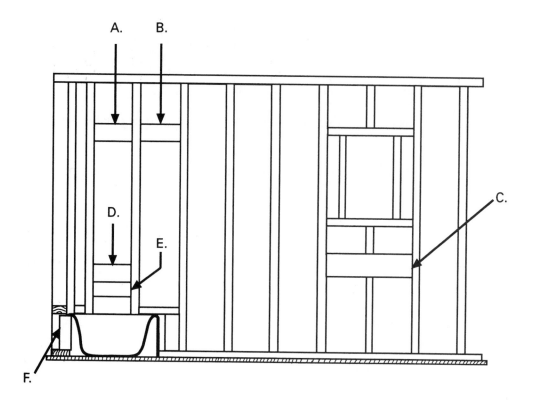

Figure 37.1

CHAPTER **38** METAL FRAMING

Completion

Complete each sentence by inserting the correct answer on the line near the number.

_____ 1. All steel framing members are coated with material that resists _____ .

_____ 2. Studs for interior nonload-bearing applications are manufactured from 25-, 22-, and _____ -gauge steel.

_____ 3. Pipes and conduit can be ran through punchouts that are located at intervals in the studs _____ .

_____ 4. The top and bottom horizontal members of a steel frame wall are called _____ .

_____ 5. Steel channels are used in suspended ceilings and for _____ of walls.

_____ 6. One and a quarter inch oval head screws are used to fasten tracks to _____ .

_____ 7. To cut metal framing to length, tin snips can be used on _____ gauge steel.

_____ 8. Maximum spacing for metal furring channels is _____ inches on center.

Discussion

Write your answer(s) on the lines below.

1. What are some of the factors that could lead to steel framing members being used more frequently in the future?

_____

_____

_____

2. What usually determines whether specialists in light steel or carpenters do the framing?

_____

_____

_____

3. Over an extended period of time, which type of stud—steel or wood—is more environmentally favorable? Explain your answer.

_____

_____

_____

CHAPTER 39 WOOD, METAL, AND PUMP JACK SCAFFOLDS

Multiple Choice

Write the letter for the correct answer on the line next to the number of the sentence.

_____ 1. All scaffolds must be capable of supporting without failure at least _____ .
   A. the maximum intended load
   B. two times the maximum intended load
   C. three times the maximum intended load
   D. four times the maximum intended load

_____ 2. _____ should never be used as a means of access or egress on metal frame scaffolding.
   A. Cross braces
   B. End frames
   C. Extension ladders
   D. A and B

_____ 3. Vertical members of a scaffold are called _____ .
   A. ledgers
   B. bearers
   C. braces
   D. poles

_____ 4. To prevent excessive checking, scaffold planks should _____ .
   A. be painted
   B. not exceed 6′ in length
   C. have their ends banded with steel
   D. be replaced yearly

_____ 5. All scaffold planks must _____ .
   A. be scaffold grade or its equivalent
   B. be laid with their edges close together
   C. not overhang the bearer by more than 12″
   D. A, B, and C

_____ 6. On scaffolds that are more than ten feet high, _____ are installed on all open sides.
   A. bearers
   B. outriggers
   C. bucks
   D. guardrails

_____ 7. Pipe scaffolds should be set _____ .
   A. up tight against the wall
   B. as far from the wall as the worker can comfortably reach
   C. as close to the wall as is possible without interfering with the work
   D. without braces on the inside face on medium duty scaffolds

_____ 8. Scaffolding should be erected _____.

    A. by an OSHA inspector

    B. under supervision of a competent person

    C. by a subcontractor

    D. using new equipment

_____ 9. With metal scaffolding, _____.

    A. only one set of braces is needed

    B. braces must be forced on to fit correctly

    C. each section consists of two end pieces and two folding braces

    D. more time is needed to erect it, due to its difficulty to work with

_____ 10. Pump jack scaffolds should not be used when _____.

    A. the working level exceeds 500 lbs.

    B. more than two people are needed to do the job

    C. the poles exceed 30′ in height

    D. A, B, and C

Completion

Complete each sentence by inserting the correct answer on the line near the number.

_____ 1. Wood scaffolds are designated as light, medium, or heavy duty according to the _____ they are required to support.

_____ 2. The work area of a scaffold must be _____ between the outside uprights and the guardrail system.

_____ 3. _____ are diagonal members that stiffen the scaffolding and prevent the poles from moving or buckling.

_____ 4. The top guardrail should be _____ inches above the working platform.

_____ 5. Scaffold _____ are allowed to do their work under less restrictive safety requirements than scaffold users.

_____ 6. Scaffold planks should be of equal lengths so that the ends are _____ with each other.

_____ 7. Mobile scaffold towers can easily _____ if used incorrectly.

_____ 8. When erecting metal scaffolding, always level it until the _____ fit easily.

_____ 9. Casters for mobile scaffolding must be able to support _____ times the maximum intended load.

_____ 10. On pump jack scaffold poles, the braces must be installed at vertical intervals not exceeding _____ feet.

Identification: Scaffold Parts

Identify each term, and write the letter of the correct answer on the line next to each number.

_____ 1. scaffold pole

_____ 2. bearer

_____ 3. top rail

_____ 4. mid-rail

_____ 5. toe board

_____ 6. ledger

_____ 7. scaffold plank

_____ 8. wall ledger

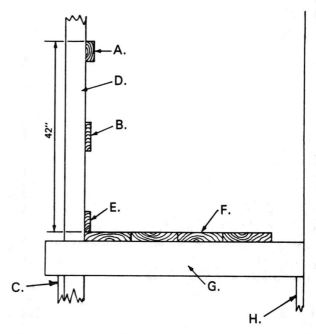

Figure 39.1

CHAPTER 40 BRACKETS, HORSES, AND LADDERS

Completion

Complete each sentence by inserting the correct answer on the line near the number.

_____ 1. Roof brackets are usually required whenever the roof has more than a _____-inch vertical rise per horizontal unit of run.

_____ 2. Roof brackets should be placed at about _____-foot horizontal intervals.

_____ 3. When nailing roof brackets, use three 8d common nails driven home; try to get at least one nail into a _____ .

_____ 4. A _____ is a low working platform supported by a bearer with spreading legs at each end.

_____ 5. For light duty work, horses and trestle jacks should not be spaced more than _____ feet apart.

_____ 6. If a horse scaffold is arranged in tiers, no more than _____ tiers should be used.

_____ 7. The base of an extension ladder should be held a distance out from the wall equal to _____ the ladder's vertical height.

_____ 8. When used to reach a roof or a working platform, the top of the ladder must extend at least _____ feet above the top support.

_____ 9. Always be careful of overhead electric lines, especially when using a/an _____ ladder.

_____ 10. Metal brackets installed on ladders to hold scaffold planks are called _____ .

_____ 11. A typical saw horse is 36" wide with 24" _____ .

_____ 12. _____ are another name for ladder rungs.

Discussion

Write your answer(s) on the lines below.

1. What are some of the things those responsible for erecting scaffolds must be aware of?

   _____

   _____

   _____

2. Do you think it would be advisable for construction firms to use professional scaffold erectors? If so, when and why?

   _____

   _____

   _____

CHAPTER 41 ROOF TYPES AND TERMS

Matching

Write the letter for the correct answer on the line near the number to which it corresponds.

_____ 1. gable roof

_____ 2. shed roof

_____ 3. hip roof

_____ 4. gambrel roof

_____ 5. span

_____ 6. rafter

_____ 7. total run

_____ 8. ridge

_____ 9. total rise

_____ 10. line length

_____ 11. pitch

_____ 12. slope of the roof

_____ 13. plumb cut

_____ 14. level cut

_____ 15. framing square

A. the longer side is 2 inches wide

B. uppermost horizontal line of the roof

C. usually the width of the building

D. inches of rise per foot of run

E. two sloping roofs meeting at the top

F. slopes in one direction only

G. sloping member of the roof frame

H. vertical when the rafter is in position

I. slopes upward from all walls of the building to the top

J. vertical distance that the rafter rises

K. horizontal when the rafter is in position

L. gives no consideration to the thickness of the stock

M. horizontal travel of the rafter

N. a variation of the gable roof

O. a fractional ratio of rise to span

Identification: Roofs

Referring to the figure on the following page, identify each term and write the letter of the correct answer on the line next to each number.

_____ 1. gable roof

_____ 2. shed roof

_____ 3. hip roof

_____ 4. intersecting roof

_____ 5. gambrel roof

_____ 6. mansard roof

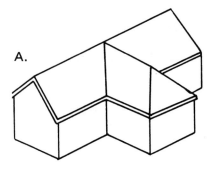

A.

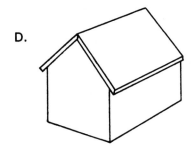

D.

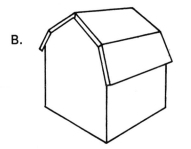

B.

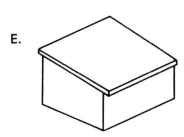

E.

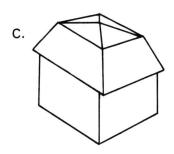

C.

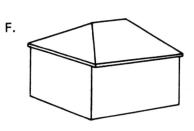

F.

Discussion

Write your answer on the lines below each instruction.

1. Describe the line length method of calculating rough rafter lengths. Include a sketch of the process in your description.

    _____

    _____

    _____

2. When would the above process be acceptable to use? When would it not be acceptable to use?

    _____

    _____

    _____

CHAPTER 42 GABLE AND GAMBREL ROOFS

Completion

Complete each sentence by inserting the correct answer on the line near the number.

_____ 1. The most common style of roof used is the _____ roof.

_____ 2. On an equal-pitched gable roof, the _____ rafter is the only type of rafter needed to be laid out.

_____ 3. Although not absolutely necessary, the _____ simplifies roof erection.

_____ 4. When laying out the rafter that is to be used as a pattern, be sure to select the _____ piece possible.

_____ 5. The faster, more accurate method for laying out a rafter uses a _____ and the rafter tables to find rafter length.

_____ 6. Rafter tables come in booklet form and are also stamped on one side of a _____ .

_____ 7. On roofs with moderate slopes, the length of the level cut of the seat is usually the width of the _____ .

_____ 8. In most plans, the rafter projection is given in terms of a _____ measurement.

_____ 9. If a ridge board is used, the rafter must be _____ a distance equal to one-half the width of the ridge board.

_____ 10. All ridge board joints should be centered on a _____ .

_____ 11. End rafters are commonly called _____ rafters.

_____ 12. When an overhang is required at the rakes, horizontal structural members called _____ must be installed.

_____ 13. When installing _____ , care must be taken not to force the end rafters up and create a crown in them.

_____ 14. Usually gambrel roof rafters meet at a continuous member called a _____ .

Identification: Gable and Gambrel Roof Parts

Identify each term, and write the letter of the correct answer on the line next to each number.

_____ 1. ridge

_____ 2. common rafter

_____ 3. plumb cut or ridge cut

_____ 4. seat cut or bird's mouth

_____ 5. tail or overhang

_____ 6. collar ties

_____ 7. gable studs

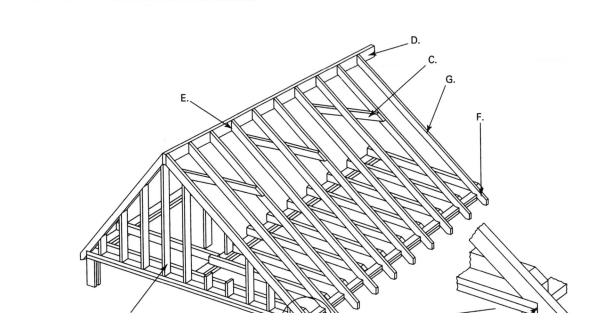

Math

The following rafter line lengths contain decimals of a foot. Convert the decimals of a foot to inches and sixteenths of an inch as found on a rule.

1. 12.37' _____

2. 19.22' _____

3. 17.69' _____

4. 14.76' _____

5. 13.42' _____

6. 8.95' _____

7. 13.40' _____

8. 21.63' _____

CHAPTER 43 HIP ROOFS

Multiple Choice

Write the letter for the correct answer on the line next to the number of the sentence.

_____ 1. Hip roofs are _____ .
A. easier to frame than gable roofs
B. more complicated than gable roofs to frame
C. the most common style of roof used
D. sloped in one direction only

_____ 2. Hip rafters are required _____ .
A. where the slopes of a hip roof meet
B. on all roof framing
C. on saltbox style roofs
D. at right angles from the plates to the common rafters

_____ 3. In comparison to the common rafters on the same roof, _____ .
A. hip rafters must rise the same but with fewer steps
B. hip rafters have a decreased unit of run
C. the slope of a hip rafter is much steeper
D. the unit of run of the hip rafter is increased

_____ 4. If the pitch of a hip roof is a 6″ rise per unit of run, the hip rafter would be laid out
by holding the square at _____ .
A. 6 and 12
B. 6 and 14
C. 6 and 17
D. 6 and 24

_____ 5. The ridge cut of a hip rafter _____ .
A. is a compound angle
B. is called the cheek cut
C. may be called a side cut
D. A, B, and C

_____ 6. When finding the length of a hip rafter using the tables on the framing square,
_____ .
A. the figure found on the square is divided by the overall run of the rafter
B. the figures from the second line are used
C. the common difference must first be determined
D. A, B, and C

_____ 7. When laying out the seat cut of a hip rafter,_____ .
A. consideration must be given to fitting it around the corner of the wall
B. consideration must be given to dropping the hip rafter
C. the next to the last plumb line laid out is used as the plumb cut for the seat of
the rafter
D. the figures from the third line of the framing square are used

_____ 8. When the corners of a hip rafter are beveled flush with the roof, it is called _____ .
   A. raising the hip
   B. dropping the hip
   C. backing the hip
   D. opposing the hip

_____ 9. A double-cheek cut is usually made at the _____ .
   A. tail cut of a hip rafter
   B. seat cut of a hip rafter
   C. seat cut of a hip-jack rafter
   D. tail cut of a hip-jack rafter

_____ 10. The hip-jack rafter _____ .
   A. runs at right angles from the hip rafter to the plate
   B. has the same unit of run as the hip rafter
   C. is actually a shortened common rafter
   D. has a double-cheek cut

_____ 11. The hip-jack rafter meets the hip roof at _____ .
   A. 22½°
   B. 45°
   C. 60°
   D. 90°

_____ 12. The line length of a hip roof ridge is _____ .
   A. the same as the overall length of the building
   B. found by subtracting one-half the width of the building from its length
   C. the length of the building minus its width
   D. determined from information on the rafter tables of the framing square

Identification: Hip Roof Parts

Identify each term, and write the letter of the correct answer on the line next to each number.

_____ 1. hip jack rafter   _____ 4. hip rafter

_____ 2. ridge   _____ 5. plate

_____ 3. common rafter

Discussion

Write your answer(s) on the lines below.

1. When planning a home design, what factors might go into the decision of choosing a hip roof?

_____

_____

_____

CHAPTER **44** INTERSECTING ROOFS

Multiple Choice

Write the letter for the correct answer on the line next to the number of the sentence.

_____ 1. Intersecting roofs must always have _____ .
   A. hip rafters
   B. valley rafters
   C. purlins
   D. kneewalls

_____ 2. If the heights of two intersecting roofs are different, _____ .
   A. supporting and shortened valley rafters must be used
   B. a valley cripple-jack rafter must be used
   C. valley-jack rafters must be used
   D. A, B, and C

_____ 3. The unit of run for valley rafters is _____ .
   A. 12
   B. the same as common rafters
   C. called the minor span
   D. the same as the hip rafter

_____ 4. In order for the valley rafter to clear the inside corner of the wall, _____ .
   A. it must be dropped like the hip rafter
   B. the seat cut must be extended
   C. the seat cut must be raised
   D. the wall plate is notched

_____ 5. The supporting valley rafter is shortened _____ .
   A. by ½ the thickness of the ridge board
   B. by the thickness of the ridge board
   C. by ½ the 45° thickness of the ridge board
   D. only if a shortened valley rafter is needed

_____ 6. The total run of the supporting valley rafter is _____ .
   A. the run of the common rafter of the main roof
   B. the run of the common rafter of the smaller roof
   C. known as the major span
   D. A and C

_____ 7. The tail cut of the valley rafter is _____ .
   A. identical to that of a hip rafter
   B. a single cheek cut
   C. a square cut
   D. a double cheek cut that angles inward

_____ 8. The unit of run used to determine the length of the valley-jack rafter is _____ .
    A. the same one used for valley rafters
    B. the same one used for hip rafters
    C. the same one used for common rafters
    D. 17″ if the step-off method is used

_____ 9. The total run of any valley-jack rafter is _____ .
    A. the same as the common rafters
    B. known as the minor span
    C. that of the common rafter minus the horizontal distance it is located from the corner of the building
    D. that of the supporting valley rafter minus the horizontal distance it is located from the end of the building

_____ 10. Hip valley cripple-jack rafters cut between the same hip and valley rafters _____ .
    A. are the same length
    B. have square cheek cuts
    C. differ in size by the same common difference found on the rafter table
    D. A and B

Identification: Intersecting Roof Parts

Identify each term, and write the letter of the correct answer on the line next to each number.

_____ 1. ridge of major span   _____ 6. valley cripple-jack rafter

_____ 2. supporting valley rafter   _____ 7. hip-jack rafter

_____ 3. shortened valley rafter   _____ 8. valley-jack rafter

_____ 4. common rafter   _____ 9. hip valley cripple-jack rafter

_____ 5. ridge of minor span   _____ 10. hip rafter

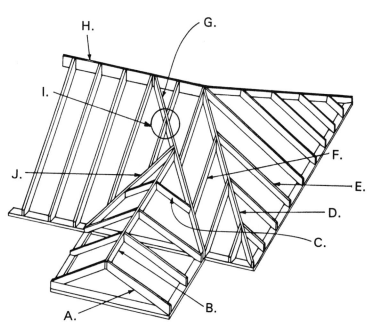

Discussion

Write your answer(s) on the lines below.

1. What are the three main things to be remembered that will help eliminate confusion concerning the layout of so many different types of rafters?

_____

_____

_____

CHAPTER 45 SHED ROOFS, DORMERS, AND SPECIAL FRAMING PROBLEMS

Completion

Complete each sentence by inserting the correct answer on the line near the number.

_____ 1. The shed roof slopes in only _____ direction.

_____ 2. The unit of run for a shed roof is _____ inches.

_____ 3. A _____ is a framed projection above the plane of the roof containing one or more windows.

_____ 4. The length of a shed roof rafter can be determined by using the rafter tables for a _____ rafter.

_____ 5. Shed roofs are framed by _____ the rafters into the plate at the designated spacing.

_____ 6. When framing a shed roof, it is important that the plumb cut of the seat be kept snug against the _____.

_____ 7. The rafters on both sides of a dormer opening must be _____ .

_____ 8. Top and bottom _____ of sufficient strength must be installed when dormers are framed with their front wall partway up the main roof.

_____ 9. In most cases, shed dormer roofs extend to the ridge of the main roof in order to gain enough _____.

Discussion

Write your answer(s) on the lines below.

1. What is the main disadvantage of building an intersecting roof after the main roof has been framed and sheathed?

_____

_____

_____

CHAPTER 46 TRUSSED ROOFS

Multiple Choice

Write the letter for the correct answer on the line next to the number of the sentence.

_____ 1. Truss use in roof framing _____ .
   A. increases the home's usable attic space
   B. slows down the home's construction
   C. eliminates the need for load-bearing interior partitions below
   D. A, B, and C

_____ 2. The diagonal parts of roof trusses are called _____ .
   A. web members
   B. knee supports
   C. stringers
   D. sleepers

_____ 3. The upper cords of a roof truss act as _____ .
   A. ceiling joists
   B. rafters
   C. collar ties
   D. a ridge board

_____ 4. Most trusses used today _____ .
   A. are designed by the carpenter
   B. are made in fabricating plants
   C. are built on the job
   D. do not contain gusset plates

_____ 5. Approved designs and instructions for job-built trusses are available from the
   _____ .
   A. American Plywood Association
   B. Truss Plate Institute
   C. American Hardwood Association
   D. A and B

_____ 6. The most common truss design is the _____ truss.
   A. howe
   B. pratt
   C. fink or W
   D. scissors

_____ 7. Carpenters are more involved in the _____ of trusses.
   A. erection
   B. design
   C. construction
   D. fabrication

_____ 8. Failure to properly erect and brace a trussed roof could result in _____ .
   A. collapse of the structure
   B. loss of life or serious injury
   C. loss of time and material
   D. A, B, and C

_____ 9. The truss bracing system depends a great deal on _____ .
   A. the use of 1" × 4" temporary bracing
   B. scabs nailed to the end of the building
   C. how well the first truss is braced
   D. 8d duplex finish nails

_____ 10. As bracing is installed, it is important that _____ .
   A. exact spacing be maintained
   B. spacing be continually readjusted
   C. it is only applied to two planes of the truss assembly
   D. it has a maximum length of no more than 8'

Completion

Complete each sentence by inserting the correct answer on the line near the number.

_____ 1. The plane of the top cord is known as the _____ plane.

_____ 2. The plane of the bottom cord is known as the _____ plane.

_____ 3. It is recommended that continuous lateral bracing be placed within _____ inches of the ridge on the top cord plane.

_____ 4. Diagonal bracing between the rows of lateral bracing should be placed on the _____ of the top plane.

_____ 5. Continuous lateral bracing of the bottom cord must be applied to maintain the proper _____ .

_____ 6. Bottom cord bracing is nailed to the _____ of the bottom cord.

____ _____ 7. Bottom cord bracing should be installed at intervals no greater than _____ to _____ feet along the width of the building.

_____ 8. Rated panels of plywood and _____ are commonly used to sheath roofs.

_____ 9. In post and beam construction where roof supports are spaced further apart, _____ is used for roof sheathing.

_____ 10. Panel clips, tongue and groove edges, or other adequate blocking must be used when _____ exceed the indicated value of the plywood roof sheathing.

Discussion

Write your answer(s) on the lines below.

1. List the advantages of using trusses over conventional roof framing.

    _____

    _____

    _____

2. What is the major disadvantage to using roof trusses? How might this affect future remodeling or sale of the home?

    _____

    _____

    _____

CHAPTER 47 STAIRWAYS AND STAIRWELLS

Multiple Choice

Write the letter for the correct answer on the line next to the number of the sentence.

_____ 1. The tread run is _____ .
   A. the part of the tread that extends beyond the riser
   B. the horizontal distance between the faces of the risers
   C. the finish material that covers the vertical distance from one step to another
   D. a nonskid material applied to tread

_____ 2. The housed finished stringer is _____ .
   A. usually fabricated in a shop
   B. usually built on the job site
   C. always used on service stairs
   D. installed by the framing crew

_____ 3. Dadoes routed into the sides of the housed finished stringer _____ .
   A. reduce the stair's rise
   B. increase the headroom
   C. support and house the risers and treads
   D. A, B, and C

_____ 4. The preferred angle for ease of stair climbing is between _____ degrees.
   A. 20 and 25
   B. 25 and 30
   C. 30 and 35
   D. 35 and 40

_____ 5. To determine the individual rise, the _____ must be known.
   A. total run
   B. total rise
   C. riser thickness
   D. tread thickness

_____ 6. To determine riser height without mathematics, _____ used.
   A. a sliding T bevel and a level are
   B. the common rafter table on the framing square is
   C. a story pole and a set of dividers are
   D. a plumb bob and a line level are

_____ 7. The sum of one rise and one tread should equal _____ .
   A. between 17 and 18
   B. between 18 and 19
   C. between 19 and 20
   D. less than 17

_____ 8. Decreasing riser height _____ .
    A. decreases the run of the stairs
    B. increases the run of the stairs
    C. uses less space
    D. makes the stairs more difficult to climb

_____ 9. Increasing stair riser height typically _____ .
    A. decreases the run of the stairs
    B. makes the stairs more difficult to climb
    C. decreases the overall space occupied by the stairs
    D. A, B, and C

_____ 10. Most building codes call for a minimum of _____ of headroom for stairways.
    A. 6'-2"
    B. 6'-4"
    C. 6'-6"
    D. 6'-8"

Completion

Complete each sentence by inserting the correct answer on the line near the number.

_____ 1. The stairwell is framed at the same time as the _____ .

_____ 2. _____ stairs extend from one habitable level of the house to another.

_____ 3. _____ stairs extend from a habitable level to a nonhabitable level.

_____ 4. In residential construction, stairways should not be less than _____ inch(es) wide.

_____ 5. A _____ stairway is continuous from one floor to another without any turns or landings.

_____ 6. Stairs that have intermediate landings between floors are called _____ stairs.

_____ 7. An L-type platform stair changes direction _____ degrees.

_____ 8. A platform stairway that changes directions 180° is called a _____ -type stairway.

_____ 9. A _____ staircase gradually changes directions as it ascends from one floor to another.

_____ 10. A _____ stairway is constructed between walls.

_____ 11. _____ stairways have one or both sides open to a room.

_____ 12. The vertical distance between finished floors is the total _____ of the stairway.

_____ 13. The total horizontal distance that the stairway covers is known as the total _____ .

_____ 14. The vertical distance from one step to another is the _____ .

_____ 15. The opening in the floor that the stairway passes through is the _____ .

Math

Determine the riser height for straight stairways that have the following total rises.

1. 8'-7" _____

2. 8'-5½" _____

3. 8'-10¾" _____

CHAPTER 48 STAIR LAYOUT AND CONSTRUCTION

Multiple Choice

Write the letter for the correct answer on the line next to the number of the sentence.

_____ 1. When laying out stair carriages, make sure _____ .
   A. riser heights are greater than tread widths
   B. all riser heights are the same
   C. all tread widths are the same
   D. B and C

_____ 2. When scaling across a framing square to determine the rough length of a stair carriage, use the side of the square that is graduated in _____ of an inch.
   A. sixteenths
   B. eighths
   C. tenths
   D. twelfths

_____ 3. When stepping off the stair carriage with a framing square, _____ .
   A. use stair gauges
   B. lay out the rise with the square's tongue
   C. lay out the tread run with the square's blade
   D. A, B, and C

_____ 4. To be sure the bottom riser is the same height as all the other risers it may be necessary to _____ .
   A. add blocking under the stair carriage bottom
   B. cut a certain amount off the stair carriage bottom
   C. alter the thickness of the first tread
   D. alter the thickness of all treads but the first

_____ 5. The top riser is equalized by _____ .
   A. lowering and cutting the level line at the top of the stair carriage
   B. altering the top treads thickness
   C. fastening the stair carriage at the proper height in relation to tread and finish floor thickness
   D. adding blocking to the top of the stair carriage

_____ 6. Residential staircases of average width usually_____ .
   A. require three carriages
   B. only need two carriages
   C. are less than 36″ wide
   D. are more than 48″ wide

7. Built-up stair carriages are used to _____ .
   A. simplify drywall application
   B. conserve wood
   C. avoid dropping the stair carriage
   D. increase the stairs' strength

8. If drywall is applied after the stairs are framed, _____ .
   A. repair or remodeling work becomes more difficult than if it were applied before framing
   B. time is saved
   C. blocking is required between studs in back of the stair carriage
   D. no blocking is needed

9. U-type stairways usually have the landing _____ of the stairs.
   A. near the bottom
   B. in the middle
   C. near the top
   D. A and C

10. According to most codes, any flight of stairs that has a vertical distance of 12' or more must have _____ .
    A. double railings on each side
    B. a width of at least 4'
    C. at least one landing
    D. a tread run of at least 12"

Discussion

Write your answer(s) on the lines below.

1. What important safety rules must be considered when laying out stairs?

   _____

   _____

   _____

2. Although winding stairs are not recommended, what are some of the rules that must be followed if they are used?

   _____

   _____

   _____

CHAPTER 49 THERMAL AND ACOUSTICAL INSULATION

Multiple Choice

Write the letter for the correct answer on the line next to the number of the sentence.

_____ 1. Organic insulation materials are treated to make them resistant to _____ .
   A. fire
   B. insects
   C. vermin
   D. A, B, and C

_____ 2. _____ insulation would be a good choice for insulating the sidewalls of an older, uninsulated home.
   A. Loose-fill
   B. Rigid
   C. Flexible
   D. Reflective

_____ 3. Rigid insulation is usually made of _____ .
   A. vermiculite
   B. glass wool
   C. fiber or foamed plastic material
   D. rock wool

_____ 4. Reflective insulation should be installed _____ .
   A. tight against the siding
   B. facing an air space with a depth of ¾" or more
   C. in contact with the foundation wall when used in basements or crawl spaces
   D. only in homes without air conditioning

_____ 5. Foamed-in-place insulation _____ .
   A. expands on contact with the surface
   B. is made from organic fibers
   C. contains glass wool
   D. is commonly used for sheathing and decorative purposes

_____ 6. To reduce heat loss, all _____ that separate heated from unheated areas must be insulated.
   A. walls
   B. ceilings
   C. roofs and floors
   D. A, B, and C

_____ 7. When installing flexible insulation between floor joists over crawl spaces, _____ .

    A. the vapor barrier faces the heated area
    B. the vapor barrier faces the ground
    C. remove the vapor barrier
    D. at least a ¾″ air space must be maintained between the joists and the insulation

_____ 8. The resistance to the passage of sound through a building section is rated by its _____ .

    A. Sound Transmission Class
    B. Impact Noise Rating
    C. Sound Absorption Class
    D. Impact Transmission Class

Completion

Complete each sentence by inserting the correct answer on the line near the number.

_____ 1. _____ insulation prevents the loss of heat in cold seasons and resists the passage of heat into air-conditioned areas in the hot seasons.

_____ 2. _____ insulation reduces the passage of sound from one area to another.

_____ 3. Proper ventilation must be provided within the building to remove _____ that forms in the space between the cold surface and the thermal insulation.

_____ 4. If confined in small spaces in which it is still, _____ is an excellent insulator.

_____ 5. Aluminum foil is used as an insulating material that works by _____ heat.

_____ 6. The higher the R-value number of insulation, the more _____ the material is.

_____ 7. The use of _____ studs in exterior walls permits the installation of R-19 insulation.

_____ 8. _____ insulation is manufactured in blanket and batt form.

_____ 9. The _____ on both sides of blanket insulation facing are used for fastening it to studs or joists.

_____ 10. Batt insulation is available in thicknesses of up to _____ inches.

CHAPTER 50 CONDENSATION AND VENTILATION

Multiple Choice

Write the letter for the correct answer on the line next to the number of the sentence.

_____ 1. When the temperature of moisture-laden air drops below its dew point, _____ occurs.
   A. evaporation
   B. condensation
   C. vaporization
   D. dehydration

_____ 2. Condensation of water vapor in walls, attics, roofs, and floors _____ .
   A. increases the R-value of any insulation it comes in contact with
   B. prevents the wood from rotting
   C. leads to serious problems
   D. only occurs in warmer climates

_____ 3. To prevent the condensation of moisture in a building, _____ .
   A. reduce the moisture in the warm, inside air
   B. ventilate the attic
   C. install a barrier to the passage of water vapor
   D. A, B, and C

_____ 4. In a well-ventilated area, _____ .
   A. condensed moisture is removed by evaporation
   B. moisture is forced back into the insulation
   C. insulation is not necessary
   D. condensation is at its worst

_____ 5. Virtually all moisture migration into insulation layers can be eliminated by _____ .
   A. airtight construction techniques
   B. not using a vapor retarder on the ceiling
   C. ventilation
   D. A, B, and C

_____ 6. On roofs where the ceiling finish is attached to the rafters and insulation is installed, _____ .
   A. an air space is not needed
   B. a moisture barrier should be placed on the cold side of the insulation
   C. a well-vented air space of at least 1½" is necessary between the insulation and the roof sheathing
   D. no ventilation is needed

_____ 7. The most effective method of ventilating an attic is to install _____ .
  A. continuous soffit vents
  B. continuous ridge vents
  C. larger triangular gable end louvers
  D. A and B

_____ 8. A variation of a hip roof known as the Dutch hip is specifically designed to house _____ on both ends.
  A. globe type ventilators
  B. large triangular louvers
  C. continuous hip vents
  D. two rectangular louvers

_____ 9. The use of a ground cover in crawl spaces _____ .
  A. is not recommended
  B. contributes to the decay of framing members
  C. eliminates the need for ventilators
  D. allows for the use of a smaller number of ventilators

_____ 10. The minimum free-air area for attic ventilators is based on the _____ .
  A. total square footage of the home
  B. ceiling area of the rooms below
  C. attic floor area
  D. total roof surface

Completion

Complete each sentence by inserting the correct answer on the line near the number.

_____ 1. If a vapor barrier ground cover is used in a crawl space, the total net area of crawl space ventilators should be _____ of the ground area.

_____ 2. _____ on ventilators should have as coarse a mesh as conditions permit.

_____ 3. The use of _____ prevents moisture from entering areas where condensation can occur.

_____ 4. The most commonly used material for a vapor barrier is _____ .

_____ 5. _____ allow for ventilation of cavities created by hip-jack rafters.

_____ 6. _____ the seams of the exterior wall sheathing is an effective method of airtight construction.

_____ 7. The minimum free-air area of attic ventilators needed for a home with a ceiling area of 1,500 square feet is _____ square feet.

_____ 8. The minimum free-air area of ventilators needed for a crawl space that has a ground area of 3,200 square feet is _____ square feet if a vapor barrier ground cover is used.

Discussion

Write your answer(s) on the lines below.

1. List the necessary steps that must be done during the construction process to eliminate condensation problems in a home.

   _____

   _____

   _____

CHAPTER 51 ASPHALT SHINGLES

Multiple Choice

Write the letter for the correct answer on the line next to the number of the sentence.

_____ 1. When installing metal drip edge, _____ .
   A. tightly butt the end joints
   B. only use 1¼″ roofing nails
   C. the roofing nails must be the same material as the drip edge
   D. space the nails every 12″

_____ 2. Asphalt shingle underlayment should _____ .
   A. be an entirely moisture-proof membrane
   B. allow the passage of water vapor
   C. be applied in vertical rows
   D. usually be as heavy a weight of felt as is available

_____ 3. After the application of underlayment, it is recommended that _____ .
   A. metal drip edge be applied to the rakes
   B. metal drip edge be applied to the eaves
   C. the ridge vent be installed
   D. A, B, and C

_____ 4. Organic shingles have a base made of _____ .
   A. glass fibers
   B. heavy asphalt-saturated paper felt
   C. shredded thatching straw
   D. rubber

_____ 5. Mineral granules are used on the surface of asphalt shingles to _____ .
   A. provide weatherproofing qualities
   B. provide a good surface for asphalt cement to adhere to
   C. reduce its weight
   D. protect the shingle from the sun

_____ 6. _____ is generally determined by weight per square.
   A. Fire resistance
   B. Shingle quality
   C. Self-sealing ability
   D. Coverage

_____ 7. On long roofs, accurate vertical alignment is ensured by _____ .
   A. starting from either rake
   B. working right to left
   C. working left to right
   D. starting at the center and working both ways

_____ 8. It is recommended that no rake tab be less than _____ in width.
   A. 2″
   B. 3″
   C. 4″
   D. 5″

_____ 9. The purpose of the starter course is to _____ .
   A. back up and fill in the spaces between the tabs on the first row of shingles
   B. eliminate the need of installing a drip edge
   C. reduce frost build up underneath the shingles
   D. A, B, and C

_____ 10. When fastening asphalt shingles, it is important to _____ .
   A. use a minimum of three fasteners in each strip shingle
   B. follow the manufacturer's recommendations for application
   C. use a fastener long enough to penetrate the sheathing at least ⅜″
   D. not use power nailers

_____ 11. The most commonly used asphalt shingles have a maximum exposure of _____ inches.
   A. 3
   B. 5
   C. 7
   D. 9

_____ 12. When snapping a long chalk line, many times it is necessary to _____ .
   A. first wet the line
   B. snap the line from the side closest to the chalk box
   C. hold the line against the roof with your thumb at about center and strike of the line
   D. simultaneously strike both sides of the line at the same time

_____ 13. When installing the ridge caps _____ .
   A. coat the last two fasteners with asphalt cement
   B. start the shingles on the end away from the prevailing winds
   C. it may be necessary to warm them in cold weather
   D. A, B, and C

_____ 14. The maximum roof angle recommended for normal asphalt shingle application is _____ degrees.
   A. 45
   B. 50
   C. 55
   D. 60

Matching

Write the letter for the correct answer on the line near the number to which it corresponds.

_____ 1. square

_____ 2. electrolysis

_____ 3. end lap

_____ 4. deck

_____ 5. course

_____ 6. flashing

_____ 7. asphalt cements

_____ 8. top or head lap

_____ 9. exposure

A. horizontal rows of shingles or roofing

B. strips of thin sheet metal used to make watertight joints

C. trowel applied adhesives used to bond asphalt roofing products

D. the amount of roofing required to cover 100 square feet

E. a reaction that occurs between unlike metals when wet

F. horizontal distance the ends of roofing in the same course overlap

G. the amount of roofing in each course subjected to the weather

H. the wood roof surface to which roofing is applied

I. shingle height minus the exposure

CHAPTER **52** ROLL ROOFING

Completion

Complete each sentence by inserting the correct answer on the line near the number.

_____ 1. Roll roofing can be installed on roofs that slope as little as _____ inch of rise per foot of run.

_____ 2. A concealed nail type of rolled roofing called _____ has a top lap of 19 inches.

_____ 3. All kinds of rolled roofing come in rolls that are _____ inches wide.

_____ 4. When roofs have a pitch that is less than _____ inches rise per foot, it is recommended that rolled roofing be used.

_____ 5. On roof slopes that are less than 2 inches of rise per foot, the _____ type of roofing should not be used.

_____ 6. The same type and length of _____ as are used on asphalt shingles should be used on rolled roofing.

_____ 7. Rolled roofing's coat can crack if it is applied at temperatures below _____ degrees Fahrenheit.

_____ 8. Use only the lap or quick setting cement recommended by the _____ .

_____ 9. Strips of rolled roofing 9" wide should be applied along the eaves and rakes with about a _____ inch overhang.

_____ 10. All rolled roofing end laps should be _____ inches wide and cement should be applied the full width of the lap.

Discussion

Write your answer(s) on the lines below.

1. Due to the fact that rolled roofing is made by several different manufacturers, the builder must be aware of what things when applying it?

_____

_____

_____

CHAPTER 53 WOOD SHINGLES AND SHAKES

Multiple Choice

Write the letter for the correct answer on the line next to the number of the sentence.

_____ 1. Most shingles and shakes are produced from _____ .
   A. white pine
   B. poplar
   C. western red cedar
   D. redwood

_____ 2. Wood shingles have a _____ surface.
   A. somewhat rough
   B. relatively smooth sawn
   C. highly textured, natural grain, split
   D. very smooth

_____ 3. There are _____ standard grades of wood shingles.
   A. 2
   B. 3
   C. 4
   D. 5

_____ 4. The area covered by one square of shingles or shakes depends on the _____ .
   A. amount of shingle or shake exposed to the weather
   B. weight of the square
   C. choice of underlayment
   D. choice of deck material

_____ 5. Shingles and shakes may be applied _____ .
   A. over spaced or solid roof sheathing
   B. on roofs with slopes under 3" of rise per foot
   C. only if extra heavy underlayment is used
   D. A, B, and C

_____ 6. The sliding gauge on a shingling hatchet is used _____ .
   A. to split shakes
   B. for checking the shingle exposure
   C. to extract fasteners
   D. to trim shingles and shakes

_____ 7. The use of a power nailer on wood shingles and shakes _____ .
   A. is a tremendous time saver
   B. is not permitted
   C. could result in more time lost than gained
   D. lengthens the life expectancy of the roof

_____ 8. _____ nails are corrosion-resistant.
   A. Stainless steel
   B. Hot-dipped galvanized
   C. Aluminum
   D. A, B, and C

_____ 9. If staples are used to fasten wood shingles or shakes, they should be _____ .
   A. at least 20 gauge with a ⅜″ minimum crown
   B. long enough to penetrate the sheathing by at least ¼″
   C. driven with the crown across the grain
   D. long enough to penetrate the sheathing by at least ⅜″

_____ 10. If a gutter is used, overhang the wood shingle starter course _____ .
   A. ½″ past the fascia
   B. plumb with the center of the gutter
   C. 1″ past the inside edge of the gutter
   D. 1½″ past the fascia

Completion

Complete each sentence by inserting the correct answer on the line near the number.

_____ 1. Place each fastener about _____ inch in from the edge of the wood shingle and not more than 1″ above the exposure line.

_____ 2. Do not allow the head of the fastener to _____ the surface of the shingle.

_____ 3. In regions of heavy snowfall, it is recommended that the starter course be _____ .

_____ 4. Joints in adjacent courses of wood shingles should be staggered at least _____ inches.

_____ 5. No joint in any _____ adjacent courses should be in alignment.

_____ 6. On intersecting roofs, do not break joints in the _____ .

_____ 7. Hip and ridge caps are usually _____ to_____ inches wide.

_____ 8. When laying wood shakes, a/an _____ consisting of strips of 18″ wide, #30 roofing felt is used.

_____ 9. Straight-split shakes should be laid with their _____ end toward the ridge.

_____ 10. It is important to regularly check the _____ of wood shakes with the hatchet handle since there is a tendency for the course to angle toward the ground.

_____ 11. Divide the total square feet of the roof area by _____ to determine the total number of squares needed for the job.

_____ 12. At standard exposure, estimate _____ pounds of nails per square of shingles.

CHAPTER **54** FLASHING

Multiple Choice

Write the letter for the correct answer on the line next to the number of the sentence.

_____ 1. The woven valley method of flashing _____ .
    A. is an open valley method
    B. is a closed valley method
    C. should have the course end joints occurring on the valley center line
    D. requires that sheet metal flashing be used under it

_____ 2. The closed cut method of valley flashing _____ .
    A. requires the use of fasteners at the valley's center
    B. does not require the use of 50 pound per square rolled roofing
    C. is an open valley method
    D. requires the use of asphalt cement

_____ 3. When using step flashing in a valley, each piece of flashing should be at least _____wide, if the roof has less than a 6″ rise.
    A. 6″
    B. 12″
    C. 18″
    D. 24″

_____ 4. The height of each piece of step valley flashing should be at least 3″ more than the shingle _____ .
    A. head lap
    B. top lap
    C. exposure
    D. salvage

_____ 5. When the valley is completely flashed with the step flashing method, _____ .
    A. a 6″ wide strip of metal flashing the length of the valley is visible
    B. rolled roofing is applied over the top of it
    C. no metal flashing surface is exposed
    D. a coating of asphalt cement is applied on top of the shingles

_____ 6. The usual method of making the joint between a vertical wall and a roof watertight is the use of _____ .
    A. a saddle
    B. an apron
    C. a heavy coating of asphalt cement
    D. step flashing

_____ 7. On steep roofs between the upper side of the chimney and the roof deck, a saddle or _____ is built.
    A. heel
    B. frog
    C. cricket
    D. gusset

_____ 8. Chimney flashings are usually installed by _____ .
    A. carpenters
    B. brick masons
    C. roofers
    D. laborers

_____ 9. The upper ends of chimney flashing is _____ .
    A. fastened to the chimney with concrete nails driven through the flashing and into the mortar joints
    B. imbedded in asphalt cement against the chimney
    C. bent around and mortared in between the courses of brick
    D. bent over and bedded to the shingles with asphalt cement

_____ 10. When installing flashing over a stack vent, _____ .
    A. shingle over top of the lower end of the stack vent flashing
    B. the flashing is attached with one fastener in each upper corner
    C. be sure the shingle fasteners penetrate the flashing
    D. A, B, and C

Completion

Complete each sentence by inserting the correct answer on the line near the number.

_____ 1. _____ and zinc are expensive but high quality flashing material.

_____ 2. When reroofing, it is a good practice to replace all the _____ .

_____ 3. It is necessary to install an eaves flashing whenever there is a possibility of _____ forming.

_____ 4. Roof _____ are especially vulnerable to leaking due to the great volume of water that flows down through them.

_____ 5. When using rolled roofing as valley flashing, the first layer should be laid with its mineral surface side _____ .

_____ 6. When the end courses are properly trimmed on a valley that is 16' long, its width at the ridge will be 6" and at the eaves _____ inches.

_____ 7. The metal flashing in an open valley between a low-pitched roof and a much steeper one, should have a _____-inch high crimped standing seam in its center.

_____ 8. _____ valleys are those where the shingles meet in the center of the valley covering the valley flashing completely.

_____ 9. The rolled roofing required in closed valleys must be _____ pound per square or more.

_____ 10. On woven valleys, be sure that no _____ is located within 6" of the centerline.

Discussion

Write your answer(s) on the lines below.

1. Perhaps the most important thing to keep in mind when applying any roofing material is that water always runs downhill. Write a short paragraph explaining the importance of this statement to the application of roofing materials.

_____

_____

_____

CHAPTER 55 WINDOW TERMS AND TYPES

Multiple Choice

Write the letter for the correct answer on the line next to the number of the sentence.

_____ 1. Wooden windows are primed _____ with their first coat of paint.
   A. after installation
   B. at the factory
   C. by the retailer
   D. when the siding is applied

_____ 2. Vinyl-clad wood windows _____ .
   A. come in a large variety of colors
   B. are designed to eliminate painting
   C. must be primed before installation
   D. are only available in fixed windows

_____ 3. Screens are attached to the outside of the window frame on _____ windows.
   A. awning
   B. sliding
   C. double-hung
   D. jalousie

_____ 4. _____ fixed windows are widely used in combination with other window types.
   A. elliptical
   B. half rounds
   C. quarter rounds
   D. A, B, and C

_____ 5. The single-hung window is similar to the double-hung window except _____ .
   A. the lower sash swings outward
   B. the parting bead is eliminated
   C. the upper sash is fixed
   D. it only has one sash

_____ 6. When the sashes are closed on double-hung windows, specially shaped _____ come together to form a weather-tight joint.
   A. parting beads
   B. meeting rails
   C. blind stops
   D. sash locks

_____ 7. The _____ window consists of a sash hinged at the side and swings outward by means of a crank or lever.
   A. casement
   B. awning
   C. hopper
   D. jalousie

167

_____ 8. An advantage of the casement type window is that _____ .
    A. the entire sash can be opened for maximum ventilation
    B. its system of springs and balances makes it easy to open
    C. it comes with removable sashes for easy cleaning
    D. the screens are installed on the outside of the frame

_____ 9. An awning window consists of a frame in which a sash _____ .
    A. hinged at the bottom swings inward
    B. slides horizontally left or right in a set of tracks
    C. hinged at the side swings inward
    D. hinged at the top swings outward

_____ 10. A major disadvantage to jalousie windows is that _____ .
    A. ventilation is poor with this window type
    B. they are not very energy efficient
    C. they are not recommended in warmer climates
    D. screens cannot be used with them

Completion

Complete each sentence by inserting the correct answer on the line near the number.

_____ 1. Wood windows, doors, and cabinets fabricated in woodworking plants are referred to as _____ .

_____ 2. The _____ is the frame that holds the glass in the window.

_____ 3. _____ are the vertical edge members of the sash.

_____ 4. Small strips of wood that divide the glass into smaller lights are called _____ .

_____ 5. Many windows come with false muntin called _____ .

_____ 6. The installation of glass in a window sash is called _____ .

_____ 7. Skylights and roof windows are generally required to be glazed with _____ .

_____ 8. To raise the R-value of insulating glass, the space between the glass is filled with _____ gas.

_____ 9. An invisible, thin _____ coating is bonded to the air space side of the inner glass of solar control insulating glass.

_____ 10. The bottom horizontal member of the window frame is called a _____ .

_____ 11. The _____ are the vertical sides of the window frame.

_____ 12. A _____ is formed where the two side jambs on side by side windows are joined together.

Identification: Windows

Identify each term, and write the letter of the correct answer on the line next to each number.

_____ 1. top rail

_____ 2. bottom rail

_____ 3. stile

_____ 4. muntin

_____ 5. light

_____ 6. double-hung window

_____ 7. casement window

_____ 8. awning window

_____ 9. sliding windows

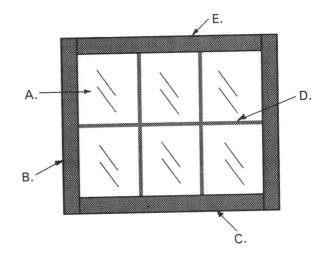

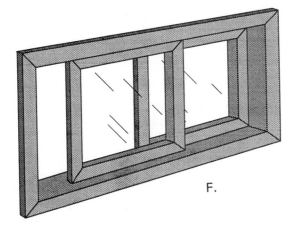

F.

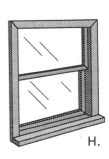

H.

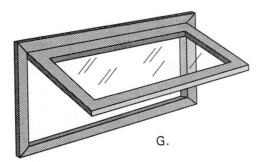

G.

I.

CHAPTER 56 WINDOW INSTALLATION AND GLAZING

Multiple Choice

Write the letter for the correct answer on the line next to the number of the sentence.

_____ 1. Those responsible for planning the location or selection of windows need to be aware of building code requirements for minimum _____ .
A. areas of natural light
B. ventilation by windows
C. window size in regard to emergency egress
D. A, B, and C

_____ 2. _____ windows should not be located above porches or decks unless they are high enough to allow people to travel under them.
A. Double- and single-hung
B. Sliding and hopper
C. Awning and casement
D. Fixed

_____ 3. The builder should refer to the window _____ to determine the window style, size, manufacturer's name, and unit number.
A. schedule
B. agenda
C. program
D. plan

_____ 4. In order for the builder to better understand the construction of a particular window unit, he should refer to the _____ .
A. local building codes
B. Sweets register
C. manufacturer's catalog
D. window syllabus

_____ 5. The major purpose of applying building paper or a housewrap prior to siding application is to make the building more _____ proof.
A. air
B. weather
C. moisture
D. vapor

_____ 6. _____ will survive the longest period of exposure to the weather.
A. Building paper
B. House wrap
C. Polyethylene film
D. Asphalt felt

_____ 7. If building paper is to be used, it must be applied _____ .
    A. prior to the installation of the doors and windows
    B. immediately after framing is completed
    C. after the doors and windows are installed
    D. after the insulation is installed

_____ 8. When using housewrap, overlap all joints by at least _____ inch(es).
    A. 1
    B. 3
    C. 6
    D. 9

_____ 9. Most windows are installed so that _____ .
    A. their tops are all at different levels
    B. their header casings lie at the same elevation
    C. the same size window is on each story
    D. the double-hung windows are on the first floor and the single-hung windows are on the second floor

_____ 10. When installing windows, _____ .
    A. remove any diagonal braces applied at the factory
    B. unlock and open the sash
    C. leave all protection blocks on the the window unit
    D. be sure to shim, level, and plumb the unit

Completion

Complete each sentence by inserting the correct answer on the line near the number.

_____ 1. When it is necessary to shim the bottom of a window to level it, the shim is placed between the rough sill and the bottom end of the window's side _____ .

_____ 2. To avoid splitting the casing, all nails should be at least _____ inches back from casing's end.

_____ 3. Nails driven through the window casing should be _____ casing or common nails.

_____ 4. On vinyl-clad windows, large head _____ nails are driven through the nailing phalange instead of the casing.

_____ 5. Windows are installed in masonry openings against wood _____ .

_____ 6. Tradespeople who perform the work of cutting and installing lights of glass in sashes or doors are known as _____ .

_____ 7. _____ are small triangular or diamond-shaped pieces of thin metal used to hold glass in place.

_____ 8. A light of glass is installed with its crown side _____ in a thin bed of compound against the rabbet of the opening.

_____ 9. Going over the scored line a second time with the glass cutter will _____ the glass cutter.

_____ 10. Prior to scoring a line on glass, it is recommended to brush some _____ along the line of cut.

CHAPTER 57 DOOR FRAME CONSTRUCTION AND INSTALLATION

Completion

Complete each sentence by inserting the correct answer on the line near the number.

_____ 1. Exterior doors, like windows, are manufactured in _____ plants in a wide variety of styles and sizes.

_____ 2. Many entrance doors come _____ in frames, with complete exterior casings applied, ready for installation.

_____ 3. The bottom member of an exterior door is the _____ .

_____ 4. Vertical side members of an exterior door are known as _____ .

_____ 5. In residential construction, exterior doors usually swing _____ .

_____ 6. In order to ensure an exact fit between the sill and the door, sometimes the _____ at the bottom of the door is adjustable.

_____ 7. For walls of odd thicknesses, _____ may be ripped to any desired width.

_____ 8. To construct an accurately sized exterior door frame, it is advisable to have the door available for _____ .

_____ 9. Jamb _____ is equal to the overall wall thickness from the outside of the wall sheathing to the inside surface of the interior wall covering.

_____ 10. If jamb stock must be ripped, rip the edge opposite the _____ .

_____ 11. Side jambs are usually _____ to receive the ends of the header jamb and the sill.

_____ 12. On each side of the door, a _____-inch joint should be allowed between the door and the frame.

_____ 13. Drive a _____ between the back sides of both the sill and header jamb and the shoulders of the dado before nailing to ensure a tight fit on the face side.

_____ 14. The _____ is the amount of setback of the casing from the inside face of the door jamb.

_____ 15. When square-edged casings are used, a _____ makes a weather-tight joint between them.

_____ 16. When an exterior molded casing is subjected to severe weather, a _____ miter joint is used.

_____ 17. When setting a door frame, cut off the _____ which project(s) beyond the sill and header jamb.

_____ 18. If it is necessary to level the sill when setting the door frame, the shims are placed under the _____ .

_____ 19. A _____ is a twist in the door frame caused when the side jambs do not line up vertically with each other.

Identification: Exterior Door Components

Identify each term, and write the letter of the correct answer on the line next to each number.

_____ 1. threshold

_____ 2. head casing

_____ 3. side casing

_____ 4. head jamb

_____ 5. sill

_____ 6. band mold

_____ 7. side jamb

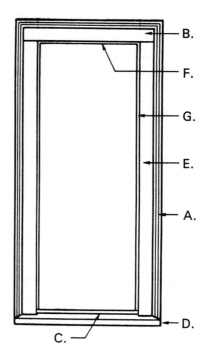

Discussion

Write your answer(s) on the lines below.

1. In buildings used by the general public that have an occupancy load exceeding fifty, building codes require exterior doors used as exits to swing outward. Why is this so?

_____

_____

_____

CHAPTER 58 DOOR FITTING AND HANGING

Multiple Choice

Write the letter for the correct answer on the line next to the number of the sentence.

_____ 1. _____ doors are highly crafted designer doors with a variety of cut-glass designs.
A. French
B. Dutch
C. High-style
D. Sash

_____ 2. _____ doors consist of top and bottom units, hinged independently of each other.
A. Dutch
B. Flush
C. French
D. Ventilating

_____ 3. A panel door consists of a frame that surrounds panels of _____ .
A. solid wood
B. glass
C. louvers
D. A, B, and C

_____ 4. The outside vertical members of a panel door are called _____ .
A. mullions
B. rails
C. stiles
D. jambs

_____ 5. The widest of all rails in a panel door is the _____ rail.
A. bottom
B. top
C. lock
D. intermediate

_____ 6. Practically all exterior entrance doors are manufactured with a thickness of _____ inches.
A. ¾
B. 1
C. 1½
D. 1¾

_____ 7. Prehung exterior doors come _____ .
A. already fixed and hinged in the door frame
B. with the threshold installed
C. with the outside casing installed
D. A, B, and C

_____ 8. When installing a prehung door unit, _____ .
   A. remove the factory installed spacers between the door and the jamb before leveling and shimming
   B. avoid nailing the side jambs through the shims
   C. make sure the outside edge of the jamb is flush with the finished wall surface
   D. it is good practice to hammer the nails completely flush with the finish

_____ 9. The first step in fitting a door is to _____ .
   A. determine the side that will close against the stops on the door frame
   B. install the lockset
   C. apply the hinges
   D. attach ¼" spacers to the door's stiles

_____ 10. Exterior doors containing lights of glass must be hung with the _____ .
   A. removable glass bead facing the exterior
   B. glass bead first removed
   C. removable glass bead facing the interior
   D. lights of glass removed

Completion

Complete each sentence by inserting the correct answer on the line near the number.

_____ 1. When a sash door is manufactured with _____ glazing, the possibility of any water seeping through the joints is virtually eliminated.

_____ 2. The _____ of the door is designated as being either left-hand or right-hand.

_____ 3. A left-handed door has its hinges on the left side if you are standing on the side that swings _____ from you.

_____ 4. The process of fitting a door into a frame is called _____ .

_____ 5. The lock edge of a door must be planned on a _____ .

_____ 6. When fitting doors, extreme care must be taken not to get them _____ .

_____ 7. To _____ sharp corners means to round them over slightly.

_____ 8. Use _____ 4" × 4" hinges on 1¾" doors 7'-0" or less in height.

_____ 9. The recess in a door for the hinge is called the_____ , or sometimes a hinge mortise.

_____ 10. When laying out hinges, use a _____ instead of a pencil to mark the line.

_____ 11. When many doors need to be hung, a butt hinge template and a portable electric _____ are used, cut hinge gains.

_____ 12. A(n) _____ is a molding that is rabbeted on both edges and designed to cover the joint between double doors.

CHAPTER **59** DOOR LOCK INSTALLATION

Completion

Complete each sentence by inserting the correct answer on the line near the number.

_____   1. Key-in-knob is another name for _____ locksets.

_____   2. A distinguishing difference between the two major categories of locksets are their basic _____ .

_____   3. A/An _____ lock combines deadbolt locking action with a standard key-in-knob set.

_____   4. _____ locks are not usually used in residential construction because of their high cost, and the increased amount of time installation takes.

_____   5. _____ are decorative plates of various shapes that are installed between the lock handle or knob.

_____   6. Measuring up from the floor, the recommended distance to the centerline of a lock is usually _____ inches.

_____   7. The _____ of the lock is the distance from the edge of the door to the center of the hole through the side of the door.

_____   8. When boring the holes for a lockset, the hole through the _____ of the door should be bored first.

_____   9. The striker plate is installed on the door _____ .

_____   10. After the door is fitted, hung, and locked, remove all _____ and prime the door and all exposed parts of the door frame.

Discussion

Write your answer(s) on the lines below.

1. When laying out hinges, face plates, and striker plates, it is recommended that a sharp knife be used instead of a pencil. Why is this so?

_____

_____

_____

CHAPTER 60 WOOD SIDING TYPES AND SIZES

Multiple Choice

Write the letter for the correct answer on the line next to the number of the sentence.

_____ 1. Most redwood siding is produced by mills that belong to _____ .
   A. WWPA
   B. CRA
   C. APA
   D. AHWA

_____ 2. In sidings classified as _____ , the annual growth rings must form an angle of 45° or more with the surface.
   A. flat grain
   B. vertical grain
   C. mixed grain
   D. cross grain

_____ 3. Vertical grain siding is the highest quality because it _____ .
   A. warps less
   B. takes and holds finishes better
   C. has less defects and is easier to work
   D. A, B, and C

_____ 4. _____ surfaces generally hold finishes longer than other types of surfaces.
   A. Smooth
   B. Flat-grained
   C. Saw-textured
   D. Double-planed

_____ 5. Knotty grade siding is divided into #1, #2, and #3 common depending on _____ .
   A. the type and number of knots
   B. its approved method of application
   C. the species of tree it comes from
   D. the thickness it is cut to

_____ 6. The best grades of redwood siding are grouped in a category called _____ .
   A. structural
   B. edifical
   C. clear
   D. architectural

_____ 7. Bevel siding is more commonly known as _____ .
   A. drop
   B. tongue and groove
   C. clapboard
   D. channel rustic

_____ 8. Most panel and lap siding is manufactured from _____ .
   A. plywood and hardboard
   B. cedar and redwood
   C. hemlock and poplar
   D. A, B, and C

_____ 9. Most panel siding is shaped with _____ edges for weathertight joints.
   A. back beveled
   B. chamfered
   C. shiplapped
   D. mitered

_____ 10. Lap siding comes in thicknesses from 7/16 to 9/16 of an inch, widths of 6, 8, and 12 inches and lengths of _____ feet.
   A. 4
   B. 8
   C. 12
   D. 16

Math

Without subtracting for window and door openings, estimate how many square feet of area is to be covered with siding on the house below.

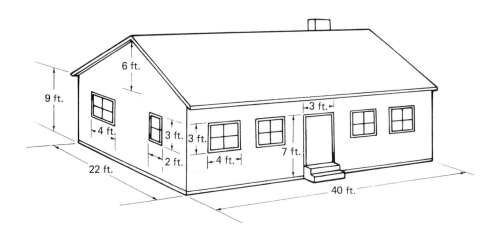

CHAPTER **61** APPLYING HORIZONTAL AND VERTICAL WOOD SIDING

Multiple Choice

Write the letter for the correct answer on the line next to the number of the sentence.

_____ 1. Corner boards are not usually used when wood siding is applied _____ .
   A. vertically
   B. horizontally
   C. diagonally
   D. A, B, and C

_____ 2. When applying tongue and groove siding vertically, fasten by _____ .
   A. face nailing into the groove edge of each piece
   B. toenailing into the groove edge of each piece
   C. toenailing into the tongue edge of each piece
   D. face nailing through the groove edge and into the tongue edge of the next piece

_____ 3. If necessary to make horizontal joints between lengths of vertical siding, _____ .
   A. a butt joint alone is acceptable
   B. install building paper beneath the joint
   C. use mitered or rabbeted end joints
   D. leave a $\frac{1}{16}''$ gap to receive caulking

_____ 4. When applying short lengths of vertical siding under a window, _____ .
   A. leave an ample margin for expansion of the window
   B. apply a bead of exterior glue between the top of the siding and the window's bottom
   C. rabbet the top of the siding to fit into the weather groove on the window's bottom
   D. butt the pieces against the window's bottom

_____ 5. The last piece of vertical siding should be _____ .
   A. much narrower than the rest
   B. wider than the rest
   C. fastened with screws instead of nails
   D. as close as possible in width to the pieces previously installed

_____ 6. When installing vertical panel siding that is thicker than $\frac{1}{2}''$, use _____ siding nails.
   A. 4d
   B. 6d
   C. 8d
   D. 10d

_____ 7. When installing horizontal or vertical panel siding, it is important that all horizontal joints be _____ .
   A. offset and lapped
   B. rabbeted
   C. flashed if a butt joint
   D. A, B, and C

_____ 8. Many times metal or plastic corners are used on siding made up of composition material because _____ .
   A. composition material does not miter well
   B. corner boards are not permitted
   C. composition material weathers poorly
   D. A, B, and C

Completion

Complete each sentence by inserting the correct answer on the line near the number.

_____ 1. A _____ is finish work that may be installed around the perimeter of the building slightly below the top of the foundation.

_____ 2. If the siding terminates against the soffit and no frieze is used, the joint between them is covered by a _____ molding.

_____ 3. If neither corner boards nor metal corners are used, then horizontal siding may be _____ around exterior corners.

_____ 4. On interior corners, the siding courses may butt against a square corner _____ .

_____ 5. One of the two pieces making up an outside corner board should be narrower than the other by the thickness of the _____ .

_____ 6. Before installing corner boards, _____ both sides of the corner with #15 felt applied vertically on each side.

_____ 7. A major advantage of bevel siding over other types is the ability to vary the siding's _____ .

_____ 8. The furring strip, which is applied before the first course of siding, must be the same thickness and width as the siding _____ .

_____ 9. A _____ is often used for accurate layout of siding where it butts against corner boards, casings, and similar trim.

_____ 10. For weather-tightness when fitting siding under a window, it is important that siding fits snugly in the _____ on the underside of the window sill.

_____ 11. Bevel and Dolly Varden siding are only to be applied in the _____ position.

_____ 12. When installing vertical tongue and groove siding directly to the frame, _____ must be provided between the studs.

CHAPTER 62 WOOD SHINGLE AND SHAKE SIDING

Completion

Complete each sentence by inserting the correct answer on the line near the number.

_____ 1. Rebutted and rejointed machine-grooved sidewall shakes have _____ faces.

_____ 2. Fancy butt shingles were widely used in the 19th century on _____ style buildings.

_____ 3. Red cedar shingles are available in several styles and exposures on factory applied 4- and 8- foot _____ .

_____ 4. When applying shingles to _____ , greater exposures are permitted than on roofs.

_____ 5. When more than one layer of shingles is needed, less expensive _____ shingles are used for the underlayers.

_____ 6. Untreated shingles should be spaced ⅛" to ¼" apart to allow for _____ and to prevent buckling.

_____ 7. Use a _____ when it is necessary to trim and fit the edges of wooden shingles.

_____ 8. If rebutted and rejointed shingles are used, no _____ should be necessary.

_____ 9. Shingles should be fastened with two nails or staples about _____ in from the edge.

_____ 10. Fasteners used on shingles should be hot-dipped galvanized, stainless steel, or aluminum and driven about 1" above the butt line of the next _____ .

_____ 11. Shingles in panelized form are applied in the same manner as horizontal _____ .

_____ 12. On outside corners, shingles may be applied by alternately _____ each course in the same manner as applying a wood shingle ridge.

_____ 13. When double coursing wood shingles, the first course is _____.

_____ 14. The number of squares of shingles needed to cover a certain area depends on how much of them are _____ to the weather.

_____ 15. One square of shingles will cover 100 square feet when 16" shingles are exposed _____ inches.

Identification: Fancy Butt Shingles

Identify each term, and write the letter of the correct answer on the line next to each number.

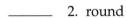 1. arrow

_____ 2. round

_____ 3. diagonal

_____ 4. octagonal

_____ 5. square

_____ 6. diamond

_____ 7. hexagonal

_____ 8. fish scale

_____ 9. half cove

A.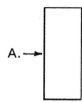

B.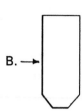

C.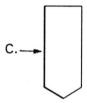

D.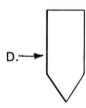

E.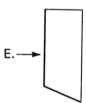

F.

G.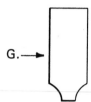

H.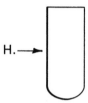

I.

CHAPTER **63** ALUMINUM AND VINYL SIDING

Multiple Choice

Write the letter for the correct answer on the line next to the number of the sentence.

_____ 1. Aluminum and vinyl siding systems are _____ .
A. both finished with baked-on enamel
B. similar to each other except for the material
C. expansion resistant
D. only available for horizontal applications

_____ 2. Aluminum and vinyl siding panels for horizontal applications are _____ .
A. made in 8″ and 12″ widths
B. also used for soffits
C. made in 6″ and 9″ widths
D. made in configurations to resemble 4, 5, or 6 courses of Dolly Varden siding

_____ 3. Panels designed for vertical application come in _____ widths and are shaped to resemble boards.
A. 6″
B. 8″
C. 10″
D. 12″

_____ 4. With changes in temperature, siding may contract and expand as much as _____ in a 12′-6″ section.
A. ⅛″
B. ¼″
C. ⅜″
D. ½″

_____ 5. Fasteners should be driven _____ the siding.
A. very tightly against
B. not too tightly into
C. every 24″ along
D. to the left of center in the slots on

_____ 6. Starter strips must be applied _____ .
A. tightly against corner posts
B. at vertical intervals of every four feet
C. as straight as possible
D. only on siding that is installed vertically

_____ 7. Install _____ across the tops and along the sides of window and door casings.
  A. starter strips
  B. corner posts
  C. undersill
  D. J-channel

_____ 8. When marking the cutout of a siding panel under a window, allow for _____ clearance under and on either side of the window.
  A. $\frac{1}{16}$"
  B. $\frac{1}{8}$"
  C. $\frac{1}{4}$"
  D. $\frac{3}{8}$"

_____ 9. _____ applied on the wall up against the soffit prior to the installation of the last course of siding panel.
  A. Starter strips are
  B. Corner posts are
  C. Undersill trim is
  D. J-channel is

_____ 10. The layout for vertical siding should be planned so that _____ .
  A. the same panel width is exposed at both ends of the wall
  B. any panels that need to have their edges cut to size are placed in the rear of the building
  C. any width adjustment made in the panels come in the center of the wall
  D. no panels are to have their edges trimmed

Identification: Vinyl Siding Systems

Identify each term, and write the letter of the correct answer on the line next to each number.

_____ 1. horizontal siding starter strip

_____ 2. vertical siding or soffit

_____ 3. fascia

_____ 4. undersill trim

_____ 5. outside corner post

_____ 6. J-channel

_____ 7. inside corner post

_____ 8. perforated soffit

_____ 9. undersill finish trim

_____ 10. "F" trim

_____ 11. horizontal siding

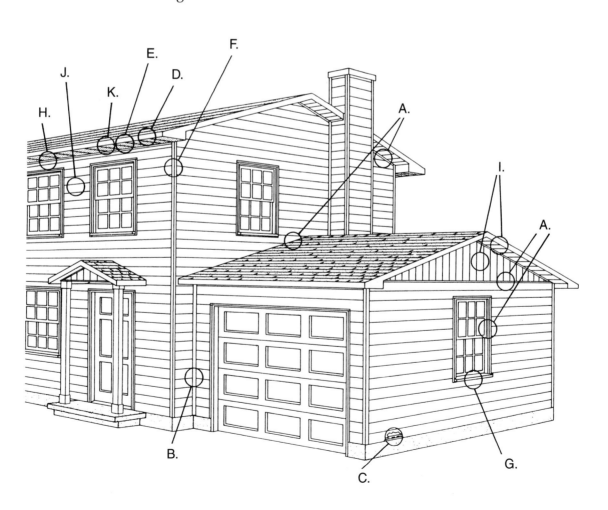

CHAPTER 64 CORNICE TERMS AND DESIGN

Completion

Complete each sentence by inserting the correct answer on the line near the number.

_____ 1. Lookouts are framing members used to provide a nailing surface for the _____ of a wide cornice.

_____ 2. The soffit is an ideal location for the placement of _____ .

_____ 3. The subfascia is usually of _____ inch nominal thickness.

_____ 4. The portion of the fascia that extends below the soffit is called the _____ .

_____ 5. If the frieze is not used, the _____ is used to cover the joint between the siding and the soffit.

_____ 6. The most commonly used cornice design is the _____ cornice.

_____ 7. The cornice design that lacks a soffit is the _____ cornice.

_____ 8. The least attractive cornice design is the _____ cornice.

_____ 9. A rake cornice would be found on a home with a _____ or gambrel roof.

_____ 10. A _____ is constructed to change the direction of a level box cornice to the angle of the roof.

Identification: Cornice Components

Identify each term, and write the letter of the correct answer on the line next to each number.

_____ 1. rafter

_____ 2. lookouts

_____ 3. soffit

_____ 4. fascia

_____ 5. frieze

_____ 6. cornice molding

_____ 7. plate

_____ 8. roof sheathing

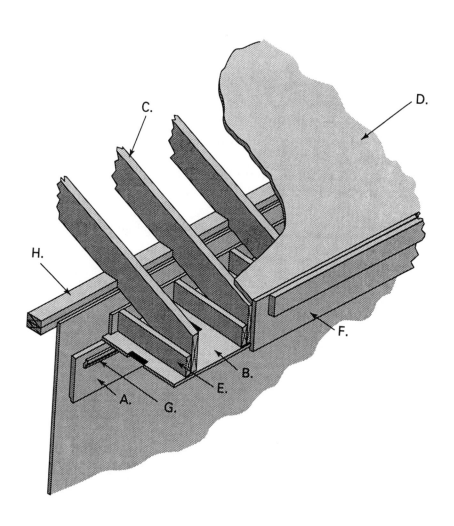

192

CHAPTER 65   GUTTERS AND DOWNSPOUTS

Completion

Complete each sentence by inserting the correct answer on the line near the number.

_____   1. The _____ carries water from the gutter downward and away from the foundation.

_____   2. No type of finish whatsoever is required on _____ gutters.

_____   3. For every _____ square feet of roof area, one square inch of gutter cross-section is needed.

_____   4. _____ gutters can be formed to practically any length when forming machines are brought to the job site.

_____   5. In order for water to drain toward the downspout, gutters should be installed with a pitch of about _____ inch(es) to 10 feet.

_____   6. On long buildings, the gutter is usually _____ in the center.

_____   7. To prevent _____ from occurring on metal gutters, be sure that the screws you are using are the same metal as the brackets.

_____   8. Aluminum brackets may be spaced up to _____ inches on center.

_____   9. _____ connectors are used to join the sections of metal or vinyl gutters.

_____   10. Round corrugated galvanized iron downspouts are fastened to the wall by galvanized iron rings called _____ .

_____   11. If downspouts are connected to the foundation, drain strainer caps must be placed over the gutter _____ .

Identification: Gutter and Downspout Parts

Identify each term, and write the letter of the correct answer on the line next to each number.

_____ 1. end cap

_____ 2. slip connector

_____ 3. strap hanger

_____ 4. gutter

_____ 5. downspout

_____ 6. fascia bracket

_____ 7. spike and ferrule

_____ 8. conductor pipe band

_____ 9. end piece

_____ 10. strainer cap

_____ 11. elbow-style A

_____ 12. elbow-style B

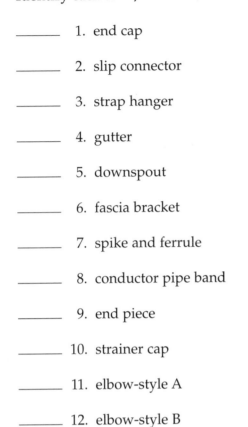

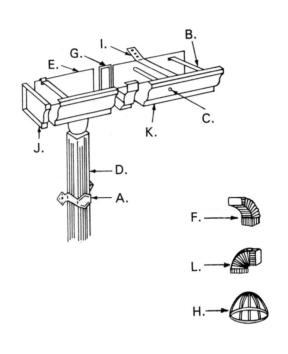

CHAPTER 66 PORCH AND DECK CONSTRUCTION

Multiple Choice

Write the letter for the correct answer on the line next to the number of the sentence.

_____ 1. Girders are installed on the beams using _____ .
   A. post and beam metal connectors
   B. fiber tube forms
   C. post anchors
   D. joist hangers

_____ 2. When joists are hung between the girders, _____ .
   A. joist hangers are not necessary
   B. the overall length of the deck must be decreased
   C. the overall depth of the deck is decreased
   D. they must be installed with the crown down

_____ 3. When decking is run _____ to the joists, the spacing of the joists may be 24″ on center.
   A. at right angles
   B. parallel
   C. diagonal
   D. A, B, and C

_____ 4. If the deck is less than _____ above the ground, the supporting posts will not need to be permanently braced.
   A. 4′
   B. 6′
   C. 8′
   D. 10′

_____ 5. When applying the deck boards, _____ .
   A. lay them with the bark side down
   B. it is advisable to start at the inside edge
   C. maintain about ½″ between them
   D. make tight fitting end joints and stagger them between adjacent rows

_____ 6. A _____ board may be fastened around the perimeter of the deck with its top edge flush with the top of the deck.
   A. ledger
   B. fascia
   C. batter
   D. skirt

_____ 7. If the deck is more than 30″ above the ground, most codes require _____ high railing around the exposed sides.
   A. 24″
   B. 28″
   C. 32″
   D. 36″

_____ 8. _____ are another name for railing posts.
   A. Stanchions
   B. Balusters
   C. Preachers
   D. Rails

_____ 9. The space between the top and bottom rail may be filled with _____ .
   A. intermediate rails
   B. balusters
   C. lattice work
   D. A, B, or C

_____ 10. If benches are built into the deck, their seat height should be _____ above the deck.
   A. 14″
   B. 16″
   C. 18″
   D. 20″

Completion

Complete each sentence by inserting the correct answer on the line near the number.

_____ 1. Lumber used in deck construction must be made either from a decay resistant species or be _____ .

_____ 2. It is the _____ of redwood and cedar that is resistant to decay.

_____ 3. If pressure-treated southern pine is used in deck construction, the grade of _____ is structurally adequate for most applications.

_____ 4. _____ is the most suitable and economical grade of California redwood for deck posts, beams, and joists.

_____ 5. All nails, fasteners, and hardware should be stainless steel, aluminum, or _____ galvanized.

_____ 6. When a deck is constructed against a building, a _____ is nailed or bolted against the wall for the entire length of the deck.

_____ 7. After the deck is applied, a _____ is installed under the siding and on top of the deck board.

_____ 8. Deck footings may require digging a hole and filling it with _____ .

_____ 9. In cold climates all deck footings must extend below the _____ .

_____ 10. All supporting posts are set on footings, then braced _____ in both directions.

CHAPTER 67 FENCE DESIGN AND ERECTION

Multiple Choice

Write the letter for the correct answer on the line next to the number of the sentence.

_____ 1. For the strongest fences, set the posts in _____ .
    A. clay
    B. gravel
    C. concrete
    D. mortar

_____ 2. Filling the bottom of the fence post hole with gravel _____ .
    A. reduces the required depth of the hole
    B. strengthens the post
    C. eliminates the need to brace the post
    D. helps extend the life of the post

_____ 3. When placing concrete around fence posts, _____ .
    A. form a slight depression around the post
    B. form the top so it pitches away from the post
    C. tamp it level
    D. use a very wet mix that has been allowed to partially harden

_____ 4. An alternative to embedding the fence posts in concrete is to _____ .
    A. pack gravel around the post
    B. attach the post to a metal anchor embedded in the concrete
    C. pack the post in sand
    D. A, B, or C

_____ 5. When installing rails on fences, keep the bottom rail at least _____ above the ground.
    A. 2"
    B. 4"
    C. 6"
    D. 8"

_____ 6. When the situation exists where the faces of the wooden posts are not in the same line as the rails, then the _____ .
    A. posts must be reset
    B. rail ends must be cut out of square to match the posts
    C. rail ends must be perfectly square
    D. rails must be slightly bowed to align them

_____ 7. If iron posts are boxed with wood, then the rails are installed _____ .
    A. in the same manner as for wood posts
    B. with special metal pipe grips
    C. by boring holes in the rails and sliding them over the posts
    D. with porcelain insulators

_____ 8. When applying spaced pickets, _____ .
        A. use a picket or a ripped piece of lumber for a spacer
        B. cut only the bottom end of the pickets when trimming their height
        C. the bottom of the pickets should not touch the ground when installed
        D. A, B, and C

Completion

Complete each sentence by inserting the correct answer on the line near the number.

_____ 1. Because fences are not _____ structures, knotty, lower grades of lumber may be used to build them.

_____ 2. Parts of the fence that are set in the ground or exposed to constant moisture should be _____ or all-heart decay resistant wood.

_____ 3. When moisture comes in contact with inferior hardware or fasteners used on fences, corrosion results, causing unsightly _____ on the fence.

_____ 4. Placement or height of fences sometimes is restricted by _____ regulations.

_____ 5. When pickets are applied with their edges tightly together, the assembly is called a _____ fence.

_____ 6. The board-on-board fence is similar to the picket fence except the boards are _____ from side to side.

_____ 7. The _____ fence creates a solid barrier with boards or panels fitted between top and bottom rails.

_____ 8. The _____ fence permits the flow of air through it and yet provides privacy.

_____ 9. Because most post and rail designs have large _____ , they are not intended to be used as barriers to prevent passage through them.

_____ 10. Iron fence posts should be _____ or otherwise coated to prevent corrosion.

_____ 11. The first step in building a fence is to set the _____ .

_____ 12. If steep, sloping land prohibits the use of a line when setting fence posts, it may be necessary to use a _____ to lay out a straight line.

_____ 13. When building on a property line, be sure the exact locations of the _____ are known.

_____ 14. Fence posts are generally set about _____ feet apart.

CHAPTER 68 GYPSUM BOARD

Multiple Choice

Write the letter for the correct answer on the line next to the number of the sentence.

_____ 1. Another name for gypsum board is _____ .
   A. drywall
   B. sheetrock
   C. plasterboard
   D. A, B, and C

_____ 2. Gypsum board is composed of _____ .
   A. compressed paper coated with a gypsum surface
   B. wood fibers coated with a gypsum surface
   C. 100% gypsum
   D. a gypsum core encased in paper

_____ 3. The long edges of the most commonly used gypsum board panels are _____ .
   A. tongue and groove
   B. rabbeted
   C. tapered
   D. mitered

_____ 4. Eased-edge gypsum board has a special _____ .
   A. tapered rounded edge
   B. thickened rounded edge
   C. tapered square edge
   D. thickened square edge

_____ 5. Type X gypsum board is typically known as _____ .
   A. fire code board
   B. gypsum lath
   C. red board
   D. backing board

_____ 6. Water-resistant gypsum board is easily recognized by its distinctive _____ face.
   A. brown
   B. green
   C. yellow
   D. orange

_____ 7. Blue board is the common name for _____ .
   A. gypsum lath
   B. veneer plaster base
   C. aluminum foil-backed gypsum board
   D. predecorated panels

_____ 8. The most commonly used thickness of gypsum board for walls and ceilings in manufactured housing is _____ .
   A. ¼"
   B. ⁵⁄₁₆"
   C. ⅜"
   D. ½"

_____ 9. _____ is used extensively as a base for ceramic tile.
   A. Coreboard
   B. Linerboard
   C. Brown board
   D. Cement board

_____ 10. Staples are an approved fastener for gypsum panels _____ .
   A. in all circumstances
   B. on base layers of multilayer applications when they penetrate the supports at least ⅝"
   C. only along tapered edges on regular gypsum board
   D. in warmer climates only

Completion

Complete each sentence by inserting the correct answer on the line near the number.

_____ 1. The heads on gypsum board nails must be at least _____ inch in diameter.

_____ 2. A drywall hammer has a face that is _____ .

_____ 3. Care should be taken to drive nails at a right angle into gypsum board panels to prevent breaking the _____ .

_____ 4. Type _____ drywall screws are used for fastening into wood.

_____ 5. Type _____ drywall screws are used for fastening into gypsum backing boards.

_____ 6. Type _____ drywall screws are used for fastening into heavier gauge metal framing.

_____ 7. It is especially important to wear eye protection when driving drywall screws into _____ framing.

_____ 8. For bonding gypsum board directly to supports, special drywall _____ adhesive or approved construction adhesive is used.

_____ 9. Caution must be exercised when using some types of drywall adhesives that contain a _____ solvent.

_____ 10. When laminating gypsum boards to each other, no supplemental fasteners are needed if _____ adhesives are used.

CHAPTER 69 SINGLE AND MULTI-LAYER DRYWALL APPLICATION

Multiple Choice

Write the letter for the correct answer on the line next to the number of the sentence.

_____ 1. Drywall should be delivered to the job site _____ .
A. as soon as the roof is on
B. when all the rough carpentry is complete
C. shortly before installation begins and the building is watertight
D. anytime after construction begins

_____ 2. Drywall should be stored _____ .
A. on its edge leaning against a wall
B. under cover and stacked flat on supports
C. on three supports at least 2" wide
D. under cover and on its edge

_____ 3. The _____ is a tool for making cuts in gypsum board.
A. utility knife
B. drywall saw
C. electric drywall cutout tool
D. A, B, and C

_____ 4. Stud edges that are to have gypsum panels installed on them must not be out of alignment more than _____ to adjacent studs.
A. $\frac{1}{16}$"
B. $\frac{1}{8}$"
C. $\frac{1}{4}$"
D. $\frac{3}{8}$"

_____ 5. When the single nailing method is used, nails are spaced a maximum of _____ on center for walls.
A. 4"
B. 6"
C. 8"
D. 10"

_____ 6. With double-nailing, the first nail must be _____ after driving the second nail of each set.
A. removed
B. reseated
C. partially withdrawn
D. set flush to the surface of the panel

_____ 7. When fastening drywall ceilings with screws to framing members that are 16" on center, the screws should be spaced _____ on center.
A. 4"
B. 8"
C. 12"
D. 16"

_____ 8. When applying adhesives to studs where two panels are joined, _____ .
A. apply one straight bead to the centerline of the stud
B. zigzag the bead across the stud's centerline
C. apply two parallel beads to either side of the centerline
D. cover the entire stud with adhesive

_____ 9. On ceilings where adhesive is used, the field is fastened at about _____ intervals.
A. 8"
B. 12"
C. 16"
D. 24"

_____ 10. The reason for prebowing gypsum panels is to _____ .
A. compensate for misaligned studs
B. eliminate the need for adhesives
C. eliminate the need for fasteners at the top and bottom plates
D. reduce the number of supplemental fasteners required

_____ 11. _____ are supports made in the form of a "T" that are used to help hold ceiling drywall panels in position when fastening.
A. Deadmen
B. Strong backs
C. Ledger boards
D. Sleepers

_____ 12. If a fastener misses a support, _____ .
A. continue driving it until it is flush with the surface of the panel
B. remove it and dimple the hole
C. set it beneath the panel's surface
D. drive its head clear through the panel, then patch the hole

Completion

Complete each sentence by inserting the correct answer on the line near the number.

_____ 1. When walls are less than 8'-1" high, wallboard is usually installed _____ .

_____ 2. The best way to minimize end joints when hanging drywall is to use the _____ panel of drywall as possible.

_____ 3. End joints should not fall on the same _____ as those on the opposite side of the partition.

_____ 4. To be less conspicuous, end joints should be as far from the _____ of the wall as possible.

_____ 5. When using a drywall cutout tool, care must be taken not to plunge too deeply and contact _____ .

_____ 6. When walls are more than 8'-1" high, _____ application of wallboard is more practical.

_____ 7. The _____ method of drywall application helps prevent nail popping and cracking where walls and ceilings meet.

_____ 8. When applying gypsum panels to curved surfaces, _____ the panels enable them to bend easier.

_____ 9. _____ gypsum board and cement board panels are used in bath and shower areas as bases for the application of ceramic tile.

_____ 10. With multilayer application of gypsum board, the joints of the face layer are offset at least _____ inches from the joints in the base layer.

CHAPTER 70   CONCEALING FASTENERS AND JOINTS

Multiple Choice

Write the letter for the correct answer on the line next to the number of the sentence.

_____ 1. For 24 hours before, during, and for at least 4 days after the application of joint compound, the temperature should be maintained at a minimum of _____ .
   A. 40°
   B. 50°
   C. 60°
   D. 70°

_____ 2. Joints between panels that are ¼" or more should be _____ .
   A. prefilled with compound
   B. filled with insulation
   C. moistened prior to filling
   D. primed with a latex primer

_____ 3. When embedding the tape in compound, be sure _____ .
   A. to center the tape on the joint
   B. there are no air bubbles under the tape
   C. there is not over ⅟₃₂" of joint compound under the edges
   D. A, B, and C

_____ 4. Immediately after embedding the tape in compound, _____ .
   A. moisten it with a fine spray of water
   B. wipe it with a damp sponge
   C. lift the edges and apply additional compound
   D. apply another thin coat of compound to the tape

_____ 5. The term spotting in drywall work refers to _____ .
   A. the application of compound to conceal fastener heads
   B. air bubbles under the tape
   C. stains that appear as a result of using contaminated compound
   D. compound that drops to the floor during application

_____ 6. When applying compound to corner beads, _____ .
   A. use the nose of the bead to serve as a guide for applying the trim
   B. apply the compound about 6" wide from the nose of the bead to a feather edge on the wall
   C. each subsequent finishing coat is applied about 2" wider than the previous one
   D. A, B, and C

_____ 7. The second coat of compound is sometimes called the _____ coat.
   A. fill
   B. pack
   C. plug
   D. supply

_____ 8. Professional drywall finishers _____ .
   A. sand between each coat
   B. moisten the compound before sanding
   C. rarely sand any excess between coats
   D. only have to apply one coat

_____ 9. When finishing interior corners, _____ .
   A. a setting compound is usually applied to one side only of each corner
   B. joint reinforcing tape is not necessary
   C. the first coat is applied approximately 16″ wide
   D. A, B, and C

_____ 10. For every 1,000 square feet of drywall area, _____ lbs. of conventional joint compound are needed.
   A. 105
   B. 115
   C. 135
   D. 155

Completion

Complete each sentence by inserting the correct answer on the line near the number.

_____ 1. Joints are reinforced with _____ .

_____ 2. Exterior corners are reinforced with _____ .

_____ 3. Taping compound is used to embed and adhere tape to the board over the _____ .

_____ 4. Second and third coats over tapped joints are covered with a _____ compound.

_____ 5. An all purpose compound may be convenient, but it lacks the _____ and workability that a two-step compound system has.

_____ 6. Setting-type joint compounds are only available in a _____ form.

_____ 7. Setting type joint compounds permit the _____ of drywall interiors in the same day.

_____ 8. To simplify its application to corners, joint tape has a _____ along its center.

_____ 9. Glass fiber mesh tape is available with a plain back or with a(n) _____ backing for quick application.

_____ 10. Instead of using fasteners on corner beads, a(n) _____ tool may be used to lock the bead to the corner.

_____ 11. Control joints are placed in large drywall areas to relieve _____ from expansion and contraction.

CHAPTER 71 TYPES OF WALL PANELING

Completion

Complete each sentence by inserting the correct answer on the line near the number.

_____ 1. The most widely used kind of sheet paneling is _____ .

_____ 2. Less expensive plywood paneling is prefinished with a _____ wood grain or other design on a vinyl covering.

_____ 3. The most commonly used length of paneling is the _____ foot length.

_____ 4. Matching _____ is available to cover panel edges, corners, and joints.

_____ 5. When exposed fastening is necessary, matching colored ring-shanked nails called _____ are used.

_____ 6. _____ is a hardboard panel with a baked-on plastic finish that is embossed to simulate ceramic wall tile.

_____ 7. Commonly used thicknesses of hardboard paneling range from ⅛" to _____ inch(es).

_____ 8. Particleboard panels must only be applied to a wall backing that is _____ .

_____ 9. Unfinished particleboard paneling made from aromatic cedar chips is used to cover walls in _____ .

_____ 10. Kitchen cabinets and countertops are widely surfaced with plastic _____ .

_____ 11. _____-type laminate is used on cabinet sides and walls.

_____ 12. Regular or standard laminate is generally used on _____ surfaces.

_____ 13. Once a sheet of laminate comes in contact with the adhesive, it can no longer be _____ .

_____ 14. Most board paneling comes in a _____-inch thickness.

_____ 15. To avoid shrinkage, board paneling, like all interior finish, must be dried to a _____ content.

Identification: Solid Wood Paneling Patterns

Identify each term, and write the letter of the correct answer on the line next to each number.

_____ 1. matched and eased channel

_____ 2. matched, edge and center grooved

_____ 3. matched and V-grooved

_____ 4. pickwick

_____ 5. channel rustic

_____ 6. shiplapped and V-grooved

_____ 7. tongue and grooved

_____ 8. matched, V-grooved, and beaded

A. ⟶

B. ⟶

C. ⟶

D. ⟶

E. ⟶

F. ⟶

G. ⟶

H. ⟶

CHAPTER 72 APPLICATION OF WALL PANELING

Multiple Choice

Write the letter for the correct answer on the line next to the number of the sentence.

_____ 1. Sheet paneling is usually applied to walls with the long edges _____ .
   A. vertical
   B. horizontal
   C. diagonal
   D. tight against the ceiling

_____ 2. The installation of a gypsum board base layer beneath sheet paneling is done so that _____ .
   A. the wall is stronger and more fire resistant
   B. sound transmission is deadened
   C. there will be a rigid finished surface for application of paneling
   D. A, B, and C

_____ 3. Before the installation of paneling to masonry walls, _____ .
   A. contact adhesive must be applied to the masonry
   B. furring strips must be applied to the masonry
   C. the wall must be parged with portland cement
   D. the back of the paneling sheet must be sealed

_____ 4. Paneling edges must fall _____ .
   A. midway between studs
   B. in line with the left side of the stud
   C. in line with the right side of the stud
   D. on stud centers

_____ 5. Panels are usually fastened with _____ .
   A. screws
   B. finish nails
   C. contact adhesive
   D. color pins and adhesive

_____ 6. Paneling that only covers the lower portion of the wall is called _____ .
   A. wainscoting
   B. louvering
   C. ledgering
   D. garthcoting

_____ 7. When cutting to a scribed line that must be made on the face side of prefinished paneling, it is recommended that a _____ be used.
   A. circular saw
   B. hand ripsaw
   C. fine-toothed hand crosscut saw
   D. saber saw

_____ 8. When using adhesive on paneling, _____ .
   A. apply beads about 4" long and 16" apart where panel edges and ends make contact
   B. do not allow the panel to move once it has made contact with the wall
   C. apply a ⅛" continuous bead to the intermediate studs only
   D. after the initial contact is made between the wall and the panel, the sheet is pulled a short distance away from the wall and then pressed back into position

_____ 9. When cutting openings for wall outlets, _____ .
   A. a saber saw may be used if the cut is made from the back of the panel
   B. a circular saw may be used
   C. the openings may be cut oversized to allow for error
   D. a ripsaw is used

_____ 10. When applying paneling to exterior corners, _____ corner molding may be used.
   A. wood
   B. metal
   C. vinyl
   D. A, B, and C

Completion

Complete each sentence by inserting the correct answer on the line near the number.

_____ 1. For vertical application of board paneling to a frame wall, _____ must be provided between the studs.

_____ 2. Prior to its application, board paneling should stand against the walls around the room to allow it to adjust to room temperature and _____ .

_____ 3. If tongue and groove board paneling is used, tack the first board in a plumb position with the _____ edge in the corner.

_____ 4. When fastening tongue and groove board paneling, blind nail into the _____ only.

_____ 5. If board paneling is of uniform width, the _____ of the first board must be planned to avoid ending with a small strip.

_____ 6. When fastening the last piece of vertical board siding, the cut edge goes in the _____ .

_____ 7. Blocking between studs on open walls is not necessary when siding is applied _____ .

_____ 8. Specially matched _____ is used between panels and on interior and exterior corners of plastic laminates that are prefabricated to plywood sheets.

Discussion

Write your answer(s) on the lines below.

1. Describe the process of estimating the number of sheets of paneling needed to do a room.

_____

_____

_____

CHAPTER 73 CERAMIC WALL TILE

Multiple Choice

Write the letter for the correct answer on the line next to the number of the sentence.

_____ 1. The proper backing for ceramic wall tile is _____ .
   A. water-resistant gypsum or cement board
   B. hard board
   C. plywood
   D. A, B, and C

_____ 2. The most commonly used wall tiles are nominal size _____ squares, in about ¼" thickness.
   A. 1" and 3"
   B. 2" and 5"
   C. 3½" and 4½"
   D. 4" and 6"

_____ 3. When tile is installed around a tub that lacks a showerhead, it should extend a minimum of _____ above the rim.
   A. 4"
   B. 6"
   C. 8"
   D. 10"

_____ 4. Around tubs with showerheads, the tile should extend a minimum of _____ above the rim or 6" above the showerhead, whichever is higher.
   A. 3'
   B. 4'
   C. 5'
   D. 6'

_____ 5. Before beginning the application of ceramic wall tile, the width of the _____ must be determined.
   A. border tile
   B. field tile
   C. application trowel
   D. tile saw kerf

_____ 6. When troweling adhesive to the wall in preparation for tile application, _____ .
   A. it is best to go on the heavy side
   B. a regular straight edge trowel is to be used
   C. overlap the coverage area with the adhesive
   D. be sure the trowel is the one recommended by the manufacturer

_____ 7. Whole tiles that are applied to the center of the wall are called _____ tiles.
   A. bullnose
   B. counter
   C. field
   D. court

_____ 8. A hand-operated ceramic tile cutter works in a manner that is similar to a _____ .
   A. glass cutter
   B. masonry saw
   C. rasp
   D. coping saw

_____ 9. After all tile has been applied, the joints are filled with _____ .
   A. portland cement
   B. tile grout
   C. tile mastic
   D. contact cement

_____ 10. After the joints are partially set up but not completely hardened, they then must be _____ .
   A. pointed
   B. checked
   C. glazed
   D. pitched

CHAPTER **74** SUSPENDED CEILINGS

Multiple Choice

Write the letter for the correct answer on the line next to the number of the sentence.

_____ 1. A main advantage of using a suspended ceiling is that the space above it can be utilized for _____ .
- A. recessed lighting
- B. duct work
- C. pipes and conduit
- D. A, B, and C

_____ 2. Suspended ceiling systems consist of panels that are _____ .
- A. stapled into firing strips
- B. applied with adhesive
- C. laid into a metal grid
- D. tongue and groove panels that interlock into each other

_____ 3. L-shaped pieces that are fastened to the wall to support the ends of main runners and cross tees are called _____ .
- A. wall ties
- B. wall angles
- C. support angles
- D. runner supports

_____ 4. Main runners are shaped in the form of a(n) _____ .
- A. L
- B. T
- C. upside down L
- D. upside down T

_____ 5. Slots are punched in the side of the runners at _____ intervals to receive cross tees.
- A. 4″
- B. 8″
- C. 12″
- D. 16″

_____ 6. The primary supports for the ceiling's weight are the _____ .
- A. main runners
- B. cross tees
- C. ceiling panels
- D. wall ties

_____ 7. Panels come in 2′ × 2′ and 2′ × 4′ sizes with square and _____ edges.
- A. rounded
- B. beveled
- C. concaved
- D. rabbeted

_____ 8. Main runners are usually spaced _____ apart.
    A. 2'
    B. 4'
    C. 6'
    D. 8'

_____ 9. The first parts of the ceiling grid system to be installed are the _____ .
    A. main runners
    B. cross tees
    C. wall angles
    D. wall ties

_____ 10. A suspended ceiling must be installed with at least _____ clearance below the lowest air duct, pipe, or beam for enough room to insert ceiling panels in the grid.
    A. 1"
    B. 3"
    C. 5"
    D. 8"

Completion

Complete each sentence by inserting the correct answer on the line near the number.

_____ 1. Screw eyes are to be installed not over _____ feet apart.

_____ 2. Screw eyes must be long enough to penetrate wood joists by at least _____ inch(es).

_____ 3. For residential work, _____ gauge hanger wire is usually used.

_____ 4. About 6" of hanger wire is inserted through the screw eye and then securely wrapped around itself _____ times.

_____ 5. A cross tee line must be stretched across the short dimension of the room to line up the _____ in the main runners.

_____ 6. Cross tees are installed by inserting the tabs on the ends into the slots in the _____ .

_____ 7. Ceiling tiles that are cut to fit along the perimeter of the room are called _____ tiles.

_____ 8. Panels are cut with a sharp _____ .

_____ 9. Always cut ceiling panels with their finished side placed _____ .

_____ 10. To find the number of wall angles needed in a room, divide the perimeter of the room by _____ .

CHAPTER **75** CEILING TILE

Completion

Complete each sentence by inserting the correct answer on the line near the number.

_____ 1. _____ fiber tiles are the lowest in cost.

_____ 2. _____ fiber tiles are used when a more fire-resistant tile is required.

_____ 3. The most popular size square tile is the _____ inch.

_____ 4. If the short walls of a room measure 12'-6", then the border tiles along the long walls of the room would measure _____ .

_____ 5. When tiles are not being applied with adhesive to an existing ceiling, then _____ must be installed to fasten the tiles to.

_____ 6. Ceiling joists are usually _____ inches on center.

_____ 7. If the size of the tiles are 12", then the furring strips must be installed _____ inches on center.

_____ 8. Furring strip fasteners must penetrate at least _____ inch(es) into the joist.

_____ 9. Prior to installing, ceiling tiles should be allowed to adjust to normal interior room conditions for _____ hours.

_____ 10. To help prevent fingerprints and smudges on the finished ceiling, some carpenters sprinkle _____ on their hands.

_____ 11. On border tiles, all _____ edges should go against the wall.

_____ 12. The correct number of ½" or ⁹⁄₁₆" staples to use in 12" square ceiling tiles is _____ .

_____ 13. With 12" × 24" tiles, the correct number of staples to use in each tile is _____ .

_____ 14. When applying adhesive to ceiling tile, each daub of it should be about the size of a _____ .

_____ 15. When using a concealed grid system, the tiles' edges must be _____ .

_____ 16. With the concealed grid system, the tiles in the end row are held tight by inserting a _____ between each tile and the end row.

Math

Estimate the number of 12″ × 24″ ceiling tiles and the lineal feet of furring strips needed to cover the ceiling of a room that measures 12′-8″ by 23′-4″.

CHAPTER 76 DESCRIPTION OF INTERIOR DOORS

Completion

Complete each sentence by inserting the correct answer on the line near the number.

_____ 1. The interior _____ door is used when a less expensive smooth surfaced door with a plain appearance is desired.

_____ 2. Most interior residential doors are manufactured in a _____-inch thickness.

_____ 3. The most common height of manufactured doors is _____ .

_____ 4. Door widths range from 1'-0" to _____ in increments of two inches.

_____ 5. Solid core doors are generally used on _____ doors.

_____ 6. The _____ is the thin plywood that covers the frame and mesh of a hollow core door.

_____ 7. Doors that swing in both directions are known as _____ doors.

_____ 8. _____ doors are not practical in openings less than 6' wide.

_____ 9. _____ doors require more time and material to install than other kinds of doors.

_____ 10. Bifold doors on the jamb side swing on _____ installed at the top and bottom.

Matching

Write the letter for the correct answer on the line near the number to which it corresponds.

_____ 1. lauan plywood

_____ 2. folding doors

_____ 3. french doors

_____ 4. louver doors

_____ 5. bypass doors

_____ 6. pocket doors

_____ 7. cafe doors

A. obstruct vision but permit the flow of air

B. ride on rollers in a double track

C. used extensively for flush door skins

D. may contain from 1 to 15 lights of glass

E. hung in pairs that swing in both directions

F. only the door's lock edge is visible when opened

G. consist of many narrow panels each about the same width as the door jamb

Discussion

Write your answer(s) on the lines below.

1. What are some of the special conditions present in heavy commercial buildings that would require heavier and larger interior doors than those used in homes?

    _____

    _____

    _____

CHAPTER **77** INSTALLATION OF INTERIOR DOORS AND DOOR FRAMES

Multiple Choice

Write the letter for the correct answer on the line next to the number of the sentence.

_____ 1. The first step in making an interior door frame is to _____ .
A. install the stop
B. check the width and height of the rough opening
C. rabbet the edge of the jamb stock
D. install the header jamb

_____ 2. The rough opening width for single acting swinging doors should be the door width plus _____ .
A. the thickness of the jamb, plus 1"
B. double the door thickness
C. double the side jamb thickness, plus ½"
D. triple the side jamb thickness, plus ¾"

_____ 3. The rough opening height of the door should be the door's height plus _____ , plus the thickness of the finish floor, plus the desired clearance under the door.
A. the thickness of the header jamb, plus ¼"
B. double the header jamb thickness
C. double the side jamb thickness, plus ½"
D. ½"

_____ 4. Interior door frames are usually installed _____ .
A. during the rough framing process
B. after the interior wall covering is applied
C. at the same time the interior wall covering is applied
D. prior to the application of the interior wall covering

_____ 5. To find the width of the jamb stock, _____ .
A. triple the thickness of the door
B. subtract the thickness of the door jamb from that of the total wall thickness
C. measure the total wall thickness including the wall covering
D. subtract 1" from the sill width

_____ 6. Door frames must be set so that the jambs are _____ .
A. straight
B. level
C. plumb
D. A, B, and C

_____ 7. If a rabbeted frame is used, _____ .
A. the door's swing must be determined so that the rabbet faces the right direction
B. a separate stop needs to be applied to the inside of the door frame
C. the rough opening is the same width and height as the door frame
D. the horns are not to be cut from the top edge of the side jambs

_____ 8. The header jamb is leveled by placing shims between the _____ .
    A. header jamb and the header
    B. header and the horns
    C. bottom of the appropriate side jamb and the subfloor
    D. side jamb opposite the header jamb

_____ 9. When straightening side jambs by shimming at intermediate points, use a
_____ .
    A. combination square
    B. 6′ straight edge
    C. butt gauge
    D. sliding T-bevel

_____ 10. Before any nails are driven home when setting a door frame, the frame should be
checked for a _____ .
    A. wind
    B. bluster
    C. gale
    D. breeze

Completion

Complete each sentence by inserting the correct answer on the line near the number.

_____ 1. Door stops are not permanently fastened until any necessary adjustment is made when the _____ is installed.

_____ 2. The special pivoting hardware installed on double acting doors returns the door to a _____ position after being opened.

_____ 3. Bypass door tracks are installed on the _____ according to the manufacturer's directions.

_____ 4. It is important that the door pulls on bypass doors are installed _____ so as not to obstruct the bypassing door.

_____ 5. Before installing bifold door tracks into position, be sure the _____ for the door pivot pins are inserted in the track.

_____ 6. Pocket door frames are usually assembled at the _____ .

_____ 7. Because folding doors are made by many different manufacturers and come in many different styles, it is important to closely follow the _____ supplied with the unit.

_____ 8. To accommodate various wall thicknesses, prehung door units are available in various _____ widths.

_____ 9. To maintain proper clearance between the door and the frame on a prehung door, small cardboard _____ are stapled to the lock edge and the top end of the door.

_____ 10. The _____ lock is used often on bathroom and bedroom doors.

CHAPTER **78** DESCRIPTION AND APPLICATION OF MOLDING

Completion

Complete each sentence by inserting the correct answer on the line near the number.

_____ 1. In order to present a suitable appearance, moldings must be applied with _____ joints.

_____ 2. To reduce waste, door casings are available in lengths of _____ feet.

_____ 3. Finger-jointed lengths of molding should only be used when a _____ finish is to be applied.

_____ 4. Moldings are either classified by their _____ or their designated location.

_____ 5. The joint between the bottom of the base and the finish floor is usually concealed by the base _____ .

_____ 6. _____ are used to trim around windows, doors, and other openings to cover the space between the wall and the frame.

_____ 7. For a more decorative appearance, _____ may be applied to the outside edges of casings.

_____ 8. Aprons and stools are part of _____ trim.

_____ 9. Another name for outside corners is corner _____ .

_____ 10. Caps and chair rails are used to trim the top edge of _____ .

_____ 11. With the exception of prefinished molding, joints between molding lengths should be _____ flush after the molding has been fastened.

_____ 12. Molding joints on exterior corners must be _____ .

_____ 13. Joints on interior corners, especially on large moldings, are usually _____ .

_____ 14. When cutting molding in a miter box, the face side of the molding should be placed _____ .

_____ 15. When mitering bed, crown, and cove moldings, place them _____ in the miter box.

_____ 16. The _____ is a tool to use when paper-thin corrective cuts are needed when fitting miter joints.

_____ 17. A mitering _____ may be used to make miters on a table or radial arm saw quickly and easily without any change in the setup.

_____ 18. When making a coped joint, the coping saw's handle should be above the work and its teeth should face _____ from the saw's handle.

_____ 19. To assure straight application of large-size ceiling moldings, a _____ should be used as a guide.

_____ 20. Nails should be placed 2" to 3" from the molding's end to prevent _____ .

Identification: Molding

Identify each term, and write the letter of the correct answer on the line next to each number.

_____ 1. crown

_____ 2. bed

_____ 3. cove

_____ 4. quarter round

_____ 5. corner guard

_____ 6. base shoes

_____ 7. chair rail

_____ 8. base moldings

_____ 9. half round

_____ 10. hand rail

A.   B.   C.   D.   E.

F.   G.   H.   I.   J.

CHAPTER 79 APPLICATION OF DOOR CASINGS, BASE, AND WINDOW TRIM

Multiple Choice

Write the letter for the correct answer on the line next to the number of the sentence.

_____ 1. Door casings must be applied before _____ .
A. window trim
B. ceiling moldings
C. base moldings
D. corner guards

_____ 2. _____ blocks are small decorative blocks used as part of the door trim at the base and at the head.
A. Plinth
B. Batten
C. Astragal
D. Crown

_____ 3. Molded casings usually have their back sides _____ .
A. rabbeted
B. backed out
C. beveled
D. laminated

_____ 4. An alternative to using molded casings is to use _____ stock.
A. S4S
B. S3S
C. S2S
D. S1S

_____ 5. The ³⁄₁₆" to ⁵⁄₁₆" setback of door casings from the inside face of the door frame is called the _____ .
A. reveal
B. exposure
C. rake
D. salvage

_____ 6. For each interior door opening, _____ are required.
A. two side casings and two header casings
B. two side casings and four header casings
C. four side casings and four header casings
D. four side casings and two header casings

_____ 7. When fastening casing into _____ , use 6d or 8d finish nails.
A. header jambs
B. side jambs
C. framing
D. A, B, and C

_____ 8. To bring the faces of mitered casing joints flush, _____ .
   A. sand them
   B. shim between the casing back and the wall
   C. use a wood chisel to remove thin shavings from the thicker side of the joint
   D. use a flat wood file

_____ 9. Base trim should be _____ .
   A. thinner than the door casing
   B. molded or S2S stock
   C. back mitered to outline the cope for interior corners
   D. A, B, and C

_____ 10. When fastening base molding, use _____ finishing nail(s) of sufficient length at each stud location.
   A. one
   B. two
   C. three
   D. four

Completion

Complete each sentence by inserting the correct answer on the line near the number.

_____ 1. When scribing lines on baseboard, be sure to hold the dividers so that a line between the two points is _____ to the floor.

_____ 2. When cutting baseboard to a scribed line, be sure to give the cut a slight _____ .

_____ 3. On outside corners of baseboard, make regular _____ joints.

_____ 4. The base shoe is usually nailed into the _____ .

_____ 5. No base shoe is required if _____ is used as a finish floor.

_____ 6. The bottom side of the stool is _____ at an angle, so its top side will be level after it is fit on the window's sill.

_____ 7. The _____ covers the joint between the sill and the wall.

_____ 8. Jamb _____ must be used when windows are installed with jambs that are narrower than the walls.

_____ 9. Window casings are installed with their inside edges flush with the inside face of the _____ .

_____ 10. The _____ is a piece of 1" × 5" stock installed around the walls of a closet to support the rod and the shelf.

_____ 11. Closet pole sockets should be located at least _____ inches from the back wall.

_____ 12. When sanding interior trim, always sand with the _____ .

_____ 13. All traces of excess glue must be removed if the trim is to be _____ .

_____ 14. To help prevent the hammer from glancing off the head of a nail, occasionally clean the hammer's face by rubbing it with _____ .

CHAPTER **80** DESCRIPTION OF STAIR FINISH

Multiple Choice

Write the letter for the correct answer on the line next to the number of the sentence.

_____ 1. The _____ is a component of the stair body finish.
   A. newel post
   B. riser
   C. handrail
   D. baluster

_____ 2. With an open staircase, _____ .
   A. tread ends butt against the wall
   B. one or more ends of the treads are exposed to view
   C. the area under the stair body is exposed to view
   D. both sides of the treads must be exposed to view

_____ 3. The part of the stair tread that extends beyond the riser is the _____ .
   A. nosing
   B. tread molding
   C. stringer
   D. half newel

_____ 4. Finish stringers are sometimes called _____ .
   A. preachers
   B. skirt boards
   C. carriages
   D. aprons

_____ 5. Open finish stringers are placed on the _____ .
   A. open side of the stairway above the treads
   B. closed side of an open stairway above the treads
   C. open side of a stairway below the treads
   D. closed side of an open stairway below the treads

_____ 6. When the staircase is open on one or more sides, _____ .
   A. a starting step may be used
   B. return nosing is used
   C. an open finish stringer is used
   D. A, B, and C

_____ 7. In post to post balustrades _____ .
   A. the newel posts fit into the bottom of the handrail
   B. the newel posts have flat square surfaces near the top
   C. goosenecks must always be used
   D. the newel posts are made with a pin in their tops

_____ 8. Narrow strips called _____ are used between balusters to fill the plowed groove on handrails and shoe rails.
   A. fillets
   B. rossettes
   C. mullions
   D. scabs

_____ 9. Short sections of specialty curved handrail are called _____ .
   A. stiles
   B. fittings
   C. heels
   D. crickets

_____ 10. _____ are vertical, usually decorative, pieces between newel posts and spaced close together, supporting the handrail.
   A. Volutes
   B. Cleats
   C. Battens
   D. Balusters

Identification: Balustrade Components

Identify each term, and write the letter of the correct answer on the line next to each number.

_____ 1. baluster

_____ 2. rake handrail

_____ 3. landing newel

_____ 4. closed finish stringer

_____ 5. half newel

_____ 6. starting newel

_____ 7. landing rail

_____ 8. balcony handrail

_____ 9. landing baluster

_____ 10. balcony baluster

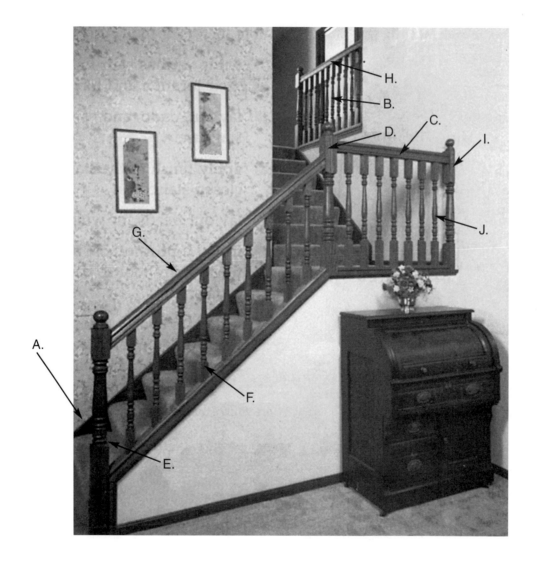

CHAPTER **81** FINISHING THE STAIR BODY OF OPEN AND CLOSED STAIRCASES

Multiple Choice

Write the letter for the correct answer on the line next to the number of the sentence.

_____ 1. Use a _____ when cutting the level and plumb cuts on a closed finish stringer.
A. 7- or 8-point crosscut handsaw
B. fine tooth crosscut handsaw
C. 5½-point hand ripsaw
D. coping saw

_____ 2. The nosed edge of the tread usually extends beyond the face of the riser by _____ .
A. ⅝″
B. ⅞″
C. 1⅛″
D. 1⅝″

_____ 3. Prior to placing the treads between the finish stringers, _____ .
A. rub wax on one end
B. liberally apply glue to the tread's end grain
C. spray the treads with a light mist of water
D. seal the treads with a varnish

_____ 4. When fastening treads, to prevent splitting the wood, _____ .
A. predrill the nail holes
B. use only 12d finish nails
C. be sure to use galvanized 10d casing nails
D. use only glue and no nails

_____ 5. Tread molding is attached using _____ finish nails.
A. 3d
B. 4d
C. 6d
D. 8d

_____ 6. On a staircase that has one side open and the other side closed, the _____ the first item(s) of finish to be applied.
A. risers are
B. closed finish stringer is
C. open finish stringer is
D. treads are

_____ 7. When laying out the plumb lines on an open finish stringer, a helpful device to use is a _____ .
A. chalk line
B. plumb bob
C. line level
D. preacher

_____ 8. When fastening a mitered riser to a mitered stringer, _____ .
    A. sand all pieces before installation
    B. apply a small amount of glue to the joint
    C. drive finish nails both ways through the miter
    D. A, B, and C

_____ 9. When ripping treads to width, _____ .
    A. bevel the back edge
    B. make allowances for the rabbeted back edge
    C. bevel the front edge of the tread
    D. only a hand ripsaw should be used

_____ 10. Treads on winding steps _____ .
    A. are more challenging to fit
    B. have the same angle on both ends
    C. are wider on the inside than the outside
    D. A, B, and C

Completion

Complete each sentence by inserting the correct answer on the line near the number.

_____ 1. Instead of a framing square, a _____ may be used to lay out a housed stringer.

_____ 2. The _____ is joined to the housed stringer at the top and bottom of the staircase.

_____ 3. A _____ is used to guide the router when housing the stringer.

_____ 4. Housed stringers are routed so that the dadoes are the exact width at the nosing and wider toward the inside so the treads and risers can be _____ against the shoulders of the dadoes.

_____ 5. An open stringer is also referred to as a _____ stringer.

_____ 6. The vertical layout line on an open stringer is mitered to fit the mitered end of the _____ .

_____ 7. On open stringers, a _____ cut is made through the stringer's thickness for the tread.

_____ 8. A ⅜″ by ⅜″ groove to receive the rabbeted inner edge of the _____ may be cut on the face side of all but the first riser.

_____ 9. If the staircase is open, a return _____ is mitered to the end of the tread.

_____ 10. _____ are usually the first members applied to the stair carriage in a closed staircase.

_____ 11. The top edge of a closed finished stringer is usually about _____ inches above the tread nosing.

_____ 12. When cutting along the layout lines for a closed finished stringer, extreme care must be made on the _____ cut.

CHAPTER 82 BALUSTRADE INSTALLATION

Multiple Choice

Write the letter for the correct answer on the line next to the number of the sentence.

_____ 1. The first step in laying out balustrades is to _____ .
   A. lay out the handrail
   B. determine the rake of the handrail
   C. lay out the balustrade's centerline
   D. determine the height of the starting newel

_____ 2. Most building codes require that balusters be spaced so that _____ .
   A. a small child's foot cannot fit between them
   B. there is no more than one per tread
   C. the space between them equals their width
   D. no object 5" in diameter can pass through

_____ 3. On open treads, the center of the front baluster is located _____ .
   A. a distance equal to ½ its thickness back from the riser's face
   B. flush with the riser's face
   C. on the center of the tread's outside edge
   D. 2" from the riser face

_____ 4. Rake handrail height is the vertical distance from the tread nosing to the _____ .
   A. handrail bottom side
   B. handrail center
   C. top of the handrail
   D. top of the newel post

_____ 5. On a stairway more than 88" in width, a handrail _____ .
   A. is needed on only one side
   B. is needed on both sides
   C. must be provided in the stairway's center
   D. B and C

_____ 6. The starting newel post is notched over the _____ .
   A. inside corner of the second step
   B. inside corner of the first step
   C. outside corner of the first step
   D. outside corner of the second step

_____ 7. Generally, codes require that balcony rails for homes be not less than _____ in length.
   A. 18"
   B. 24"
   C. 36"
   D. 42"

_____ 8. To determine the height of a balcony newel, you must know the _____ .
   A. height of the balcony handrail plus 1″ for the block reveal
   B. height of the newel's turned top
   C. distance the newel extends below the floor
   D. A, B, and C

_____ 9. When square top balusters are used, _____ .
   A. holes must be bored in the bottom side of the handrail at least ¾″ deep
   B. the balusters must be trimmed to length at the rake angle
   C. holes need not be bored in the treads
   D. A, B, and C

_____ 10. Instead of a half newel, a _____ is sometimes used to end the balcony handrail.
   A. landing fitting
   B. gooseneck
   C. half baluster
   D. rosette

Completion

Complete each sentence by inserting the correct answer on the line near the number.

_____ 1. Square top balusters are fastened to the handrail with finish nails and _____ .

_____ 2. When using square top balusters, _____ are installed between the balusters in the plow of the handrail.

_____ 3. When installing an over-the-post balustrade, the first step is to lay out the balustrade and baluster _____ on the stair treads.

_____ 4. A _____ is a piece of wood cut in the shape of a right triangle, whose sides are equal in length to the rise and tread run of the stairs.

_____ 5. When laying out the starting fitting, mark it at the _____ point, where its curve touches the pitch block.

_____ 6. When cutting handrail fittings on a power miter box, be sure to securely _____ the fitting and the pitch block.

_____ 7. To mark the hole locations for handrail bolts, a _____ should be used to assure proper alignment.

_____ 8. A one-riser balcony gooseneck fitting is used when the balcony rails are _____ inches high.

_____ 9. On over-the-post balustrades, the height of the rake handrail is calculated from the height of the starting _____ .

_____ 10. The height of a balcony newel on an over-the-post balustrade is found by subtracting the handrail thickness from the handrail _____ .

234

CHAPTER 83 DESCRIPTION OF WOOD FINISH FLOORS

Multiple Choice

Write the letter for the correct answer on the line next to the number of the sentence.

_____ 1. Most hardwood finish flooring is made from _____ .
   A. Douglas fir
   B. white or red oak
   C. hemlock
   D. southern yellow pine

_____ 2. The most widely used type of solid wood flooring is _____ .
   A. strip
   B. laminated parquet blocks
   C. laminated strip
   D. parquet strip

_____ 3. Unfinished strip flooring _____ .
   A. has a chamfer machined between the face and edge sides
   B. cannot be sanded after installation
   C. is milled with square sharp corners at the intersection of the face and the edges
   D. is waxed at the factory

_____ 4. Laminated strip flooring _____ .
   A. is easily recognizable by the V-grooves on the floor's surface after it is laid
   B. is a 5-ply prefinished wood assembly
   C. must be sanded after it is installed
   D. is chamfered on its edges

_____ 5. Plank flooring is similar to _____ flooring.
   A. strip
   B. parquet strip
   C. Monticello
   D. Marie Antoinette

_____ 6. The highest quality parquet block flooring is made with _____-thick, tongue and groove solid hardwood flooring.
   A. 3⁄8″
   B. 1⁄2″
   C. 5⁄8″
   D. 3⁄4″

_____ 7. Monticello is the name of a parquet originally designed by _____ .
   A. Benjamin Franklin
   B. George Washington
   C. Thomas Jefferson
   D. Samuel Adams

_____ 8. Laminated blocks are generally made of 3-ply laminated oak in a _____ thickness.
    A. ⅜"
    B. ½"
    C. ⅝"
    D. ¾"

_____ 9. Finger blocks are another name for _____ .
    A. laminated blocks
    B. slat blocks
    C. unit blocks
    D. A, B, and C

_____ 10. _____ is the top grade of unfinished oak flooring.
    A. No. 1
    B. No. 2
    C. Clear
    D. Select

Completion

Complete each sentence by inserting the correct answer on the line near the number.

_____ 1. In addition to appearance, grades are based on _____ .

_____ 2. Red grades of unfinished pecan flooring contain all _____ .

_____ 3. White grades of unfinished pecan flooring contain all _____ .

_____ 4. The lowest grade of unfinished hard maple flooring is called _____ grade.

_____ 5. The average length of clear bundles of flooring is _____ feet.

_____ 6. A bundle of flooring may contain pieces from 6" under to 6" over the _____ length of the bundle.

_____ 7. No pieces shorter than _____ inches in length are allowed in a bundle.

_____ 8. _____ is the lowest grade of prefinished flooring.

CHAPTER **84** LAYING WOOD FINISH FLOORS

Multiple Choice

Write the letter for the correct answer on the line next to the number of the sentence.

_____ 1. When fastening flooring to ½" plywood subfloors, it is required that _____ .
   A. screws be used as fasteners
   B. the fasteners penetrate into the joists
   C. rigid insulation be placed over the subfloor
   D. A, B, and C

_____ 2. When laying the first course of strip flooring, it is placed with its _____ from the starting wall.
   A. tongue side ¾"
   B. groove side ½"
   C. tongue side ½"
   D. groove side ¾"

_____ 3. When blind nailing flooring, drive the nails at about a _____ angle.
   A. 90°
   B. 60°
   C. 45°
   D. 30°

_____ 4. When nailing strip flooring by hand, _____ is used to set hardened flooring nails.
   A. the head of the next nail to be driven
   B. a nail set
   C. a screwdriver laid on its side
   D. a center punch

_____ 5. Laying out loose flooring ahead of time to assure efficient installation is known as _____ .
   A. cribbing the stock
   B. racking the floor
   C. grouping the strips
   D. clustering the stock

_____ 6. When using a power nailer to fasten flooring, _____ .
   A. an air compressor must be used
   B. holes for the fasteners must be predrilled
   C. one blow must be used to drive the fastener
   D. the floor layer must not stand on the flooring

_____ 7. The last course of strip flooring must be _____ .
   A. fastened with a power nailer
   B. blind nailed
   C. face nailed
   D. glued and not nailed

_____ 8. Laminated strip flooring _____ .
   A. needs an ⅛" foam underlayment
   B. is not fastened or cemented to the floor
   C. is brought up tight against the previous course with a hammer and tapping block
   D. A, B, and C

_____ 9. When installing parquet flooring, it is usually _____ .
   A. face nailed
   B. blind nailed
   C. laid in mastic
   D. fastened with a power nailer

_____ 10. When laying unit blocks in a square pattern, two layout lines are snapped _____ .
   A. at right angles to each other and diagonal to the walls
   B. with one parallel and one diagonal to the walls
   C. at right angles to each other parallel to the walls
   D. parallel to each other and diagonal to the walls

Completion

Complete each sentence by inserting the correct answer on the line near the number.

_____ 1. The installation of wood finish floors on _____ slabs is not recommended.

_____ 2. New concrete slabs should be allowed to age at least _____ days prior to the installation of a wood finish floor.

_____ 3. When preforming a rubber mat moisture test on a concrete slab, allow the mat to remain in place at least _____ hours.

_____ 4. To ensure a trouble-free finish floor installation, a _____ must be installed over all concrete slabs.

_____ 5. Prior to the application of polyethylene film to a concrete slab, a skim coat of _____ is troweled over the entire area.

_____ 6. Exterior grade sheathing plywood may be used for a subfloor if it is at least _____ inch(es) thick.

_____ 7. Strips of wood laid over a concrete floor that finish flooring is attached to are known as _____ .

_____ 8. The National Oak Flooring Manufacturers Association does not recommend fastening finish flooring to subfloors of _____ panels.

_____ 9. For its best appearance, strip flooring should be laid in the direction of the room's _____ dimension.

_____ 10. To help keep out dust, prevent squeaks, and retard moisture from below, _____ is applied over the subflooring.

Discussion

Write your answer(s) on the lines below.

1. Describe the recommended procedures that are necessary to maintain the proper moisture content of hardwood flooring prior to its installation.

_____

_____

_____

CHAPTER 85   UNDERLAYMENT AND RESILIENT TILE

Completion

Complete each sentence by inserting the correct answer on the line near the number.

_____ 1. _____ is installed on top of the subfloor to provide a base for the application of resilient sheet or tile flooring.

_____ 2. All joints between the subfloor and the underlayment should be _____ .

_____ 3. To allow for expansion, leave about _____ inch(es) between underlayment panels.

_____ 4. Unless underlayment is installed over a board subfloor, its face grain should run _____ the floor joists.

_____ 5. If _____ is used as a subfloor, no underlayment is needed.

_____ 6. Resilient floor tiles are applied to the floor in a manner similar to applying _____ .

_____ 7. Long strips called _____ strips are used between the tiles to create unique floor patterns.

_____ 8. Caution must be exercised when removing existing resilient floor covering because it may contain _____ .

_____ 9. Before installing resilient tile, make sure underlayment _____ are not projecting above the surface.

_____ 10. If border tiles are a half width or more, then the layout lines are _____ .

_____ 11. Peel-and-stick floor tiles are manufactured with the _____ applied at the factory.

_____ 12. When applying adhesive for floor tile, it is important that the trowel has the proper size _____ .

_____ 13. When laying tiles, start at the _____ of the layout lines.

_____ 14. Tiles are to be laid in place instead of _____ them into position.

_____ 15. Border tiles may be cut by scoring with a sharp _____ and bending.

_____ 16. Many times a vinyl _____ is used to trim a tile floor.

_____ 17. The number of 12″ × 12″ tiles needed to cover a floor is equal to the floor's _____ in square feet.

Discussion

Write your answer(s) on the lines below.

1. Unless we know for sure that it does not, why should we assume that existing flooring contains asbestos?

_____

_____

_____

CHAPTER **86** DESCRIPTION AND INSTALLATION OF MANUFACTURED CABINETS

Multiple Choice

Write the letter for the correct answer on the line next to the number of the sentence.

_____   1. The method of cabinet construction that has a traditional look is called _____ .
- A. face-framed
- B. European
- C. modular
- D. prosaic

_____   2. The two basic kinds of kitchen cabinet units are _____ .
- A. supporting and shelf
- B. standing and attached
- C. base and wall
- D. case and drawer

_____   3. Countertops are usually_____ from the floor.
- A. 28″
- B. 32″
- C. 36″
- D. 40″

_____   4. The usual overall height of a kitchen cabinet installation is _____ .
- A. 6′-6″
- B. 7′-0″
- C. 7′-6″
- D. 8′-0″

_____   5. Standard wall cabinets are _____ deep.
- A. 8″
- B. 10″
- C. 12″
- D. 14″

_____   6. The usual countertop thickness is _____ .
- A. ¾″
- B. 1″
- C. 1¼″
- D. 1½″

_____   7. A recess called a _____ is provided at the bottom of the base cabinet.
- A. toe kick
- B. foot area
- C. counter base
- D. floor cove

_____ 8. Cabinets that provide access from both sides are called _____ .
   A. dual-sided
   B. twin-entry
   C. bi-frontal
   D. double-faced

_____ 9. Double door pantry cabinets are made _____ wide.
   A. 28"
   B. 36"
   C. 42"
   D. 48"

_____ 10. Wall cabinets with a 24" depth are usually installed _____ .
   A. when a contemporary appearance is desired
   B. above refrigerators and tall cabinets
   C. above ranges
   D. A, B, and C

Completion

Complete each sentence by inserting the correct answer on the line near the number.

_____ 1. Most vanity base cabinets are manufactured _____ inches high.

_____ 2. The first step in drawing a cabinet layout plan is to carefully and accurately _____ the walls on which the cabinets are to be installed.

_____ 3. Many large kitchen cabinet distributors will, on request, provide _____ .

_____ 4. Scribbing and fitting cabinets to an uneven floor eliminates the need for a _____ .

_____ 5. When laying out the wall, a level line is drawn _____ up the wall to indicate the top of the base cabinets.

_____ 6. When installing cabinets, most installers prefer to mount the _____ units first.

_____ 7. The installation of wall cabinets is started in a _____ .

_____ 8. If base cabinets are to be fitted to the floor, then their level layout line is measured from the _____ of the floor.

_____ 9. Countertops are covered with a thin, tough, high-pressure plastic surface known as _____ .

_____ 10. To prevent scratching the countertop when making the sink cutout, apply _____ to the base of the saber saw.

CHAPTER **87** COUNTERTOPS AND CABINET COMPONENTS

Multiple Choice

Write the letter for the correct answer on the line next to the number of the sentence.

_____ 1. Wrought iron and other decorative hinges are usually _____ hinges.
   A. pivot
   B. concealed offset
   C. European-style
   D. surface

_____ 2. Offset hinges are used on _____ doors.
   A. overlay
   B. flush
   C. lipped
   D. European-style

_____ 3. Pivot hinges are usually used on _____ doors.
   A. overlay
   B. flush
   C. lipped
   D. European-style

_____ 4. Many carpenters use a self-centering tool, called a _____ , when drilling pilot holes for a screw fastening of cabinet door hinges.
   A. VIX bit
   B. expansive bit
   C. butt gauge
   D. butt marker

_____ 5. When two screws are used to fasten a pull, drill the holes _____ the diameter of the screw.
   A. smaller than
   B. the same size as
   C. slightly larger than
   D. twice

Completion

Complete each sentence by inserting the correct answer on the line near the number.

_____ 1. Most countertops are covered with _____ .

_____ 2. Before laminating a countertop, lightly hand or power sand all joints, making sure they are _____ .

_____ 3. When trimming laminate with a router or a laminate trimmer, it is recommended to use a _____ trimming bit.

_____ 4. _____ cement must be dry before the laminate is bonded to the core.

_____ 5. To test the cement for dryness, you can check it with your _____ .

_____ 6. If the cement is allowed to dry more than _____ hours, the laminate will not bond properly.

_____ 7. When using a trimming bit with a dead pilot, the laminate must be _____ where the pilot will ride.

_____ 8. To prevent water from seeping between the backsplash and the countertop, apply _____ to the joint.

_____ 9. If heated to 325°F, the laminate can be bent to a minimum radius of _____ inches.

_____ 10. The most widely used method of hanging cabinet doors is the _____ .

_____ 11. Face frames are not used on _____-style cabinets.

_____ 12. The _____ door has rabbeted edges that overlap the opening by about ⅜" on all sides.

_____ 13. The _____-type door must be fitted to the door opening.

_____ 14. Drawer fronts are generally made from the same material as the cabinet _____ .

_____ 15. Drawer sides and backs are usually _____ inch thick.

_____ 16. Drawer bottoms are usually made of _____-inch-thick plywood or particleboard.

_____ 17. The _____ joint is the strongest used in drawer construction.

_____ 18. The _____ joint is the easiest joint to make that is used between the drawer front and side.

_____ 19. To provide added strength, the drawer back is usually set _____ inch(es) from the rear of the sides.

_____ 20. The simplest type of wood drawer guide is probably the _____ .

Identification: Wood Joints

Identify each term, and write the letter of the correct answer on the line next to each number.

_____ 1. dovetail joint

_____ 2. dado joint

_____ 3. dado and rabbet joint

_____ 4. butt joint

_____ 5. lock joint

_____ 6. rabbeted joint

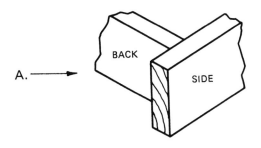

A.

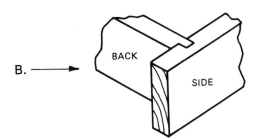

B.

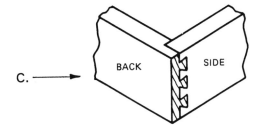

C.

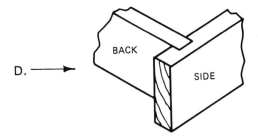

D.

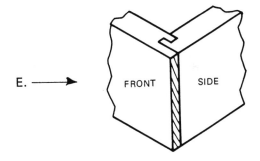

E.

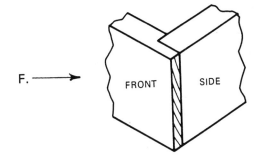

F.